EDIBLE
NORTH CAROLINA

EDIBLE NORTH CAROLINA

A Journey across a State of Flavor

Edited by Marcie Cohen Ferris

Foreword by **VIVIAN HOWARD**

K. C. Hysmith, *Associate Editor*

Photography by **Baxter Miller**

THE UNIVERSITY OF NORTH CAROLINA PRESS

Chapel Hill

The photography program in this book was supported by a gift from John Powell.

Set in Miller, Caslon Ionic, and Bodoni by April Leidig
Manufactured in the United States of America

The University of North Carolina Press has been a member of the Green Press Initiative since 2003.

Cover illustration: Carrboro Farmers' Market sampler. Photo by Baxter Miller.

Library of Congress Cataloging-in-Publication Data
Names: Ferris, Marcie Cohen, editor. | Hysmith, K. C. (Katherine C.), editor. | Miller, Baxter, photographer (expression) | Howard, Vivian (Vivian S.), 1978– writer of foreword.
Title: Edible North Carolina : a journey across a state of flavor / edited by Marcie Cohen Ferris ; K.C. Hysmith, associate editor ; photography by Baxter Miller ; foreword by Vivian Howard.
Description: Chapel Hill : The University of North Carolina Press, 2022. | Includes bibliographical references and index.
Identifiers: LCCN 2021046314 | ISBN 9781469667799 (cloth ; alk. paper) | ISBN 9781469667805 (ebook)
Subjects: LCSH: Cooking—North Carolina. | Local foods—North Carolina. | Food—Social aspects—North Carolina. | LCGFT: Cookbooks.
Classification: LCC TX715 .E2456 2022 | DDC 641.59756—dc23
LC record available at https://lccn.loc.gov/2021046314

To RANDALL KENAN,

who cherished and shared

the flavors of his North Carolina

home with the world

Contents

VIVIAN HOWARD

Foreword

I grew up on a working farm in rural eastern North Carolina. Tobacco, corn, cotton, and hogs organized our year and made the rules for where we could go and when. Tobacco, the cash crop without a rival, required every hand in the family from June to September. Cotton and corn siphoned up spring and early fall. Pigs squealed for attention every dang day. We didn't travel far, and we didn't travel a lot. Aside from sporadic road trips to Florida to visit my aunt, I didn't leave the state of North Carolina until I was fifteen (except for that time we crossed over into Gatlinburg, Tennessee, for just a minute when I was eight).

I wasn't happy about it. I saw the rest of the world on TV and I wanted a taste of it. I wanted to go to London and nosh on fish and chips with Princess Di. I wanted to flit up to Martha's Vineyard and flirt with JFK Junior over a clambake. I had a deep desire to order take-out that came with chopsticks. My parents heard none of it. With every request for a plane ticket, Mom met me with, "North Carolina's got it all, Vivian. We've got beaches. We've got rolling hills, AND we've got mountains. You could live your whole life and never leave here."

I heard none of that. Actually, I heard all of it loud and clear, and looking back I think the fear of doing what my mom suggested—living my whole life *trapped* inside North Carolina—closed my eyes and dulled my senses to the variety of tastes, smells, and natural majesty my state did in fact offer. There were moments when North Carolina did successfully grab my attention—vignettes that live in my memory, scenes that rush forward when triggered and to this day confirm my mom's mantra about North Carolina.

I'll never forget the January morning in the mid-eighties when my dad spontaneously decided we'd skip church and take a day trip to Ocracoke. The long, desolate drive from the flat farmland of eastern North Carolina followed by a foggy, cold ferry ride made landing on the sliver of an island in the Atlantic feel as if we had stepped into another world. I panicked as my dad drove around looking for somewhere to eat. Everything was closed, boarded up even. I was seven years old and irritably hungry. And then there was a place, a general store with flickering light and warm, steamy insides. We got hot chocolates and something the woman at the counter called light rolls. She said they were fresh out of the oven. They smelled like butter and yeast and had shiny, slick tops. The three of us huddled around a tall table and ate standing up: the rolls' soft, puffy crumb and faint sweetness tasted like the best and last thing on earth.

There were our annual family vacations snatched over a weekend between harvest season and the holidays. Three teenagers, one kid (me), two parents, and a pile of sausage biscuits lumbered out of the driveway at 3:00 A.M. headed for the North Carolina mountains. We did the same thing every year, leaving far before dawn so we could gawk at the leaves, swing by Tweetsie Railroad, pick up baskets of apples and gallons of cider, then turn around and head home before sunset. In line before they opened, we always stopped first at the Daniel Boone Inn. There we traded our region's sausage biscuits for the mountains' country ham. Served family style, breakfast at the Daniel Boone Inn was the rare occasion I was master of my destiny, building a plate with the absolute best thing about the mountains—a mound of fried apples and a trio of ham biscuits.

Other moments stand out, too—snapshots from my North Carolina childhood. There was the port wine cheese with crackers and my first bite of chocolate chess pie at the Angus Barn in Raleigh. Both marked my earliest brush with sophisticated tastes. The cheese was luxurious and spreadable. Its sharp notes woke my nose and made my tongue tingle. The pie was rich, earthy, and creamy and reminded me of something from France, *if* I had ever eaten anything from France. At once the fanciest, grandest place I had ever seen and the only time I had been allowed to order dessert in a restaurant, the Angus Barn highlighted a city's ability to provide a more refined experience than the country ever could.

There was the time my seventeen-year-old sister was forced to bring me along with her to Emerald Isle for the day. She had hoped to spend the afternoon at the beach drinking wine coolers and smoking cigarettes with her friends. Instead she had a seven-year-old in tow who, despite living just an hour from the North Carolina coast, had never so much as dipped a toe in the Atlantic Ocean. While a loss for my sister, this trip was a definite win for me. Headed back home in my sister's red Somerset Regal, hungry, sunburned, and sandy, I stared up through the driver's side window as my sister ordered two shrimp burgers, two fries, and two Pepsis from a woman with a notepad and a visor that read "El's Drive In." I wondered if that was El herself, and I wondered if I'd feel good about this. When the woman returned and my sister pitched my burger into the back, I gobbled it up and marveled at how tiny fried shrimp smashed together with slaw and cocktail sauce between a soft white bun was so much more than the sum of its parts. It was my first taste of the beach and, from then on, the perfect end of a day spent in the sun and sand.

Like I promised myself, I moved away from North Carolina as soon as possible. I went to boarding school in Virginia. I spent a summer in Connecticut. I studied abroad in Argentina, backpacked through Europe, and at the age of twenty-two moved to New York, where I thought I'd most definitely live forever. A lot happened during the fifteen years I spent outside of eastern North Carolina. I found that wherever I went, the food of that place was what helped me define its culture and better understand its people. And then, probably because I said I never would, I moved back home. Only now, I saw it through the prism of all the other places I had been. I tasted wood-smoked, vinegar-laced whole-hog BBQ and appreciated how distinct it was from all the other 'Q out there. I became aware of backyard gardens and marveled at how many people still grew the food they ate. I went to covered-dish lunches at my mom's church and noted the variety in the everyday—deviled eggs adorned with a dozen different garnishes, chicken pastry, chicken slick, and chicken and rice, turnip greens stewed with sausage, collard greens simmered with ham hock, and salad "kilt" with hot bacon grease.

I saw new influences, too. Taco trucks, Chinese buffets, and Asian markets dotted strip malls and roadsides in large and small towns across the state. Restaurants with a laser focus on the food of other cultures thrived and drove the collective excitement around dining out. Consecutive waves of new North Carolinians were adding depth and variety to the state's food landscape. And although I grew up here, I felt like one of these new North Carolinians with fresh perspective and a point of view that had the potential to push our state's food culture forward. This book is a collection of voices much like my own. Farmers, chefs, artisans, writers, and home cooks who come from different backgrounds, celebrate different ingredients, and raise up disparate foodways. These essays and the people who wrote them provide a snapshot of what it looks like when a place shapes our food traditions and when our food traditions reshape a place. In this case, that place is North Carolina. From the Outer Banks to the Blue Ridge Mountains and all the farming communities, small towns, and cities in between, I can hardly think of a more exciting place to live and eat.

MARCIE COHEN FERRIS

Introduction

An Edible North Carolina History

> *"This week in North Carolina is what the menu is going to be."*
>
> —AARON VANDERMARK, chef/owner, Pancuito, Hillsborough, North Carolina, June 4, 2019

Edible North Carolina: A Journey across a State of Flavor is the story of the contemporary food landscape in a state deeply tied to its rural heritage and, most important, to the flavor of its distinctive regions—the outer coastal plain, the inner coastal plain or what most folks call eastern North Carolina, the Piedmont, and the mountains. What sets North Carolina's food movement apart from others is its historic food heritage—a complex language of core ingredients and the interrelations of racism, land, and labor—the proximity of farm to table, the comradery of the present-day food community, and the powerful edible point of view expressed across the state. North Carolina's culinary inventiveness is fostered by the state's biodiversity (its unusual range of climate, soil, water, altitude, and year-round growing season), varied food economies, tourism, new and shifting populations, and expansive academic resources. Rural and metropolitan regions are close by, creating both challenges and opportunities for the state's many small, diversified farms and their farmers. Dynamic as the present-day food economy appears, we witness its fragility as global forces affect our daily lives and tables. The COVID pandemic, the immigration crisis, the nation's political rifts, and the strong storms spawned by a warming climate threaten the daily food supply and economic livelihoods of thousands of North Carolinians in ways unimaginable in the past.

Now more than ever we viscerally understand what it means to lose local farms, entrepreneurs, food markets, food banks, school cafeterias, beloved neighborhood restaurants, and landmark food venues. In this book, twenty diverse individuals across North Carolina take us on a journey to explore this changing state of flavor and its meaning for generations to come. Through their stories, we collectively examine how North Carolinians—despite these challenging times and, for many, *because* of these very challenges—are passionately reengaging with, reinventing, and reclaiming the vibrant food that is theirs and ours.

A generation of small-scale farmers, sustainable food system activists, food entrepreneurs, aggregators, and chef founders of what has been called New Southern cuisine in the 1980s inspired and laid the foundations of North Carolina's contemporary local food movement. Today that food movement is led by the next generation of young and midcareer people, some native to the state, others recently arrived from other states and countries. The movement is noteworthy for the number of women among its leaders. If the movement had a manifesto, it would proclaim a commitment to healthy, local, sustainable food for all that honors the great diversity of our people; protects our land, animals, plants, air, and water; fosters joy and flavor; tells a story of place through ingredients; and secures the right of all North Carolinians to food sovereignty, food equity, and food justice.

Agriculture and fisheries are the foundation of North Carolina's foodways, and both sectors face contemporary obstacles. Structural racism, sexual harassment, and inequity exist from field to processing plants to restaurants. Our state's *local* food systems—the sustainable, regional processes involved in feeding people, from growing to consuming, defined by place and people—have been diminished by a national diet bound to industrial agriculture and its production of refined and processed foods. North Carolina is losing farmland and aging farmers and fishers to debt and financial loss, increased regulation, globalization, industrial consolidation, and issues related to climate change and environmental pollution. Urban areas in North Carolina have prospered as rural counties have experienced economic and population decline—a "political-economic divide" reflected in the 2020 presidential election.[1] Land loss is much worse for Black North Carolinians. From the late 1970s to the early 2000s, the number of African American–owned farms in the state declined by 70 percent.[2] Thousands of food-insecure North Carolinians experience daily hunger and food insecurity. Food writer and scholar Kelly Alexander notes, "Our local food scene has grown at the expense of local people being able to access it."[3]

In 2018, food activist and chef Bryant Terry spoke about the power of the food movement in North Carolina at a statewide summit that brought together 150 chefs, food entrepreneurs, nonprofit leaders, and public health professionals. He urged them to recognize their role at this history-making moment in America and to address the intersection of food justice, sexism, and antiracism in their work. Increasing numbers of younger farmers and food entrepreneurs—including more women and Black, Latinx, and Asian Americans—are growing and making food in North Carolina, and their business plans lead with social change, racial and gender equity, community empowerment, and environmental sustainability.[4] Food is never distant in this state, from the coast's historic fishing operations to the industrial growers of eastern Carolina, the small-scale farms of the Piedmont, and the vineyards, orchards, and family farms of the mountains. Each era has shaped the evolving food narrative of this distinctive place and created the food landscapes we encounter in the state today. Before we explore North Carolina's contemporary food landscapes and ponder what lies beyond the rapidly shifting times in which we live, it is helpful to examine the history of our food, farming, and fishing heritage in North Carolina, including issues, innovations, and struggles that endure today. The summary that follows showcases critical moments and people who reflect North Carolina's racial and ethnic diversity and the power of women's leadership. I hope that this brief taste of place will inspire readers to explore further the long arc of North Carolina's rich culture of food, soil, and water from the Outer Banks to the Blue Ridge.

North Carolina Food—An Edible History

The first Carolinians arrived in the region more than 10,000 years ago, and food is at the heart of origin stories of both the Tuscarora and Cherokee peoples.[5] Tribal narratives include powerful accounts of famine in a cold, northern world where starvation forced a long migration eastward in search of food. That journey brought Indigenous people to the Southeast, a region with abundant food resources. Eastern Indians hunted white-tailed deer, black bear, and wild turkey; fished for freshwater and saltwater fish and shellfish; and gathered berries, nuts, greens, and seeds.[6] A transition from hunting large animals, trapping small game, fishing, and foraging occurred as farming, or the domestication of native plants into food crops such as the sunflower, was well established in precontact Carolina by the year 1200. From Mesoamerica, maize, or corn, became the staple food crop of Indigenous people in the region. Archaeologist Rachel Briggs describes this hominy foodway as "not a singular dish but rather the life-sustaining staple foodways for Native groups in the Eastern Woodlands."[7] During the first settler-colonization efforts in the 1650s in the Outer Banks and Albemarle region of North Carolina, Europeans observed the successful farming of the Tuscarora tribes and their strong agricultural economy controlled by native women who grew corn, tobacco, beans, and squash.

The Sara Indians lived in the North Carolina Piedmont near the Dan River in this same era. Archaeological studies show evidence of small-grain crops such as sumpweed, whose oily kernels were added to breads and stews. Hickory nuts were gathered in the fall and stored for later use. The crushed nut meat was used in soups and to create a nut milk high in fat and plant protein. Corn was roasted and eaten on the cob after it was picked in the late summer, but much was dried and stored. Sofkee was made from pounding dried corn kernels and, like beans and squash, was added to stews, soups, and bread. European trade with the Sara brought deadly epidemics and devastating loss of life that the tribe attempted to control with intensive communal rituals that included large feasts and purification and renewal events, such as the annual Green Corn ceremony or busk.[8] The diet of the Sara and other Indigenous peoples in the region in this era—maize, grains, beans, squashes, nuts, persimmons, grapes, other fruits, small game, and fish—are the foundational foodways of North Carolina.

Today these Indigenous foods and dishes from North Carolina's First People preserve memories of community, ingenuity, resilience, trauma, and resistance into the present. In the spring of 2021, an orchard—apple, peach, pomegranate, fig, persimmon, and blueberry—was planted at the Lumbee Tribe Cultural Center in Maxton. The orchard and grapevines, alongside a greenhouse and garden, provide locally grown, seasonal produce for the Lumbee people, building food sovereignty and reintroducing native plants important to the community.

Throughout the mid-1700s, English settler-colonists sought land to farm as they migrated south from eastern Virginia into the coastal Albemarle region, followed by Scots-Irish and German migrants, also in search of farmland. They traveled to the North Carolina Piedmont and backcountry on the long wagon road and trading paths from Pennsylvania and the Chesapeake. Historian Alfred Crosby describes the "ecological imperialism" of European settlers who permanently altered the native ecosystem as they cut down forests, built fences, and freely grazed hungry cattle and horses.[9] Their economies were extractive, and they valued land for what it could produce quickly. Their sense of impermanence was palpable, especially in the mid-1600s Albemarle region where temporary dwellings housed sparsely settled colonists as they tried to turn a fast profit from tobacco before they succumbed to disease.

A greater sense of permanence was possible as a more diversified subsistence agriculture became the livelihood of most white North Carolinians from the Piedmont west to the foothills and the mountains in the first decades of the 1700s. The typical white yeoman farmer could not afford enslaved labor. On small farms that ranged from one hundred acres to far less, families raised corn, wheat, cattle, hogs, chickens, and fruit trees. Tobacco was their cash crop, and pork was their meat of choice, given how well it stored after curing in a smokehouse. In the Piedmont and western foothills, German immigrants slow cooked pork shoulders. They valued the fatty, flavorful cut, which they basted with a lightly sweetened tomato sauce, replaced by commercially produced ketchup when it became available in the late 1800s.[10] Leftover parts of the pig mixed with cornmeal, flour, and spices became livermush, a popular sausagelike food. Turnips and other greens, squash of all kinds, beans, cucumbers, onions, peas, watermelons, Irish potatoes, and sweet potatoes were grown for the family table, and any surplus was traded in town.[11] Apple and cherry trees grew in the yard, and wild persimmon trees in neighboring woods. What corn they didn't sell or store for later use was eaten on the cob, as cornbread, hominy grits, hoecakes, and mush. They fed corn to animals and used it to make corn whiskey—cracked corn or moonshine—a critical cash crop. Small farmers sold their grain, beef, and pork through local and export markets. By the mid-twentieth century, the Piedmont was known for its dairies and dairy farms.

The barrier islands known as the Outer Banks off the coast of North Carolina were home to the Sioux, Iroquois, and Algonquian peoples, tribal groups who experienced the earliest contact with European explorers in the 1580s. Years of conflict and disease endured by Native people and the failed attempt by English colonizers to establish a settlement at Roanoke Island left the remote region sparsely settled for another century.[12] By the early 1800s, resilient Outer Bankers from the Core Sound region in Carteret County up to Corolla in Currituck County near the Virginia border provided for their families by fishing, hunting, and other water-related work on the inlets and sounds. The intersection of the northern-born cold waters of the Labrador Current and the southern warm waters of the Gulf Stream off the coast assured great varieties of fish. The commercial fishing industry came to the region later in the nineteenth century due to the Outer Banks' distance from major markets, insufficient transportation, and lack of refrigeration for perishable fish.[13] Banks families ate every sort of fish from the waters but also kept a cow, a few chickens, and always a garden patch for potatoes, onions, collards, and beets.[14] Fig trees, wild grapes, and berries were plentiful. The fig cakes of Ocracoke Island remain a beloved food tradition in the region today.

In the mountains, Scots-Irish migrated in the late 1700s to the coves and valleys near the French Broad River, where they established subsistence farms defined by the challenging topography and short growing season.[15] Small fields for corn and garden patches for vegetables were situated in flatter land that backed up to the mountain ridges. Here, as writer and western North Carolina native Sheri Castle explains, "the usefulness of a crop was measured by how well it could be preserved through the winter."[16] Green runner beans, beans for soup, beets, speckled butter beans, cowpeas, corn to ferment, dry, and grind, cabbage, carrots, cucumbers, Irish potatoes, onions, candy roaster squash or cushaw, parsnips, pumpkins, apples, grapes, summer squash, sweet potatoes, turnips, and sorghum for sweetening were core foods of mountain families.[17] Livestock ranged the woods for acorn mast and other nuts and fruits. Brook trout were abundant in mountain streams until logging damaged their habitat. Locals foraged in the spring for ramps (a wild onion) and morel mushrooms, and in the summer for blackberries and gooseberries. By the late 1820s, an important trading route along the French Broad River, the Buncombe Turnpike, was used by drovers to move cattle, hogs, mules, and fowl to regional livestock markets.[18] Railroad shipping brought the great drives to an end after the Civil War. Tobacco also became an important cash crop in the mountain hollers.

In eastern North Carolina, the sandy coastal plain provided excellent growing conditions for tobacco and cotton, where large plantations thrived, and white wealth was built. Although never as extensive here as in the bordering states of Virginia and South Carolina, the plantation system was organized around the intensive labor of enslaved workers, who also oversaw prized hogs, cattle, horses, and mules, fields of corn, additional row crops, and large vegetable gardens for the slaveholding family. Collard and other greens flourished here, as did scuppernong and muscadine grapes and chinquapins, a petite relative of the chestnut. Whole hogs were slow cooked over wood coals and flavored with a vinegary pepper sauce crafted by African American pit masters in the region. Peanuts were also important, and in 1919, a local fertilizer and farm supply company, Powell and Stokes, expanded to buy peanuts and cotton, and later founded Bertie County Peanuts in Windsor. In the lower Cape Fear River region near Wilmington—the northernmost end of the Lowcountry—rice grew on plantations, like Orton and Kendall in present-day Brunswick County. Here again, Black labor was crucial to the successful cultivation and processing of the crop, particularly because of enslaved peoples' extensive knowledge from rice-growing regions in West Africa. By the mid-1700s, many eastern North Carolina counties were majority African American.[19] The deep trauma and legacy of slavery as the engine of the region's economy reverberate into the present, where it is met by the resistance, will, and work of Black North Carolinians in the state's food movement, including farmers, chefs, award-winning pit masters, writers, scholars, food system leaders, and policy makers.

Small farms and the regional infrastructures that supported farming—gristmills, slaughterhouses, country stores, and railroads—remained at the heart of North Carolina's rural economy throughout the nineteenth and into the early twentieth century. Black and white North Carolinians raised and preserved food for personal use and participated in an active regional food economy of local merchants, entrepreneurs, and food-related businesses, rather than self-sufficiency. In 1853, the North Carolina State Agricultural Society sponsored the first annual state fair in Raleigh—for whites only—as a venue to demonstrate and showcase best farming practices. In 1879, members of the North Carolina Industrial Association created the separate Great Negro Fair, also in Raleigh, for Black North Carolinians. African American and white youth did not compete together at the fair until 1965. (In the late 1940s, North Carolina State University architect Matthew Nowicki designed the bold, modernist J. S. Dorton Arena, the livestock-judging pavilion for the fair named in honor of fair manager Dorton, who wanted "the most modern plant in the world" for the state fair facilities.)[20]

Economic and political change after the Civil War, emancipation, and Reconstruction damaged the state's and region's farming and food economy, and an agricultural depression in 1890 further weakened the economy. In eastern North Carolina, white planters divided their large farms into smaller pieces that they rented to African American freedmen and poor whites who worked as tenants and sharecroppers. By 1900, once independent farmers in the Piedmont now tended land owned by someone else.[21] Cash-strapped small farmers, both Black and white, focused solely on money crops of cotton and tobacco and paid for food on credit rather than grow it as their grandparents had done on more diversified farms.[22] Overproduction of cotton and tobacco led to depressed prices in a declining market, exhausted soil, growing farm debt, and ultimately loss of farmland.

To confront the agricultural depression, thousands of white North Carolina farmers joined the Farmers' Alliance. The alliance was inspired by a cooperative model of progressive farm management, led by Leonidas Polk, charismatic publisher of the weekly *Progressive Farmer.* A member of the new People's Party, or Populists, Polk later became North Carolina's first commissioner of agriculture and the first president of whites-only North Carolina College of Agriculture and Mechanic Arts (now North Carolina State University), which was established in 1887 in Raleigh as the state's land-grant institution. North Carolina A&T State University was created for African American students in Greensboro in 1891.

As the depression worsened, white farmers aligned with the Populists, joining with Republicans to strengthen their combined interests. Republicans largely supported equal rights for Black North Carolinians, who also aligned with the party. In 1896 this successful Fusionist movement elected middle-class Blacks to the state legislature and local government. In the 1898 campaign, white supremacists among North

Carolina Democrats—the party of the Confederacy—called for the end of "Negro Domination."[23] Brutal assaults on Black Americans were carried out by organized factions of whites in cities with significant Black populations across the country, including the deadly Wilmington, North Carolina, coup on November 10, 1898. In this overthrow of Wilmington's mixed-race government, the city's vibrant African American business community—including food-related entrepreneurs, grocers, and merchants—was destroyed, and Black residents were terrorized. Thousands of Black citizens left the city, never to return. Journalist Nikole Hannah-Jones explains how lynching, massacres, and racial terrorism were regularly used against middle-class Blacks to terrify but, even more important, to prevent them from building generational wealth.[24] The legacy of this racial violence was economic inequity, food insecurity, and substandard housing that affects low-income African Americans in Wilmington to this day. The small numbers of Black farmers, chefs, and food entrepreneurs in the larger Cape Fear region is further evidence of a history of racial disenfranchisement. In spite of this history, Black leadership in local food systems, restaurants, and farms in the region today is creating a powerful new narrative.

The Great Depression deepened the financial challenges faced by North Carolina farmers, tenants, and sharecroppers. Although many remained on the land, many others sought a way out. Historian Sydney Nathans argues that "industrialization in North Carolina was . . . born [not] in the factory but on the farm."[25] Two hundred thousand North Carolinians who left farms their families had owned for generations to work in the Piedmont's burgeoning textile mills moved frequently between mill and farm to visit family and help with seasonal farmwork.[26] New South historian Tom Hanchett describes Piedmont barbecue as the product of industrialization. Railroads that serviced mills and other industries brought cheap cuts of pork from the Midwest, as well as such manufactured foods as bottled ketchup, preferred in "Lexington-style" barbecue sauce, and Nabisco wafers and imported bananas, used in banana pudding. Chef Mike Moore, who grew up in eastern North Carolina recalls, "Tobacco farming and barbecue went hand and hand in Wilson. At the end of harvest, the pits were dug, and the same wood used as fuel in the tobacco barns was used to cook a whole hog."[27] Hot dog stands and diners founded by Greek immigrants across the state provided tasty, affordable midday meals and snacks for tobacco laborers and mill and office workers alike. West of Charlotte, working-class people ate at home, and by the 1930s and 1940s, a Friday night family meal meant platters of fried catfish, shrimp, flounder, French fries, hushpuppies, and coleslaw at one of Gaston County's fish camps on the Catawba River.[28]

Charlotte is officially in North Carolina's Piedmont, but its enterprise and sense of reinvention transformed this New South city into a stand-alone region in the state. Once the nation's top cotton manufacturing district, it became a trading center and distribution hub for the region; an early recording hub for area musicians, from gospel and bluegrass to blues and jazz; and later, a banking empire and, Hanchett notes, "an epicenter for caffeinated soft drinks." Historian Glenda Gilmore describes the dense urban vegetable and flower gardens of middle-class Black families in Charlotte—like that of painter Romare Bearden and of his great-grandparents H. B. and Rosa Kennedy, who ran a small grocery store next to their home before the Great Migration.[29] Black disenfranchisement associated with white supremacy campaigns at the turn of the twentieth century and later urban "redevelopment" created "two Charlottes" visibly divided by race, income, and access to healthy food, health care, and housing.[30] The city's connection to stock car racing and NASCAR lay in Prohibition and the fast drivers who delivered illegal moonshine to customers. Perhaps not surprising, this is also a deeply religious city and region.

Charlotte's uptown steakhouses and clubs served conservative bankers, attorneys, and finance professionals anxious to impress clients with dining that connoted taste yet also stability and wealth. In the early 2000s, entrepreneurs invested in concept restaurants designed for Charlotte diners with deep pockets. In the last decade of the twentieth century, Latinx workers, global newcomers, and refugees escaping violence and oppression settled in Charlotte, and their presence is reflected in Central Avenue's many international markets and eateries. New food events and festivals are highlighting the skill and talent of the city's Black chefs and food entrepreneurs. Journalist Kathleen Purvis says, "Charlotte is a different city now, with an exploding, diversifying population, a city that has faced tear gas and rage as it felt its way toward a more just community."[31]

As North Carolina became a leading industrialist state in the Southeast, its tobacco and furniture plants drew young people away from small farms. Those who stayed on farms grew more cotton and tobacco and less food. Nathans describes this "central paradox of the time"—"North Carolina, despite its devotion to agriculture, was a heavy importer of food."[32] This steady escalation of agricultural change distanced North Carolinians from growing, processing, preparing, and eating food that was locally grown.

For North Carolinians who farmed in the first decades of the twentieth-century South, the buzzwords of "progress," "reform," "science," "efficiency," "diversity," and "profit" were a familiar chorus from the Department of Agriculture and state agricultural colleges' corps of extension service and home demonstration agents. Working out of racially segregated agricultural extension branches, male and female agents spread the gospel of scientific agriculture and better business practices through hands-on workshops, farmers' bulletins, and the radio. Their message was simple. To survive, small farmers had to diversify. They must grow food crops and raise small livestock essential for their own use. Girls and boys organized tomato canning clubs and livestock clubs to apply lessons learned in home economics and farm management, and they raised funds to contribute to their families. Farm wives and mothers similarly honed their gardening, food preservation, and marketing skills to increase home productivity and income, often selling produce, meat, eggs, butter, and home-baked goods at local curb markets. Women also heard a strong public health message that promoted better family nutrition, health, and diet. Men attended annual farmers' institutes. Mechanization and modernization carried North Carolina farmers into the mid-twentieth century, but not the small farms touted by county extension agents. Tenant farmers and sharecroppers remained as a remnant of another time.

Between the 1920s and 1950s industrial agriculture and commercial food production came to North Carolina, as did the Civil Rights Movement. On February 1, 1960, four Black college students from North Carolina A&T staged a sit-in at the segregated lunch counter at the Woolworth's store in Greensboro. Ironically the food served at that counter—sandwiches, sodas, coffee, milkshakes, a slice of pie prepared with canned filling, the packaged foods for sale on the nearby aisles—symbolized the modern New South, while conservative white customers and store management remained tethered to a racist Jim Crow past. More sit-ins, protests, and interracial gatherings followed in North Carolina until the passage of the 1964 Civil Rights Act, which outlawed segregated "public accommodations," including restaurants, although legal compliance took much longer.

North Carolina commercial food companies manufactured snack foods, sandwich makings, and beverages enjoyed first by working-class North Carolinians and later by consumers across the country. A soft drink and a "Nab" peanut butter cracker—and, when needed, a Goody's Powder—gave a tired loom operator the boost needed to finish a ten- to twelve-hour shift at a mill. To discourage workers from leaving their machines and slowing production, "dope wagons" carried food and beverages throughout the mill—their name tied to the slang for a Coca-Cola. During World War I, soldiers training at Charlotte's Camp Greene also enjoyed Nabs for a quick snack. The Piedmont was home to Snyder's-Lance (sandwich crackers), Cheerwine (a cherry-flavored soft drink), Sun Drop (a citrusy soda), Krispy Kreme donuts, Carolina Foods' Duchess Brand "Honey Buns," Luck's beans, Star Foods, Stan's Quality Foods, and Ruth's Salads (pimento cheese and other sandwich spreads), TW Garner (Texas Pete hot sauce), and the grocery chains Food Lion, Harris Teeter, and Lowes Foods and, in Asheville, Ingles Markets.[33] Eastern Carolina had Pepsi-Cola, Bright Leaf hot dogs, House-Autry cornbread, grits, and breading mixes, and Mt. Olive pickles. Canneries such as the North State Canning Company in Boone—known for its Watauga Chopped Kraut, made from local cabbage—were a crucial piece of western North Carolina's economy.

Triad cities like Greensboro and Winston-Salem, located in the heart of the North Carolina textile industry, whose executives traveled frequently between North Carolina, New York City, and Europe, were home to a growing dining scene influenced by new American regional cuisine in the 1970s and New Southern cuisine in the 1980s. Piedmont restaurateur Nancy King Quaintance points to the era's affordable air travel, company expense accounts, the culinary gospel of Julia Child, the influence of food media, and the legalization of liquor-by-the-drink sales in 1978 (allowing restaurants and bars to sell liquor rather than having customers brown-bag their own bottles) as factors that supported a burgeoning restaurant community in the Triangle, Triad, and Charlotte.

The Angus Barn, a Raleigh institution of this era, expertly run by Chef Walter Royal, celebrated its sixtieth anniversary in 2020. Van Eure, whose parents built this rustically elegant steakhouse on fifty acres of land near the growing Raleigh-Durham International Airport and Research Triangle Park's industries, recalls, "It ended up being the perfect location in what started to be the worst location."[34] For those with means, dining out in North Carolina was no longer limited to cafeterias, meat and three cafés and lunch counters, barbecue joints, drive-ins, and segregated country clubs.

Grace Summers, an agricultural consultant who works with small-scale farmers throughout North Carolina and Virginia, grew up in the 1960s in rural Guilford County in the Piedmont, where her parents farmed tobacco and grains and raised animals. They also worked off the farm, her mother in cooperative extension and her father on the second shift at Cone Mills in nearby Greensboro. Summers describes how young people left the tobacco fields either to enter the military or to get a factory job. Some attended college. As these baby boomers left, the local food scene changed.[35] The older generation of women cooked less or not at all. Rural stores sold grab 'n go food items and operated grills to feed commuting working people who no longer raised food as their elders had. Fast food–style eating from a quick market—heat lamp–warmed fried chicken, hot dogs, burgers, barbecue, biscuit sandwiches, burritos and carnitas from a taco truck—was standard fare for many working North Carolinians.

The Raleigh Farmers Market (now the State Farmers Market) opened in 1955 and provided a central location for farmers and consumers to meet. Jim Graham, who became North Carolina's longest-serving commissioner of agriculture, was its first manager. Graham recognized farmers' need for better marketing opportunities as they transitioned from tobacco to grow and sell produce. State-run markets in Asheville, Charlotte, and the Triad were established from the 1970s through the 1990s. City councils allocated public space for community gardens and market pavilions, which over time became important gathering places, not unlike alternative town commons. These new markets coincided with the civil lawsuits against the tobacco industry and the massive federal buyout and settlement programs that compensated former tobacco growers. North Carolina farmers who had grown burley tobacco began to grow vegetables, melons, potatoes, and sweet potatoes.[36] Some farmers aged out of farming, choosing not to grow food as an alternative to tobacco. Many experienced farmers became anchor vendors who produced fruits and vegetables for the new farmers' markets. At the same time, some North Carolina farmers continued to grow tobacco and rely on it as a cash crop alongside cotton, soybeans, and one or two vegetables for commercial truck farming, and they used buyout money to expand their tobacco output.

By the early 1970s, an industrial switch in North Carolina had flipped. Farmers were advised to "get big or get out": they needed more land and less labor due to tractors and specialized machinery, herbicides and pesticides, hybrid seeds, U.S. Department of Agriculture (USDA) loans, bank financing, and contracts with agribusiness companies. Food became a super commodity of the Green Revolution, which massively expanded grain yields through selective breeding, huge inputs of fertilizer, and irrigation systems.

African American land loss increased in eastern North Carolina, the coastal plain, and the Piedmont because Black farmers were unable to secure USDA crop loans and were denied access to government farm programs—expressions of institutional structural racism locked into place by the early twentieth century. Black farmers had long pushed back against these forces through groups like the Colored Farmers'

Alliance organized in the 1870s. Black youth coming of age in the 1960s and 1970s turned away from farming because of its racist history, but Black farmers also fought the racism. In 1997, Timothy Pigford, a farmer in Cumberland County in eastern North Carolina, filed two class-action lawsuits, known as Pigford I and II, charging the USDA with racial discrimination against Black farmers. Yet settlement payment stipulations left thousands of Black farmers unable to register for the funds. The American Rescue Plan, signed into law by President Joe Biden in spring 2021, included $5 billion to address the historic economic losses of Black farmers, including debt relief.

Attorney Savonala "Savi" Horne is executive director of the Land Loss Prevention Project, a Durham-based nonprofit founded by the North Carolina Association of Black Lawyers in the 1980s to curtail the loss of Black-owned land in North Carolina. "You will find," says Horne, "that limited-resource farmers, small farmers have a resiliency that is unparalleled. . . . They care not just about their economic bottom line but about social justice and civil rights. They care about what is going on in our state. They care about the environment, and they care about young people. This is what links all the farmers in North Carolina, a pride not just of self but of place."[37] The nonprofit focuses on the legal infrastructures Black farmers must negotiate to participate in the state's emerging local food systems and food hubs and to become vested in these initiatives.

In the last decades of the twentieth century, farms located near cities like Charlotte and Durham faced exorbitant land taxes as their property was rezoned for suburban development. Small and mid-size farm income declined rapidly as higher yields lowered market prices. During the American Farm Crisis, thousands of North Carolina farmers stopped farming.[38] Many were forced to sell multigenerational family land and took jobs in manufacturing. The Rural Advancement Fund International (RAFI-USA), located in Pittsboro, North Carolina, was founded in 1990 and organized the first emergency hotline for farmers in crisis because of debt tied to global competition and disastrous farming contracts.

By the 1980s, farming in North Carolina was synonymous with big poultry (turkeys, chicken, eggs) and big pork, soybeans, peanuts, and massive growers of sweet potatoes, tomatoes, peppers, and cucumbers. Pork and poultry operations emphasized vertical integration, in which the company owns virtually every step of production. Duplin County native, farmer, and former state legislator Wendell Murphy became known as "Boss Hog" for his massive expansion of industrial hog farming in eastern North Carolina, supported by tax exemptions, subsidies, and exclusion for large poultry and hog farmers from environmental regulation. Small, family-owned slaughtering and processing facilities crucial to independent farmers closed. The efficiencies of consolidated food production created value for consumers, but cheap food came at a cost. Mexican and Central American workers were the predominant labor force for these large agroprocessors and for most of North Carolina's food production by the early twenty-first century. To help families affected by climate change and industrial agriculture in their countries, migrant workers sought better jobs and higher wages in North Carolina. America's H-2A program provided temporary guest worker visas in exchange for seasonal farm labor in the United States. Migrant labor camps were often dehumanizing. In 2004, the first union contract in the nation for H-2A workers was signed with Mt. Olive Pickle Company, following a five-year boycott backed by the National Council of Churches because of the company's mistreatment of workers.

Issues of animal welfare, environmental pollution—which severely affects people who live near hog operations that contaminate local water supply and coastal fish habitats—and the exploitation of laborers exposed to dangerous work conditions reflect the hidden cost of industrial hog production in eastern North Carolina. In 1999 devastating floods from Hurricane Floyd polluted local water and rivers with hog waste and chemicals in many eastern counties. Climate change and the COVID pandemic have exacerbated these issues. Once food from agribusinesses is processed, much of it leaves the state for national and international markets, including China, which imports huge quantities of processed pork from North Carolina. Virginia's Smithfield Foods, the number one producer and processor of pork in the world, was acquired by Hong Kong–based WH Group in 2013. Smithfield's largest slaughterhouse is located in Tar Heel, North Carolina, and by April 2020 experienced alarming COVID-19 rates among its employees. Industrial agriculture greatly increased food production in and from North Carolina, exported it for profit, and yet distanced its citizens from the local food heritage of their grandparents. "The age of agribusiness," stated Sydney Nathans, left "little room for the independent farmer."[39]

A generation of young people in the 1970s and 1980s responded to industrial agriculture and the heavily processed American diet with small-scale farming and a vision of local, sustainable food supported by farms, food venues, new markets, and organizations across North Carolina. Inspired by the politics and activism of social justice, the environmental movement, feminism, and antiwar protest in the 1960s and 1970s, many counterculture youth turned back to the land as an alternative life choice to mainstream America. Their farms and food cooperatives drew young people into the local food movement. Dining venues with progressive politics were part of this evolving landscape. In the Triangle cities of Raleigh, Durham, and Chapel Hill, Mary Bacon and Arthur Gordon were important alternative food voices who opened the region's first vegetarian restaurants.

Physician activist, community organizer, and organic farmer Bill Dow (1945–2012), the "doctor of local food," believed that good food was the key to good health.[40] After helping organize southern rural health clinics through the Student Health Coalition at Vanderbilt University in the late 1960s, Dow's activism shifted to nutrition, and he mobilized farmers' markets to increase public access to healthy local food. This work brought him to North Carolina, where in 1977 Dow, Laurie Heise, and students in public health at UNC–Chapel Hill formed the North Carolina Agricultural Marketing Project, which organized a group of farmers to start a market. In partnership with the town of Carrboro, the Carrboro Farmers' Market evolved from the late 1970s to become the heart of downtown Carrboro. Vendors were required to reside and produce their goods within fifty miles of Carrboro, and the market was distinctive for being "farmer owned, farmer run, and farmer controlled."[41] At Ayrshire Farm in Chatham County, Dow and his partner, Daryl Walker, became the first certified organic farm in North Carolina.

Charlie Thompson, a scholar of food politics and a former small farmer in Chatham County, writes about the long mid-twentieth-century exodus of farmers he knew on his family farm in rural southwestern Virginia and later witnessed in the North Carolina Piedmont in the 1970s and early 1980s. At the same time, he and his wife, Hope, and a cadre of like-minded young people believed that growing local food sustainably and selling it directly to customers and chefs would build a vibrant and deeply connected community. It did, but the people they served at the Carrboro Farmers' Market were not the diverse community they had envisioned. Their customers were from a university community willing and able to pay higher prices for high-quality food, comfortable in the predominantly white setting of the farmers' market. Despite the region's growing reputation for its excellent restaurants, chefs, and vibrant food economy, low- and moderate-income people of color as well as the white middle class had little access to these food venues. (Today Farmer Foodshare collects farm produce for families in need, who can also use federal nutrition assistance benefits at the market, but access remains difficult and unrealistic for most.)

Tobacco transition farmers like the Brinkley family (Creedmoor) and century farms such as Lyon (also in Creedmoor), McAdams (Efland), and Pine Knot (Hurdle Mills) were critical to a new market like Carrboro.

Organic tobacco and vegetable growers Stanley Hughes and Linda Leach of Pine Knot Farms were one of the market's only multigenerational Black farms. Some tobacco farmers grew organic tobacco because it brought a better price, selling their crop to Santa Fe Natural Tobacco Company in Oxford, North Carolina. Newly formed Eastern Carolina Organics (now Happy Dirt) and the Carolina Farm Stewardship Association (CFSA) encouraged those farmers to also grow organic vegetables.

The Carolina Farm Stewardship Association, founded in 1979 in Pittsboro, was one of the earliest sustainable agriculture organizations in the Southeast. It created a coalition of farmers, consumers, and businesses to build a healthy food future based on local organic farming. Food activist, educator, and organic farmer Tony Kleese (1964–2018) was a former executive director of CFSA and a leader in launching the Sustainable Farming Program at Central Carolina Community College in 1996. Kleese also helped develop the USDA's National Organic Standards in the 1990s. Since 2007, Roland McReynolds has served as CFSA's executive director, oversees their annual Sustainable Agriculture Conference—in operation for over thirty-five years—and their Piedmont Farm Tour, and is a vocal advocate for policy that supports sustainable agriculture at the state and federal levels. In 1977, the Livestock Conservancy was created to protect endangered livestock and poultry breeds from extinction. Headquartered in Pittsboro, it is the leading U.S. organization that conserves heritage breeds for future generations.

In the late 1990s, the Golden LEAF Foundation distributed funds from the tobacco settlement to support sustainable agriculture projects in rural North Carolina. Charlie Jackson of the Appalachian Sustainable Agriculture Project (ASAP) stresses that "the local food movement in North Carolina was jump-started and would not be where it is today if not for the tobacco settlement and the creation of the funds administered by Golden LEAF and the North Carolina Tobacco Trust."[42]

In 1994, agricultural commissioner Jim Graham, NC State University dean Durwood Bateman, and North Carolina A&T dean Daniel Godfrey Sr. endorsed the founding of the Center for Environmental Farming Services (CEFS) to support environmentally sound and socially responsible agriculture. This important partnership between NC State, NC A&T, and the North Carolina Department of Agriculture provided long-term field-scale research and experimentation on organic, sustainable crops and integrated extension and academic programming as an integral aspect of research. Over the years, the W. K. Kellogg Foundation, Blue Cross Blue Shield of North Carolina Foundation, Golden LEAF Foundation, and USDA Sustainable Agriculture Research and Education (SARE) program funded significant initiatives across the state dedicated to building sustainable food systems. Today CEFS is one of the country's most important sustainable food and farming programs and was led by founding director Nancy Creamer for over twenty-five years until her recent retirement. "The biggest challenge," says Creamer, is "how do you have affordable food without furthering consolidation in agriculture and driving more and more farmers further from the land?"[43]

In Asheville, the Appalachian Sustainable Agriculture Project was organized in the mid-1990s to reverse farm loss in western North Carolina and to help small farmers transition away from tobacco. North Carolina native Charlie Jackson was a founding farmer and the first executive director of ASAP. (Upon his retirement in 2022, Molly Nicholie became ASAP's new executive director.) While in graduate school in Maine, Jackson wrote about the back-to-the-land movement and Helen and Scott Nearing, whose book, *Living the Good Life* (1954), became a manifesto for homesteading—living simply and sustainably—as a path to social change and economic justice. ASAP published the region's first "Local Food Guide" and has organized the Asheville City Market, area farm tours, farmer training programs, and a local food certification program, "Appalachian Grown." Early funding from Golden LEAF Foundation allowed ASAP to build a local food economy with the region's small-scale farmers and retailers. ASAP's "Growing Minds Farm to School" program was one of the first in the country and remains an important leader in the National Farm to School Network, a grantee of the W. K. Kellogg Foundation. These programs strengthen local food sourcing for school food programs, promote working gardens on school campuses, and integrate food and agriculture education into the curriculum. A 2018 ASAP study that focused on western North Carolina concluded, "While local food has not replaced tobacco as a means of livelihood for the farmers of the region, it has emerged as a significant new direction for agriculture."[44]

"We were on the back end of the back-to-the-land movement."

—ALEX HITT, Peregrine Farm, Graham, North Carolina, January 30, 2019

In the early 1990s, farmers Alex and Betsy Hitt of Peregrine Farm in Alamance County formed a working partnership and lifelong friendship with chef and baker Ben and Karen Barker of Magnolia Grill restaurant in Durham. "Organic" was still a little-known word at the time, as was the meaning of local food. Alex Hitt explains, "We wanted to do the most environmentally sound job we could do growing local food for local people."[45] The Hitts were early leaders at the Carrboro Farmers' Market, and the Barkers were loyal chef customers. "We were picking and selling to wine and cheese stores and tried knocking on the door of restaurants," says Hitt. "Ben and Karen and Bill Smith were at La Res[idence]. We knocked on the door and Karen was there, smiling, making desserts. She said, 'Yes, I'll buy blackberries from you!'"[46] Their relationship represents the strong farmer/chef symbiosis that was crucial to the birth of New Southern cuisine, a regional expression of the nascent farm-to-table movement launched by Alice Waters in California in the 1970s and in the American South through the seminal voices of chef-writer Edna Lewis, Frank Stitt in Alabama, and Bill and Moreton Neal in North Carolina. Chef Scott Howell, who opened Nana's in Durham in 1992, states, "North Carolina was ready to start happening. It just needed a little push."[47] In 1990 and 1991, Sammy and Melinda Koenigsberg created New Town Farms, a small organic farm in Waxhaw, outside of Charlotte, with a community-supported agriculture (CSA) seasonal subscription program. Sammy was a cofounder of the nearby Matthews Community Farmers' Market, now a much-loved institution in the local food and farming scene. "A Barker at the table was the only chef who made me cry," remarks Koenigsberg, "and Alex Hitt was my farmer inspiration."[48] Chef Gabe Barker of Pizzeria Mercado in Carrboro says of his parents' award-winning restaurant, "I see snapshots in my head of dishes from the Grill, and I remember what they taste like. I remember the fried oysters with butter bean salad like it was yesterday."[49]

The presence and proliferation of so many award-winning restaurants in Durham, Chapel Hill, Carrboro, Hillsborough, and Raleigh today—passionately committed to local food—is grounded in this earlier generation of chefs, farmers, writers, and entrepreneurs, who experienced rapidly changing city and townscapes. As tobacco declined, Durham's growth shifted to white suburbs and suburban shopping centers as retail businesses left downtown. In the 1950s, urban renewal—racially targeted municipal programs put in place to remove urban poverty—destroyed many of Durham's historic Black neighborhoods and their food scene, while new downtown traffic patterns, expressways, demolition, and construction obliterated street life. Redevelopment initiatives in the 1980s and 1990s slowly brought urban Durham back to life but dramatically changed the city's residents. The new economy downtown was split between a workforce of high-wage earners in research and technology and low-paid employees in service jobs.[50]

In 1981, Lex and Ann Alexander opened Wellspring Grocery in Durham, modeled after a European-style greengrocer–natural food grocery that featured seasonal, locally grown produce. Flo Hawley and Portia McKnight were important early team members at Wellspring and later created Chapel Hill Creamery, known for its award-winning artisanal cheeses and whey-fed pork. Sheila Dalton Neal, longtime food leader, first full-time manager of the Carrboro Farmers' Market, and owner of

Neal's Deli in Carrboro, describes the food community's intricate networks in this era as connected by "six degrees of separation through Wellspring."[51] Veteran alumni of Magnolia Grill, Billy and Kelli Cotter opened Toast, an Italian-style sandwich shop, in downtown Durham in 2008, just months before the global financial crisis. Kelli says, "We were not going to be in a shopping center. We weren't going to be in a mall. We were going to be downtown proper. We believed in it and believed it would come back." Billy responds, "We got lucky. It did."[52]

In Carrboro, Weaver Street Market, a community-owned cooperative grocery store, opened in 1988, focused on local, sustainably produced products. Durham-based Counter Culture, one of the state's first independent coffee roasters, launched in 1995. Little Waves Coffee Roasters—the coffee-roasting and wholesale arm of Cocoa Cinnamon, a trio of "Latina-owned, women-forward" coffee shops in Durham—was founded by Areli Barrera Grodski and Leon Grodski Barrera in 2017. A North Carolina–sponsored chapter of SlowFood—a global initiative to preserve local food cultures—was launched in the late 1990s by NC State University professor David Auerbach. The Durham Farmers' Market got its start in 1999 when several farmers met in the parking lot of the Durham Bulls stadium. In the early 2000s, Eliza MacLean became known in the state and the region for her innovative work in sustainable small-scale, pasture-raised pork, beginning with a herd of Ossabaw Island hogs. In 2004, the Asheville Bread Festival was organized, the first of its kind in the Southeast. This same era is noteworthy for the rise of local cheesemakers across the state, such as Boxcarr Handmade Cheese (Cedar Grove), Celebrity Dairy (Siler City), and Looking Glass Creamery (Fairview and Columbus). Several are located on farms that once grew tobacco.

Many of the leading grain farmers, millers, and bakers who are part of a larger grain renaissance in the contemporary South live and work in North Carolina. The state's milling history stretches from eighteenth-century gristmills like Lindley Mills in the Piedmont to the 2009 North Carolina Organic Bread Flour Project, an initiative of the Carolina Farm Stewardship Association and Jennifer Lapidus's Carolina Ground (2012), an Asheville milling facility that provides bakers across the region with southern flours, including organic grains grown in North Carolina milled using the cold stone method. In *Southern Ground* (2021), Lapidus's seminal book on southern grains, growers, and bakers, she writes, "It is through breads and pastries made with that flour that bakeries are making an economic and social impact on their communities. And it is through flavor and story that they engage their customers in reclaiming this fundamental piece of a sustainable food system."[53] Dave Bauer began his innovative western North Carolina baking and milling project, Farm and Sparrow, in 2006. At Old World Levain (OWL) Bakery in west Asheville, founder Susannah Gebhart describes a loaf prepared with Carolina Gold rice porridge, Farm and Sparrow's Turkey Red wheat flour, local miso, and apples: "It's a taste of North Carolina, mountains to sea." [54]

Innovative statewide and regional food aggregation initiatives have been critical to building North Carolina's local food economy and reflect the strength and skill of women's leadership. Happy Dirt, formerly ECO, or Eastern Carolina Organics, markets and distributes wholesale organic farm produce to retailers and restaurants in both the Carolinas and the Northeast. Founder and CEO Sandi Kronick explains, "When we started ECO back in 2004, we had a very simple purpose, which was to make it more convenient for wholesale buyers, restaurants, and grocery stores to get North Carolina organic produce into their institution. We had *no* competition—and we had *no* experience."[55] ECO was initially fostered by the Carolina Farm Stewardship Association.

Sarah Blacklin directs NC Choices (2002), an initiative of CEFS in collaboration with NC Cooperative Extension, to market and advance the local pasture-based meat supply in North Carolina. "We work across the supply chain to help get more pasture-raised meats into the marketplace—farmers, the distributor, the processor, the packer, the regulatory agency," explains Blacklin. "The more efficient that is, the more we have affordable and, hopefully, animal welfare–friendly, pasture-raised meat on the table."[56] Firsthand Foods (2010), a women-owned, Durham-based food hub that sells local meats from North Carolina farms, was incubated and launched by NC Choices. It is directed by cofounders and co-CEOs Jennifer Curtis and Tina Prevatte Levy. On the tenth anniversary of Firsthand Foods in 2020, Levy said, "We wanted to connect the dots between food producers and consumers in the uniquely challenging world of locally and humanely raised meats. And we set out to do so in a way that would be a means of rural economic development, environmental stewardship, and consumer education."[57] Jennifer Curtis remembers, "I found it thrilling when I moved here—farmer's markets, small farms, the seasonality, the ability to grow food year-round, to have both livestock and crops—the diversity from the coast to the mountains is pretty rich."[58] The first Carolina Meat Conference in 2011, organized by NC Choices and CEFS, began to rebuild the critical infrastructure of the battered local meat supply chain, bringing together farmers, chefs, butchers, and industry leaders for hands-on training and networking, including a groundbreaking "Women in Meat" initiative.

Farm to Fork: A Guide to Building North Carolina's Sustainable Food Economy, a comprehensive guide to statewide action written by

Jennifer Curtis with Nancy Creamer and Tessa Eliza Thraves, was published by CEFS in 2010 after convening more than a thousand stakeholders in the state who met over two years to discuss strategies to transform North Carolina's food systems. Many of the proposals in the study are now part of North Carolina's local food landscape, including the creation of a statewide network of county food councils—facilitated by CEFS's Community Food Strategies team—and the "Eat 10% Local Sustainable Food Campaign," an initiative of CEFS and NC Cooperative Extension that encourages consumers and businesses to spend 10 percent of their food dollars on locally produced foods. In 2019, a planning process was initiated by Community Food Strategies and CEFS to craft a new North Carolina Food Action Plan to address systemic food inequities across the state and to create local food economies that are community driven, sustainable, and resilient.

At UNC–Chapel Hill, Alice Ammerman, the Mildred Kaufman Distinguished Professor in the Department of Nutrition, focuses on the connection between local food and health. Working with her current and former students in public health, Ammerman has advanced many of the state's most effective programs to build a sustainable food system, along with mentoring its leaders. Her work crosses the boundaries of classroom, kitchen, and farmers' market, as seen in Good Bowls, frozen entrée grain bowls prepared simply with locally sourced ingredients, such as sweet potatoes, greens, peppers, and North Carolina eggs and grits. Recipes are based on the Med South diet—dishes blending Mediterranean-inspired nutrition with core ingredients of southern foodways, such as collard greens. This heat-and-eat meal, created in 2018, provides a tasty, healthy, affordable meal option for lower-income consumers and offers another market opportunity for local farmers and their food products.

Food studies and the interest in North Carolina foodways in particular is increasingly important at university and college campuses across the state, thanks to passionate faculty and activist students and the vibrant voice of journals like *Southern Culture* and food-focused series and scholarship from UNC Press. Appalachian State University in Boone, Warren Wilson College in Swannanoa, and Central Carolina Community College (CCCC) offer excellent programs in sustainable agriculture and agroecology, and students participate in teaching and research farms associated with many of these programs.

In 2012, chef Kris Reid and her colleagues founded the Piedmont Culinary Guild in the Charlotte metro region, a unique platform to connect chefs, restaurateurs, farmers, food entrepreneurs, craft beverage makers, educators, and other food professionals within the Piedmont of North and South Carolina. Reid recognizes the unique flavor profile of produce grown in the region—from carrots to Cherokee purple tomatoes—long ignored because of commodity crops like tobacco and corn. She argues, "There is such integrity to our food. The minerality of our soil. Our terroir, our microclimate. Our small farms. We are a strong food *landscape* rather than a food 'scene.' When we solely talk about a plate of food, we're missing 90 percent of the story. We're writing the history for food right now in the southeast in the Piedmont."[59]

In 2015, Zack Wyatt created the Carolina Farm Trust, which manages a network of small urban farms in the Charlotte metro region dedicated to strengthening the food system for neighborhoods that have long experienced food insecurity due to racism and redlining practices of the 1950s and 1960s. In Chapel Hill, Colleen Minton organized the first TerraVita food and beverage festival in 2009 to celebrate and educate the public about the regional culinary landscape. For over ten years, the highly successful event included an "East Meets West" dinner that brought North Carolina chefs from different regions of the state together to prepare a single meal shaped by their sense of place and story. In 2014, Durham chef and caterer Jacob Boehm founded Snap Pea, a pop-up dining experience featuring storied meals using local North Carolina ingredients.

In 2016, Max Trujillo and Matthew Weiss launched their Raleigh-based *North Carolina Food & Beverage Podcast*, which explores the contemporary food and beverage industry in the state, as well as the stories and history of North Carolina's diverse food cultures and experiences. Drawing on their extensive work experience in restaurants and wine service from New York to California, their interviews provide a compelling portrait of the state's working food landscape and its community.

A significant facet of North Carolina's contemporary food movement is its diverse craft beverage scene, which includes breweries, distilleries, cideries, and wineries, as well as beverage importers and distributors. In 1985 Uli Bennewitz lobbied North Carolina legislators to permit breweries to sell beer on site, and he opened the state's first brewpub, Weeping Radish, in Currituck County on the coast. In 2005, Sean Lilly Wilson, founder of Durham's Fullsteam Brewery, successfully led the "Pop the Cap" campaign, which in 2005 raised the legal alcohol content of beer in the state, changing a 1930s era law designed to keep mill workers' drinking in check. Wilson says, "I saw an opportunity for Durham to be a base, a hub for agriculture in a post-tobacco North Carolina."[60] Oscar Wong opened Highland Brewing Company in Asheville in 1994, and in 2015, his accomplished daughter Leah Wong Ashburn became president and is now CEO of the brewery. Owner Inez

Ribustello speaks of the democratizing power of breweries like Tarboro Brewing Company, where a diverse and sometimes divided community can enjoy a beer or a soft drink with an inexpensive snack from a food truck.[61] Today North Carolina is a leader in the southern beer economy with more than 300 breweries. On I-70 alone, Matt Hart of Kinston's Mother Earth Brewery—and craft spirits, too—describes the brewery corridor that stretches from Raleigh east to the coast.

Since the early 2000s, North Carolina wineries have grown in number and style, expanding from beloved native grape varieties such as scuppernongs and muscadines to designated American Viticultural Areas in the state where European grape varietals are grown. In the summer of 2020, despite the pandemic, Clara and Preston Williams Jr. and their three sons opened Seven Springs Farms and Vineyard in Warren County, transforming land where soybeans had grown into acres of muscadine vines. Their Black-owned vineyard, farm, and event venue represents a historic shift in the local ag and food economy of Black entrepreneurship and economic development. Wine entrepreneur Jay Murrie envisioned a market in North Carolina for natural and sustainable beverages and turned to wine crafted on family farms in the Italian Piedmont, where the slow-cooked, meat-rich dishes and polenta resonate with the Carolina Piedmont's barbecue, greens, and grits. The craft liquor movement in North Carolina emerged after the post-2008 economic crash as entrepreneurs sought new business opportunities. Distillers can now sell gin, vodka, whiskey, and moonshine in tasting rooms.[62] Despite North Carolina's long history of illegal liquor, today state-run ABC stores offer an impressive selection of locally crafted spirits.

North Carolina has been transformed by the labor, vision, and creativity of a new generation of immigrants, and nowhere is this more visible than in the state's contemporary food economy. Asian, Latinx, and immigrants from India and South Asia increasingly came to North Carolina following the 1965 passage of legislation that altered immigration quotas in America. The 2020 U.S. census reveals marked growth in these communities, particularly in North Carolina's urban areas. We see and taste their influence in every part of the state's local food systems, from growing and harvesting food in the large industrial farms of eastern North Carolina and apple orchards in the mountains, to the line cooks, restaurateurs, and chefs in the region's best restaurants, to immigrant-owned food markets in virtually every town across the state. Just outside of Chapel Hill, refugee farmers, originally from Burma, grow and market Southeast Asian vegetables on an eight-acre educational farm called Transplanting Traditions Community Farm.

Executive Director Kelly Owensby says, "Despite the distances traveled and the cultures traversed, our farmers have rebuilt their farm businesses as well as their lives here in North Carolina."[63] East of Asheville, at Lee's One Fortune Farm, Tou and Chue Lee—Hmong farmers who immigrated from Laos—grow several varieties of heirloom rice and Southeast Asian vegetables and fruits that they sell at area farmers' markets.[64] In Raleigh, members of Highland United Methodist Church established a Community Victory Garden on the church property in 2010 after realizing there was a greater use for their land than expanding the parking lot. Church members created a vibrant and extensive food resource enjoyed by new immigrants, volunteers, and people in need in the community. It has become a model for community gardens with its emphasis on health, social justice, and creating a place of refuge for all.

Second- and third-generation immigrant North Carolinians are now food entrepreneurs, journalists, policy makers, scholars, and strong stakeholders in their communities. They are consumers and investors. Even before the coronavirus pandemic upended the state's food economy—affecting the lives of meat and poultry processing plant workers and forcing chefs to shutter restaurants—immigrant North Carolinians struggled for economic equity, access, and opportunity. Progressive activist and chef Vimala Rajendran found fruits and vegetables not unlike those of her native Mumbai in the peanuts, sweet potatoes, okra, eggplant, tomatoes, and cauliflower of the Piedmont. "Coming to Carrboro," says Rajendran, "it just felt more like home."[65] Rajendran's ardent stance that food is an essential human right lies at the core of her Chapel Hill restaurant, where all are served regardless of their ability to pay.

Carrboro and Chapel Hill mirror the polarization of America's food economy: the big ag supply chain that controls most food bought by institutional purchasers such as corporate grocery chains, discount warehouses, hospitals, governments, universities, and schools and the curated food relationship among small farmers, food entrepreneurs, and well-to-do white consumers in high-end markets. Chef Andrea Reusing in Chapel Hill points to fault lines in these food systems: "The components of this inequality—racism, lack of access to capital, exploitation, land loss, nutritional and health disparities in communities of color—are tightly connected. Our nearly twenty-year obsession with food and chefs has neither expanded access to high-quality food nor improved nutrition in low-resource neighborhoods."[66] Food insecurity is growing in suburban Durham, Charlotte, and Raleigh. Yet, during these same twenty years, a corps of North Carolina food activists—farmers, extension agents, restaurateurs, chefs, scholars, public health experts, fisheries professionals, food bank managers, food hub coordinators, food aggregators, and food council leaders—have built a strong local food network. Alex Hitt observes how the customer base of local farmers' markets is shifting, too: "In Carrboro, it flipped from fifty and older to fifty and younger. It's families with kids now, and it happened over the last ten years."[67]

Although the next generation of North Carolina's food leaders face significant challenges from skyrocketing land prices to climate change, they are ably taking the reins of North Carolina's food movement. In 2018 Moses Ochola, Crystal Taylor, and Ja'Nell Henry organized the Black Farmers' Market, which alternates bimonthly between Durham and Raleigh. The market promotes Black farmers and Black-owned food businesses and also fosters a welcoming space for the Black community with projects like Tall Grass Food Box, a Durham-based CSA sourced from Black farmers in the Piedmont. Gabrielle E. W. Carter, Derrick Beasley, and Gerald Harris created the twice-monthly subscription box that brings seasonal vegetables, fruits, and eggs direct to members' homes. In Northampton County, Julius Tillery is the fifth generation in his family to grow cotton, as well as soybeans, timber, and fresh produce, on their land in northeastern North Carolina. A UNC–Chapel Hill economics alumnus, Tillery founded Black Cotton, which markets and sells his cotton direct to consumers as home goods and clothing. Tillery describes Black families who remain "land rich and cash poor."[68] He focuses on reinvigorating Black health through access to locally grown seasonal produce at the Garysburg Town Center Farmers' Market and helps Black farmers better monetize their farm resources.

In 2016 Kamal Bell, a farmer, former middle-school teacher, and doctoral student in agricultural and extension education at NC State University, founded Sankofa Farms near Efland in Orange County. Sankofa addresses food insecurity and racial inequity through sustainably farmed greens, beehives, and an agricultural academy for Black youth that reaffirms the cultural history of Black southerners tied to the land and the empowerment that lies in that connection. Bell is featured in Natalie Baszile's anthology *We Are Each Other's Harvest* (Amistad, 2021), a powerful celebration of Black farmers and Black-owned land across the country. "They call themselves 'the returning generation,'" writes Baszile, "and they are fierce and unapologetic in their quest to reclaim their legacy."[69] In Pinetops, North Carolina, at Golden Organic Farm, Kendrick Ransome farms land purchased by his great-grandfather more than a hundred years ago to raise hogs and grow vegetables. Today Ransome, in his late twenties, has a CSA and provides fresh fruits and vegetables to both the local hospital and programs for children, and he plans to develop his farm as a training ground for young Black farmers. Ransome honors the farming knowledge of his ancestors while creatively shaping a new, antiracist narrative for modern Black farmers that generates both health and wealth. His location in Edgecombe County is significant due to the region's historic presence of independent Black farmers and communities like Princeville, established by freed Blacks as "Freedom Hill" in 1885. In 2018, the Cooperative Extension program at NC A&T recognized Duplin County farmer Ronald Simmons as North Carolina's small farmer of the year for his work in pasture-raised pork at Master Blend Family Farms near Kenansville. The family also operates a general store at the farm where they sell pork and other locally grown products.

A 2020 ASAP survey revealed that of their member farmers in western North Carolina, 46 percent were women and 29 percent were new farmers who have farmed for ten years or less.[70] Yesod Farm + Kitchen, twenty-five miles outside Asheville, was cofounded by SJ Seldin with executive director Shani Mink of the Jewish Farmer Network, a national organization based in western North Carolina that provides retreat space and experiential education at the intersection of Judaism and farming. Focused on regenerative agriculture, they steward sixteen acres of land whose deep history lies in the Catawba and Cherokee people who once lived here.

Dallas Robinson moved back home to farm family-owned land in Whitakers, North Carolina, in 2019. She named it the Harriet Tubman Freedom Farm. After studying the destructive history of America's globalized food system at Vassar College and apprenticing in a farm immersion program at Soul Fire Farm in New York State, Robinson turned to sustainable small-scale farming as a response to racial trauma and disparity. She grows vegetables for a CSA and sells sorghum to local breweries and plans to transition to a cooperative-run farm. Black liberation and Indigenous sovereignty are at the heart of her work. In Wake County at Oliver's AgroForest, Olivia Watkins grows organic shiitake mushrooms on land that her ancestors purchased and farmed in the 1890s. She plans to raise bees and grow produce and flowers. A Barnard College alumna with an MBA from NC State University, Watkins is the fifth generation of her North Carolina family to steward this land. Her focus lies in food sovereignty, community, and forest conservation. Watkins is cofounder and president of the Black Farmer Fund.

Vera Fabian and Gordon Jenkins started to grow organic vegetables intensively on their small Piedmont farm, Ten Mothers Farm, in 2015 with hoop houses, no tilling, and no tractor. Gordon grew up on the West Coast, and Vera is a native North Carolinian. They trained with some of the country's best farmers and leaders of the local food movement, including restaurateur and chef-activist Alice Waters of Chez Panisse in Berkeley, California, small-scale, sustainable farmers Elliot Coleman and Barbara Damrosch in Harborside, Maine, and two of the founding farmers of the Carrboro Farmers' Market, Ken Dawson and Libby Outlaw in Cedar Grove, North Carolina. "In the young farm scene these days, there are more and more of us," says Fabian, who is in her early thirties. "Our customers are part of the local food movement; they're choosing to be part of our farm. They might do it because of health or because they know that the vegetables taste better, but there's something bigger than just us that they want to be part of. People are hungry for a different life."[71]

Finding Our Way Back to North Carolina Food—A Journey from the Coast to the Mountains

Edible North Carolina reveals the people and places of North Carolina's contemporary food movement—an intersection of culinary excellence, creative entrepreneurship, changing populations, historic yet evolving foodways, the struggle for racial justice and equity, and a commitment to protect and sustain food resources for generations to come. This collection is written by journalists, farmers, chefs, entrepreneurs, scholars, and food activists. Its photographs are the work of photographer Baxter Miller, whose family roots are in Hatteras, and her partner and collaborator, Ryan Stancil, a native of eastern North Carolina. Together they have documented the state's diverse foodways, landscapes, and cultures. If North Carolina has a contemporary spokesperson for food and place, Chef Vivian Howard is it. Her voice opens this volume with a foreword that is grounded in the rural eastern North Carolina worlds of her youth. When she returned to North Carolina after cooking professionally in New York City, Howard began to cook and eat the iconic foods of her home place again. She realized, "I could speak its language—in fact, it was my native tongue."[72]

In coastal North Carolina, a passionate duo brings us to the heart of the state's seafood economy—Karen Willis Amspacher, director of the Core Sound Waterfowl Museum and Heritage Center in Harkers Island, and New Bern native Ricky Moore, chef-owner of Saltbox Seafood Joint in Durham. Moore's daily fish offerings are *so* local, a chalkboard rather than a printed menu lists the day's freshest, seasonal offerings from the North Carolina coast. Amspacher, an eighth-generation [Outer] Banker, argues that North Carolinians should appreciate local fish from the coast as their rightful inheritance.

Moving from the coast to the coastal plain of eastern North Carolina, Shorlette Ammons, an extension associate at NC State University's

Center for Environmental Farming Systems, reflects on her experiences as a Black Country woman from rural North Carolina and how her home place, its people, and the region's history forged her relationship to food and farming. Eastern Carolina is the epicenter of industrial hog production. No southern state has more passionate pig-related activists, educators, small farm policy advisers, farmers, butchers, pit masters, and wholesalers. The current generation of leading barbecue makers who consciously choose pasture-raised pork for their venues from Ayden to Asheville are profiled here by journalist Andrea Weigl, who has written extensively on pork in North Carolina. Robeson County, on the southern border of the eastern coastal plain, is the ancestral home of the Lumbee Tribe in North Carolina. Historian Malinda Maynor Lowery argues that southern foodways *are* Indigenous foodways and explores the meaning and lived memory of Lumbee food in her own extended North Carolina family.

In the North Carolina Piedmont, food entrepreneur, writer, and activist April McGreger reflects on eleven years of operating her award-winning small batch preserves and pickling business and the farmers and producers who became her community and loyal customers. She asks hard questions about how dreams for a sustainable food market system have fallen short, and what must change. Chef Bill Smith, formerly of Crook's Corner in Chapel Hill, which closed in 2021, tells a powerful story from this iconic venue in the region's farm-to-table movement. Bill explores his experience with Mexican immigration in North Carolina and how a corps of young Latinx men became critically important workers in North Carolina's restaurants beginning in the late 1980s. Their presence shaped the flavor and foundations of North Carolina cuisine, resulting in what writer Sandra Gutierrez describes as the New Southern Latino culinary movement as it unfolded around her, a young Latina journalist, wife, and mother living in largely white, suburban Cary, North Carolina, in the early 1990s.

Journalist Victoria Bouloubasis introduces a new generation of Triangle-area first-generation American immigrant chefs and food entrepreneurs who complicate the stereotypes of back-of-house cooks and ethnic restaurateurs. These individuals—many who grew up as restaurant kids in North Carolina—built landmark, sophisticated food venues in their communities while confronting fraught immigration policies that threaten their families' livelihoods and their dedicated team members. Chef Andrea Reusing blends Asian flavors and North Carolina ingredients in her touted Chapel Hill restaurant, Lantern, but she is also known for her work on food policy and her activism in the North Carolina sustainable food movement. Reusing discusses the unfulfilled promise of the local food economy, and she envisions a more just food landscape for all North Carolinians. With her blended roots in India, New York City, and North Carolina, chef and musician Cheetie Kumar is the creative power behind Garland, Neptunes Parlour, and Kings, three groundbreaking venues for food, cocktail culture, and music in downtown Raleigh. Reflecting on the COVID-19 crisis that began in March 2020, Kumar considers the fate and future of independent restaurants in North Carolina.

Folklorist Katy Clune, a scholar and documentarian of Laotian food cultures, straddles the state as she examines the growing number of Laotian food and farming entrepreneurs in the Triangle metro region and in the foothills of the Blue Ridge in Morganton. Historian Michelle T. King, a historian of modern China, considers China in North Carolina as she and her students explore Chinese restaurants across the state. Though these institutions are familiar to loyal diners, little is known about the complex cultural and food history, the stories of immigration, and the creative entrepreneurship they embody. In the northeastern Piedmont, Carla Norwood and Gabe Cumming, founders of Working Landscapes, a rural development organization in Warrenton, show that even when the state's food system appears abundant and full of promise, in rural, economically distressed Warren County, the view is different. They propose to fundamentally change the ways food reaches *everyone* in our state.

Two veteran Charlotteans, historian Tom Hanchett and journalist Kathleen Purvis, carry us to the evolving food landscapes of North Carolina's largest city. Fascinated by the evolution of Charlotte as a New South urban center, Hanchett goes to the city's Central Avenue corridor to meet several immigrant food entrepreneurs in their popular markets, cafés, and bakeries. Practically mini-embassies of their countries of origin—Mexico, Columbia, Bosnia, Israel, Ethiopia, and Vietnam—these businesses reflect Charlotte's most recent immigration wave from the late 1990s to the present. Purvis examines the manufacturing base of Charlotte's development and how it shaped the food scene, including the impact of African Americans and Greek immigrants. Pie entrepreneur and writer Keia Mastrianni recounts the circuitous path of creating a small "forever farm" with her husband, chef turned farmer Jamie Swofford, in Shelby, about forty miles from Charlotte. Mastrianni offers a powerful take on how food and food media impact community and why the area's rural food economy became her chosen path.

In western North Carolina, Appalachian foodways writer Ronni Lundy tells a compelling story of Asheville through the voices of people who have built one of the state's most significant local food landscapes over the past twenty years. In this story competing forces—tourism, development, sustainable agriculture, and culinary entrepreneurship—loom large. Anthropologist Courtney Lewis examines the contemporary reclamation of native foodways among the Eastern Band of Cherokee Indians in the Qualla Boundary. Their development of hybrid chestnut trees, garden and farming initiatives, and value-added food products reflect the sustainable and sovereign Indigenous food systems that Lewis describes. The final essay—a photographic portrait by Baxter Miller and historian and baker Maia Surdam—travels to the food-related work of six contemporary makers and creators in western North Carolina. Their work, vision, and creativity are part of the current generation of farmers, bakers, brewers, cheesemakers, chefs, craftspeople, distillers, grocers, and millers who are creating the region's local food economy.

Food illuminates a world of daily ritual, want, and connection in North Carolina, one in which we all participate, perhaps even unconsciously. The bedrock of our foodways—what people eat, when, where, why, how, and with whom—is the taste of place. Eating is never as simple as we might imagine, and these voices offer a corrective. The food-focused conversations that follow reveal new ways of understanding and addressing the social, economic, and political challenges that North Carolinians encounter each day. These writers also show us how taste, story, soil, and regional waters are integrated in the state's distinctive foods and define the essence of its cuisine. Given North Carolina's geographic diversity, which reaches from the barrier islands of the Outer Banks to the Appalachian Mountains, and the state's historical breadth from the earliest Native American communities to recently arrived families, no state is better positioned to present the complex story of race, identity, migration, culture, place, food, and flavor in the United States.

NOTES

1. Editorial board, "A Startling Report on the 2020 Vote Shows a Stark Divide in North Carolina," *News and Observer* (Charlotte), November 19, 2020.

2. Jennifer Curtis et al., *From Farm to Fork: A Guide to Building North Carolina's Sustainable Local Food Economy* (Raleigh, N.C.: Center for Environmental Farming Systems, April 2010), 10.

3. Kelly Alexander, interview by Marcie Cohen Ferris, September 6, 2019.

4. Martha Quillen, "Small Farms, Big Ideas: NC Has a New Crop of Farmers Willing to Try Something Different," *News and Observer* (Charlotte), July 13, 2019.

5. Joe A. Mobley, ed., *The Way We Lived in North Carolina* (Chapel Hill: University of North Carolina Press, 2003), 3.

6. H. Trawick Ward and R. P. Stephen Davis Jr., *Time before History: The*

Archaeology of North Carolina (Chapel Hill: University of North Carolina Press, 1999), 2.

7. Rachel Briggs, "The Hominy Foodway of the Historic Native Eastern Woodlands," *Native South* 8 (2015): 112.

8. Amber M. VanDerwarker, C. Margaret Scarry, and Jane M. Eastman, "Menus for Families and Feasts: Household and Community Consumption of Plants at Upper Saratown, North Carolina," in *The Archaeology of Food and Identity*, ed. K. Twiss (Carbondale: Center for Archaeological Investigations, Southern Illinois University, Carbondale, 2007), 16–49.

9. Charles Mann, "Jamestown: The Real Story," *National Geographic*, May 2007.

10. John Shelton Reed and Dale Volberg Reed with William McKinney, *Holy Smoke: The Big Book of North Carolina Barbecue* (Chapel Hill: University of North Carolina Press, 2008), 35–37.

11. David R. Goldfield, "History," in *The North Carolina Atlas: Portrait for a New Century*, ed. Douglas M. Orr Jr. and Alfred W. Stuart (Chapel Hill: University of North Carolina Press, 2000), 56.

12. Kathy Carter, "Outer Banks," *Encyclopedia of North Carolina* (Chapel Hill: University of North Carolina Press, 2006), www.ncpedia.org/fishing-commercial.

13. David Stick, *The Outer Banks of North Carolina, 1584–1958* (Chapel Hill: University of North Carolina Press, 1958), 212–13.

14. Barbara Garrity-Blake and Karen Willis Amspacher, *Living at the Water's Edge: A Heritage Guide to the Outer Banks Byway* (Chapel Hill: University of North Carolina Press, 2017), 47–52.

15. Laura Kirby, Charlie Jackson, and Allison Perrett, "A Brief History of Farming in the Region," in *Growing Local: Expanding the Western North Carolina Food and Farming Economy* (Asheville, N.C.: Appalachian Sustainable Agriculture Project, 2007), 10.

16. Sheri Castle, conversation with Marcie Cohen Ferris, June 18, 2020.

17. Ronni Lundy and Sheri Castle, conversation with Marcie Cohen Ferris, June 18, 2020.

18. Kirby, Jackson, and Perrett, "Brief History of Farming."

19. Mobley, *Way We Lived*, 136.

20. "Matthew Nowicki," *North Carolina Architects and Builders: A Biographical Dictionary*, https://ncarchitects.lib.ncsu.edu/people/P000044.

21. Jacquelyn Dowd Hall et al., *Like a Family: The Making of a Southern Cotton Mill World* (Chapel Hill: University of North Carolina Press, 1987), 6.

22. Milton Ready, *The Tar Heel State: A History of North Carolina* (Columbia: University of South Carolina Press, 2005), 287.

23. Caleb Crain, "What a White-Supremacist Coup Looks Like," *New Yorker*, April 27, 2020.

24. Nikole Hannah-Jones, "What Is Owed," *New York Times Magazine*, June 26, 2020.

25. Sydney Nathans, "The Quest for Progress: North Carolina, 1870–1920,"

in *The Way We Lived in North Carolina*, ed. Joe A. Mobley (Chapel Hill: University of North Carolina Press, 2003), 378.

26. Nathans, 388.

27. Mike Moore, interview by Marcie Cohen Ferris, September 11, 2019.

28. Mary Helen Montgomery, "Fish Camps: Fried Seafood and Family in a North Carolina Mill Town," Gravy Podcast, June 30, 2016, www.southernfoodways.org/gravy/fish-camps-fried-seafood-and-family-in-a-north-carolina-mill-town-gravy-ep-41/; Ava Lowery, "All Fried: Carolina Fish Camps," Southern Foodways Alliance, video, 6:46, June 27, 2017, http://avalowrey.com/all-fried-carolina-fish-camps/.

29. Glenda Gilmore, "In Search of Maudell Sleet's Garden," in "Human/Nature," special issue, *Southern Cultures* 27, no. 2 (Spring 2021): 27.

30. Jennifer Zuckerman, *Charlotte Food & Social Mobility Summit Report* (Durham, N.C.: Duke Sanford World Food Policy Center, July 2019), https://wfpc.sanford.duke.edu/reports/charlotte-food-social-mobility-summit-report-recommendations.

31. Kathleen Purvis, "Dinner Reservations: Chef Jim Noble and an Ever-Changing Charlotte," *Charlotte Magazine*, December 3, 2020.

32. Nathans, "Quest for Progress," 480.

33. Emily Wallace, "It Was There for Work: Pimento Cheese in the Carolina Piedmont" (M.A. thesis, University of North Carolina at Chapel Hill, 2010); Rachel Kirby, "Tasting the North Carolina Piedmont: Agriculture, Industry, and Economy in the Region's Foodways" (unpublished paper, University of North Carolina at Chapel Hill, May 2015).

34. Van Eure, interview by Marcie Cohen Ferris, October 10, 2019.

35. Grace Summers, interview by Marcie Cohen Ferris, October 7, 2019.

36. Charlie Jackson and Allison Perrett, *The End of Tobacco and the Rise of Local Food in Western North Carolina* (Asheville, N.C.: Local Food Research Center, ASAP, March 2018), 10, https://asapconnections.org/report/end-of-tobacco/.

37. "Savi Horne on the Land Loss Prevention Project," Farm Aid, video, 2:42, October 20, 2014, https://youtu.be/ApxNctBJpeU.

38. Charles D. Thompson Jr. *Going Over Home: A Search for Rural Justice in an Unsettled Land* (White River Junction, Vt.: Chelsea Green, 2019), 35.

39. Mobley, *Way We Lived*, 490.

40. See William W. Dow Papers #5612, Southern Historical Collection, Wilson Library, University of North Carolina at Chapel Hill. See these compelling studies of the Carrboro Farmers' Market and food landscape: Whitney E. Brown, "From Cotton Mill to Co-op: The Rise of a Local Food Culture in Carrboro, North Carolina" (M.A. thesis, University of North Carolina at Chapel Hill, 2010); and Sara Camp Arnold, "What Is a Story Worth? The Value of Narrative at the Carrboro Farmers' Market" (M.A. thesis, University of North Carolina at Chapel Hill, 2012).

41. Alex and Betsy Hitt, interview by Kate Medley, Southern Foodways Alliance, August 23, 2011.

42. Charlie Jackson, interview by Marcie Cohen Ferris, April 6, 2021.

43. Nancy Creamer, interview by Marcie Cohen Ferris, January 23, 2019.

44. Jackson and Perrett, "End of Tobacco," Summary Report.

45. Alex and Betsy Hitt, interview by Marcie Cohen Ferris, January 30, 2019.

46. Hitt interview by Ferris.

47. Scott Howell, interview by Marcie Cohen Ferris, August 9, 2019.

48. Sammy Koenigsberg, interview by Marcie Cohen Ferris, April 23, 2019.

49. Gabe Barker, interview by Marcie Cohen Ferris, July 25, 2019.

50. Melissa Norton, *Power & Benefit on the Plate: The History of Food in Durham, North Carolina* (Durham, N.C.: Duke Sanford World Food Policy Center, June 2020), 93, https://wfpc.sanford.duke.edu/reports/power-benefit-plate-history-food-durham-north-carolina.

51. Sheila Dalton Neal, interview by Marcie Cohen Ferris, March 20, 2019.

52. Kelli and Billy Cotter, interview by Marcie Cohen Ferris, August 9, 2019.

53. Jennifer Lapidus, *Southern Ground: Reclaiming Flavor through Stone-Milled Flour* (Berkeley, Calif.: Ten Speed Press, 2021), 26.

54. Caroline Sanders, "Southern Bakeries on the Rise," *Garden & Gun*, April/May 2021.

55. Sandi Kronick, interview by Marcie Cohen Ferris, February 5, 2019.

56. Sarah Blacklin, interview by Marcie Cohen Ferris, January 23, 2019.

57. Jennifer Curtis, "Co-owner, Tina Prevatte Levy, Reflects on 10 Years in Business," *Firsthand Foods*, October 21, 2020, https://firsthandfoods.com/2020/10/21/co-owner-tina-prevatte-levy-reflects-on-10-years-in-business/.

58. Jennifer Curtis, interview by Marcie Cohen Ferris, March 13, 2019.

59. Kris Reid, interview by Marcie Cohen Ferris, April 26, 2019.

60. Sean Lilly Wilson, interview by Marcie Cohen Ferris, September 9, 2019.

61. Inez Ribustello, interview by Marcie Cohen Ferris, May 6, 2019.

62. Kathleen Purvis, *Distilling the South: A Guide to Southern Craft Liquors* (Chapel Hill: University of North Carolina Press, 2018), 54.

63. Kelly Owensby, email to Marcie Cohen Ferris, December 10, 2020.

64. Adam Rosen, "Rice in Appalachia? Meet the Farmers Growing Traditional Laotian Foods in North Carolina's Hills," 100 Days in Appalachia, November 23, 2020, www.100daysinappalachia.com/2020/11/rice-in-appalachia-meet-the-farmers-growing-traditional-laotian-foods-in-north-carolinas-hills/.

65. Vimala Rajendran, interview by Marcie Cohen Ferris, April 29, 2019.

66. Andrea Reusing, "Farm-to-Table May Feel Virtuous, But It's Food Labor That's Ripe for Change," *The Salt*, NPR, July 30, 2017, www.npr.org/sections/thesalt/2017/07/30/539112692/a-chefs-plea.

67. Hitt interview by Ferris.

68. Julius Tillery, interview by Marcie Cohen Ferris, June 3, 2019.

69. Natalie Baszile, *We Are Each Other's Harvest: Celebrating African American Farmers, Land, and Legacy* (New York: Amistad, 2021), 3.

70. *Appalachian Grown™ 2019 Producer Survey Report* (Asheville, N.C.: Local Food Research Center, ASAP, June 2020), https://asapconnections.org/report/2019-appalachian-grown-producer-survey-report/.

71. Vera Fabian, interview by Marcie Cohen Ferris, April 17, 2019.

72. Vivian Howard, "Introduction," in *Deep Run Roots: Stories and Recipes from My Corner of the South* (New York: Little, Brown, 2016), 15.

KAREN AMSPACHER

Are Commercial Fishermen Not Food Providers?

The Rise of the Local Seafood Movement in North Carolina

Uncle Willie didn't think he had eaten a decent meal unless he had "something out of the sound." He was raised on Harkers Island when that was all there was to eat. And Uncle Willie was determined to keep eating what he wanted even when he married Ruby Hardison from New Bern, who knew nothing of how to catch, clean, or cook seafood when she stepped off the mailboat on Harkers Island in 1923.

Aunt Ruby did all she could to accommodate his gentle (but constant) demands, learning from the women in the neighborhood how to scale, gut, and fry fish and stir up fritters with whatever was available—clams, scallops, shrimp. In the summer she stewed conchs and stew-fried baby flounders, in the fall it was mullets every day, even the roe, and in the winter, it was oysters and corned spots salted and packed earlier in the fall.

A young Ruby Hardison came to Harkers Island to teach at the island's two-room school. She loved the island children, but from her tiny kitchen she learned the island way of life that depended on the productive waters that surrounded it. She picked, cleaned, and cooked what their tiny garden and the season provided every day, keeping Uncle Willie happy and ready to go back the next day (or night) to fish, shrimp, clam, oyster, or scallop—whatever the weather would let him do. In those days, seafood was more than something to eat; it was a way of life.

THAT'S THE WORLD I KNEW. I never thought much about it, actually. We considered a nice steak or pork barbecue extraordinary. Fresh seafood was commonplace, every day, no big deal. Sometimes you ate it because that was all there was to eat. From this abundance an industry emerged, becoming the economic mainstay of North Carolina's coastal communities. Elizabeth Howard of Ocracoke remembered in 1986, "The natives feast on the ocean's bounty—drum, crabs, mackerel, and spot.

Top, **Hardy Plyler and Pattie Johnson Plyler, Ocracoke Seafood Company, Ocracoke Island, North Carolina;** *bottom*, **Ryan Speckman and Lin Peterson, Locals Seafood, Raleigh, North Carolina;** *background*, **Spanish mackerel and pompano**

What fish they didn't eat, they salted in barrels and sold to northern markets. Or they bartered their catch with inland Hyde County for fresh vegetables."[1]

Depending on the season, fishing became shrimping, scalloping, crabbing, clamming, oystering, and conching, as well as the steady search for the base ingredient of everyone's diet—finfish. Gear of differing design and engineering provided island families with bluefish, speckled trout, hogfish, mullets, spots, and whatever the Lord provided. As the industry grew, some fishermen became fish dealers. Fish houses evolved into hubs where fishermen could sell product, tie up their boats, and repack food, ice, and fuel for the next trip. Thanks to the availability of ice and trucks, seafood could more easily move to northern markets. By the 1950s and 1960s North Carolina was a major source for the legendary Fulton Fish Market in New York City. Everyone knew you could hitch a ride to New York anytime you wanted if you were willing to ride the fish truck. Trucks left communities like Atlantic and Wanchese every night, hauling bluefish, shrimp, soft crabs, or whatever was in season.

The seafood industry helped build coastal North Carolina. In 1996, Jonathan Robinson, fisherman and community leader, reminded all who attend Carteret County's annual Blessing of the Fleet each October, "This is a time to remember the fishermen, fathers, grandfathers, brothers who have gone before. . . . They were the ones who built the courthouses, built the schools, built the churches along the coast."[2] As the local economy changed and land-based work opportunities with steady incomes pulled fishermen away, many continued their commercial fishing efforts as second jobs. Often it was less about supplemental incomes and more about stocking their freezers for the winter ahead and carrying on the work of the fishermen who came before them. No matter what was needed to support their families, they were always fisherman first.

In 2000, local fishermen found themselves in competition with a global economic market. Inferior, cheaper, and unsafe seafood products flooded the markets. Retailers and consumers were blinded to the sourcing conditions of these seafood commodities. From Wanchese to Varnumtown and all along the sounds, fish houses—the epicenter of the seafood industry—were closing. An inventory of North Carolina fish houses in 2006 documented a 33 percent reduction in seafood packing capacity since 2000. The decline in the industry and decreasing profits were due to the influx of less expensive imports, higher operating costs, labor shortages, increased fishing regulations, diminished water quality, scarcer fish stocks, and development pressures.[3]

The pressures of coastal development became an even more immediate threat nationally and locally. Fish houses were replaced by condos and waterfront residential communities. Working boats competed for space with sportfishing yachts. The fishing industry's access to the water, harbors for the fleet, and the character of the fishing community were all disappearing. Led by the Island Institute in Maine, coastal efforts to save working waterfronts began to take hold in North Carolina, with strong leadership from Senator Marc Basnight of Dare County. A 2007 report argued that ensuring "existing waterfront-dependent uses of the shoreline" and retaining and enhancing "public access to coastal public trust waters" was an urgent issue confronting the people of North Carolina.[4] Resulting legislation designated $20 million to support maritime use of North Carolina's waterfront property.

As the farm-to-table movement continued to grow across North Carolina, leaders in the state's seafood industry began to see parallels. They asked, "Are commercial fishermen not food providers?" Grassroots initiatives in the seafood industry encouraged consumers to "know your fishermen" as they "know your farmer." Carteret Catch was the first to launch the "local catch" brand and, over time, to convince area restaurants that patrons would actually pay more for local seafood. North Carolina Sea Grant became a welcome partner. Visitors and locals alike began to ask, "Is it local?" Slowly, pressure mounted on seafood restaurants to bear a Carteret Catch flag affirming their commitment to serving local catch. The local foods movement finally had a foothold in North Carolina's seafood industry.

Efforts were made to help provide fishermen with much-needed processing support in order to compete with ready-to-cook product from large suppliers of imported seafood. For instance, local shrimp sales increased significantly when fishermen, because of the local food movement, began to trust that consumers would pay more for fresh shrimp. Leasing peeling machines and hiring day laborers to head and clean shrimp became feasible. "Now, we hope Carteret Catch will be a model for other coastal communities in North Carolina striving to compete in the global seafood marketplace," declares Barry Nash, NC Sea Grant's seafood marketing specialist.[5]

And that is exactly what happened.

Other regions of the state created their own local catch programs. Brunswick Catch, Ocracoke Fresh, and Outer Banks Catch carried the same message to local seafood markets and restaurants. New regions are now considering their own local catch groups, realizing the positive impact of this important branding for local fishermen. NC Catch was organized in 2011 as an umbrella for the local catch groups. Networks were extended across the state to local food advocates and seafood lovers. These efforts not only informed consumers but also helped fishermen recognize the local food movement's strong support. In 2014, North Carolina fishermen brought their local seafood to the North Carolina State Fair and have continued to do so since. They were overwhelmed by fairgoers' appreciation of North Carolina seafood and their desire to learn more about coastal fish.

Education is the centerpiece of the local catch efforts, promoting the value of local seafood not only to the consumer—taste and health—but to the coastal communities and families that depend on this industry and the economy it supports. As we have seen in the farm-to-table movement, consumers are fascinated by the stories behind the people and places that provide their seafood. As they become more knowledgeable about the benefits of eating local seafood, they are willing to pay more for a product they truly value.

And fishermen are adapting, as they always have.

Until the "buy, eat, support local" movement reached the seafood industry, North Carolina's fishing was little appreciated by the outside world. Grassroots advocacy groups have helped fishermen realize the importance of the local food movement and its value to their industry. Over the past ten years, fishermen have become not only gillnetters and shrimpers, oyster growers and crab shedders, but public relations and marketing experts. Film crews on boats and interviews with journalists are part of the job description. Websites feature profiles of fishermen and their families. Social media is critical, allowing fishermen and local seafood outlets to post the daily catch and, most important, support direct retail sales from fisherman to consumer, a business model never possible in the past.

And it is working! In 2021, NC Sea Grant published a new research report on the economic impact of North Carolina's wild-caught commercial seafood industry that confirms what local fishing communities already know: North Carolina–sourced seafood is a vital part of our state's economy and food supply. North Carolina's seafood industry supports 5,500 jobs, contributing $300 million to the state's domestic product.[6] Inland consumer demand for North Carolina seafood is also seen in growing restaurant and retail sales across the state. This is possible because consumers have learned from the local NC Catch groups and key advocates across the state that local seafood is sustainable and worth the price for its superior flavor, health value, and the North Carolina fishing communities it sustains.

"You can't have a quaint fishing village if you don't have fishermen."

—**MORTY GASKILL, fisherman, Ocracoke Island, North Carolina, June 25, 2019**

The Ocracoke Fish House has become a benchmark on the North Carolina coast, integrating the important message of the local food movement into their community's commercial fishing industry. "How can you consider yourself a fishing village without a fish house?" was

Vicki Basnight, Lone Cedar Cafe, Nags Head, North Carolina; ***background*****, wheel of the** ***Albatross*****, Hatteras, North Carolina**

the central question fishermen posed as they sought statewide support to save the last fish house on Ocracoke. Natives, newcomers, and visitors rallied local and state resources to establish the state's first association-based business model for seafood aggregation and distribution at the Ocracoke Seafood Company. It was a win for everyone: fishermen had a place to sell their fish, Ocracoke preserved a trusted seafood market, and visitors could experience a true working waterfront.

"We've managed to resurrect our fish house from a very difficult situation," says Ocracoke fisherman David Hilton. "Many of the tourists want to see the fishermen who are actually doing the work. In this day and age of everybody wondering where our food comes from, when you come to our dock you put [the fish] there."[7]

Fishing communities are adapting as they always have, but this time with consumers as their allies. Like farmers in the local food movement, fishermen are learning that the story, place, and people behind the product are increasingly valued by consumers. "Know your fishermen" efforts have grown across the industry, from the fish house to inland retail seafood markets. Many restaurants, like Basnight's Lone Cedar Cafe in Dare County, design their nightly menu around the fresh catch of the day. Co-owner Vicki Basnight explains, "We know our fishermen and they know we want only the freshest, best-quality seafood for our customers. We are dedicated to local seafood and produce, and we will only serve the best. That's the way we were raised. We are committed to the fishermen."[8]

Yet, despite the unprecedented demand for local seafood, commercial fishermen continue to fight for the right to fish, not for the volume the industry once depended on, but rather for the growing demand of consumers who want fresh, local, sustainable seafood. Direct sales, either at the fish house retail market or from the local fisherman's roadside stand, have allowed many fishermen to stay in business as demand has grown for dock-to-table seafood.

Concerns about the environmental impact of commercial fishing practices have been amplified by recreational fishing groups competing for the resource, species by species. Politically charged rather than science-based fisheries management allocates more resources to the recreational sector because of its greater economic impact. This continues to threaten North Carolina's seafood industry. A similar pattern has played out in other states such as Florida, where a net ban decimated the commercial fishing industry.

A public relations game has also occurred in which recreational groups partner with environmental organizations to further dissemble their motives. Independent commercial fishermen are portrayed as irresponsible and greedy, their practices and gear blamed for decreasing stocks, when in fact the commercial fishermen understand and respect the cycles of the fisheries and their habitat from a lifetime of working on the water. Frustration, fear, and anger complicate the conversation. The livelihood of commercial fishermen in North Carolina depends on preserving a healthy ecosystem. Commercial fishermen are the caretakers of the resource, advocating for fisheries habitat protection and pristine water quality, the most important factors for the future of seafood production. Politics—and the money that always follows politics—alongside rapid development and the subsequent environmental threat to Carolina's sounds, rivers, creeks, and marshes, have made the seafood industry an endangered species. These battles have raged for decades, dividing communities and enmeshing policy and politics so deeply that it is hard to imagine either as separate entities.

Economic impact studies funded by political interest groups justify their role in the state's economy. Campaign contributions, lobbyists, and media campaigns assure well-funded recreational user groups that allocations of finfish in particular, a public-trust resource, will be dedicated to those who have the time and money to fish for leisure, rather than those who fish for a living and provide North Carolinians with the state's best, freshest seafood. Even as the political and environmental factors surrounding the commercial fishing industry threaten its existence, fishermen remain steadfast in their commitment to provide fresh seafood for their families and local markets. Today the fleet is smaller, but it survives despite hardship and uncertainty. There is more optimism thanks to the growing numbers of consumers who want North Carolina's best local seafood when they dine out and cook at home.

Ryan Speckman and Lin Peterson, founders and owners of Locals Seafood in Raleigh, have led the charge in promoting North Carolina seafood within the state's local food movement. "The only hope is to educate the consumer," says Speckman. "It's the state's resource, our resource, everyone's resource."[9] Beginning with direct sales at area farmers' markets, Speckman and Peterson have fostered a powerful connection between fishermen and eager consumers. "Everybody's been talking how important it is to get this seafood into inland North Carolina, and now Ryan Speckman and folks like him are the ones helping us get this product to the consumers in this state," Hardy Plyler, Ocracoke Fish House manager, explains. "They call and want to know who caught it and where and how it was caught, and that's good. They want fresh, wild-caught seafood, and we have it here off Ocracoke. North Carolina is blessed with seafood; [there are] more species of fish here because this is where the northern waters and southern waters meet."[10]

Their success moving seafood from fishermen and dealers on the coast to families in the Raleigh area proves that the market is strong. Education and advocacy for North Carolina seafood is an important part of their work. Many days Speckman and Peterson join fishermen walking the halls of the state legislature in search of support for key legislation. Retail markets that deliver to the Triangle, such as Locals and Walking Fish, the state's first and longest-running community-supported fishery out of Beaufort, are helping shape the future of North Carolina's seafood industry. One of the most consequential aspects of the local food movement are the chefs who strongly support North Carolina's seafood and its fishermen. As it has for farmers, chefs' commitment to fishermen and local, sustainably harvested seafood is making a positive difference. Journalists and writers have also taken the "seafood is local" message far beyond the coast, supporting new markets and restaurants across the state and region.

"Our story is the story of Wilmington, the coast, the fish, and the season."

—DEAN NEFF, chef/owner, Seabird, Wilmington, North Carolina, March 1, 2020

Through the collective work of local seafood education, advocacy groups, marketing, new retail venues beyond the coast, chefs, restaurants, media, scholars, and consumers, the seafood industry is building its place in the local food movement. This work also honors fishing and a way of life that has long defined coastal communities in North Carolina. Due to the commitment of local food advocates and the persistence of a new generation of determined fishermen, the pursuit of seafood continues in coastal communities across Carolina's sounds and up and down the southern coast. From Smith Island in the Chesapeake Bay to the fishing community of Cortez in Florida, watermen are still fishing, yet they are struggling in the face of contemporary economic, environmental, and political challenges.

Fishermen's deep love for working the waters of coastal North Carolina and their innate knowledge of the tides and seasons lives on in the hearts of young men and women inspired by those who came before them. Working the water may again become a viable livelihood for those willing to take advantage of the new opportunities the local food movement has created.

Some things have not changed; seafood is still more than something to eat, it is a way of life, the story of people working the water, building communities, supporting families, and preserving a heritage that continues to define coastal North Carolina. The future of this industry depends in great part on consumers' continued interest in the men and women of the North Carolina coast who bring seafood to the dock, the quality of the waters that sustain this resource, and supporting an industry that guarantees North Carolinians access to seafood—in truth, their seafood.

Scallop Fritters KAREN AMSPACHER

Makes 4–6 servings

Cooking oil
16 ounces fresh scallops; frozen are okay, but make sure they are wild caught
Salt and pepper to taste
2–4 tablespoons all-purpose flour

Place a large skillet filled with ½–1 inch of cooking oil over medium-high heat.

Chop the scallops until they have a clumpy consistency. Season with salt and pepper. Gradually add flour until the scallops stick together. You may not need all the flour.

Once the oil is heated to 350°, gently drop heaping tablespoons of the scallop-flour mixture into the oil. Gently press each fritter down to flatten it slightly. Working in batches, cook the fritters, turning over once, until the edges are browned, about 1–2 minutes per side, depending on thickness. Be careful not to burn them. Drain on paper towels and serve.

NOTES

1. Nancy Davis and Kathy Hart, *Coastal Carolina Cooking* (Chapel Hill: University of North Carolina Press, 1986), 81–82.

2. North Carolina Seafood Festival Blessing of the Fleet Annual Program, North Carolina State Port, Morehead City, First Sunday in October, 1997–2019.

3. Barbara J. Garrity-Blake and Barry Nash, "An Inventory of North Carolina Fish Houses" (grant report, March 27, 2007), https://nsgl.gso.uri.edu/ncu/ncuc07001/WASC/files/wasc_bgb_fishhousefinal.pdf.

4. North Carolina Marine Fisheries Commission and the North Carolina Coastal Resources Commission, *Final Report to the North Carolina Joint Legislative Commission on Seafood & Aquaculture* (North Carolina Sea Grant and the NC Coastal Resources Law Planning and Policy Center, April 13, 2007).

5. Barry Nash, "Restaurants Denote When Seafood Is Local," *Carteret (N.C.) News-Times*, October 14, 2005.

6. Julie Leibach, "New Research Reveals Growing Economic Impact of NC Seafood," News Releases, North Carolina Sea Grant, March 5, 2021, https://ncseagrant.ncsu.edu/news/2021/03/new-research-reveals-growing-economic-impact-of-nc-seafood/.

7. Heidi Jernigan Smith, "Saving More Than a Fishhouse," *Carolina Country*, July 2007, 8–10.

8. Vicki Basnight, interview by Marcie Cohen Ferris, June 27, 2019.

9. Ryan Speckman, Panelist, 8th Annual NC Catch Summit, March 2, 2020, Transfer Co. Food Hall, Raleigh, N.C.

10. Hardy Plyler, interview by Marcie Cohen Ferris, June 24, 2019.

The Evangelfish of Craven County

From Calabash to the Outer Banks, the North Carolina coastline is 322 miles of food, people, and natural history. Within these salty waters and sandy shores is a tremendous selection of seasonal, edible wildlife that has largely gone underappreciated by most North Carolinians. I was reared in the Coastal Plains, and the genesis of my flavor memories as a chef are located in eastern North Carolina and its seafood. For my family, seafood is a symbol of survival, celebration, and good health. Our community came together around its love and appreciation of the coast. Seafood was abundant and available. I consider it true food for the soul. As a son of this place, it is my mission to uplift the fisherfolk who tend its waters and share its seafood bounty. I celebrate the joy North Carolina seafood brings to our tables, whether at home, dining out, or on the road. It is my hope to share here a bit of who I have become as a proud native of North Carolina, military veteran, chef, restaurateur, writer, and all-around cool dude from Craven County.

I was born at Marine Corps Air Station Cherry Point, and my experience growing up in a military family both stateside and abroad, coupled with my upbringing in New Bern, has shaped my understanding of food, seasonality, and sustainability. My family is rooted in the communities of New Bern, Riverdale, Harlowe, and Beaufort. With my father, Russell Moore, being in the military, my earliest years were spent overseas. We lived in Germany and then stateside in Texas and Kentucky until I was about eleven years old. I experienced foreign cuisine simultaneously with the southern home-cooked meals prepared by my parents. In Germany, we ate hahnchen and frites (roasted chicken on a spit with French fries), but the frites were dipped in mayonnaise rather than ketchup. I had my first taste of German potato salad, red cabbage, and potato pancakes, and they were delicious. My mom, Arlene McClease Moore, brought these recipes back home since we loved them so much, and we often enjoyed them with pork chops for supper or at family functions. She served the potato pancakes either with apples or sour cream and chives. This reinforced my understanding of food at an early age. After moving back to New Bern, I spent my formative years in this historic city, home to Pepsi and myself. New Bern is situated between the Neuse and Trent Rivers, an important avenue for ships and cargo. The Neuse is the largest waterway in the state, and its name comes from the Neusiok Tribe. The Trent was originally fished by the Tuscarora people, who are among the first voices in the historic foodways of eastern North Carolina.

I grew up in New Bern among a large working-class family where women and men helped gather and prepare food for the table. My grandmother Bernice McClease Lofton was the school lunch lady at a time when cafeteria food was homemade. Mom worked at the local hospital assisting nurses and cleaning the emergency rooms. My uncle Keith McClease worked at Tryon Palace as the grounds' supervisor. As a child I grew up with what people now understand as organic, local, and sustainable food. What has become trendy was natural to me back then because we always ate local, fresh, seasonal produce and seafood.

Our family and friends had small gardens where they grew hot peppers, tomatoes, green beans, carrots, and an assortment of greens. The tomatoes were canned for stews during the winter, as were other vegetables. Produce was also bought from the vegetable man, who came through the neighborhood on Saturdays. The local grocery store had a good selection of fresh vegetables, too. Roadside stands allowed people to bring their own bags and pick as much as you wanted for about two dollars a bag. This was especially the case during greens season. My mom and my father's mother, Lottie Mae Godette, always cooked greens with light cornmeal dumplings, which is still a classic dish in the coastal Carolinas. Grandma Lottie would partially brown fresh sausage and then store it in a jar in its own grease, like duck confit. A typical breakfast she cooked included eggs from the chicken coop, fried country ham, the confit sausages fried and by now steeped with flavor, cheese grits, and skillet biscuits. The biscuits were thin and tender, cooked in a greased pan, and eaten with apple preserves. Dinners in my family were mostly home cooked. A typical supper was braised turkey wings or chicken and pastry, cabbage, rice, rutabagas, and a pot of beans, served with cornbread, light rolls (yeast rolls), or flat biscuits (dough rolled out thin only once, rather than folded to create layers; these are tender and moist and feed a lot of folks with little waste). We didn't have fried chicken a lot because it required constant attention, so we only had it on special occasions. Instead, most meals were slow-cooked entrees, allowing my mom to cook and accomplish other tasks at the same time.

"Spot, croaker, mullet, Spanish mackerel. The only salmon we got back then was out of a can. We ate a lot of shrimp and crab. Vegetables were front and center. This is what most of us ate—white and Black—back then."

—**KEITH RHODES on his childhood in Cape Fear Region, chef/owner, Catch, Wilmington, North Carolina, May 22, 2019**

Although fishing in New Bern was mostly for commercial and recreational purposes, my family fished because we had to put supper on the table. If someone left the house with a pole and bait, we knew they were catching dinner. We ate whole fish, bonefish, crabs, shrimp, trout, and more. If we bought fish at the local market when I was a kid, which was B&J or Tryon Palace Seafood, it was typically bonefish, which was cheaper and more flavorful. Each week vendors came to our neighborhood and by our house to sell fresh fish on Saturday. Occasionally we had a fish fry, whether it was after church on Sunday, for a birthday celebration, or following a funeral. You often heard the words "fried hard" at these gatherings, a phrase that describes fish fresh from the Atlantic waters, transformed into a sizzling, crunchy, delicious dish. The fish were usually whole fish such as croakers, spots, butter fish, and fried hard-shell crabs. They were eaten with fried country potatoes with green peppers and onions, sliced cucumbers and onion salad, sliced tomatoes, squash casserole, Brunswick stew, mixed salad (collards, mustard, and cress greens), and always soft Merita brand white bread and Texas Pete hot sauce. Dessert was banana pudding, coconut cake, strawberries with whipped cream, or seasonal fruit such as watermelon and cantaloupe. One of my fondest memories as a child was flounder gigging. During the summer, we'd wait for the sun to set and then, at low tide, wade out into the water wearing our hefty boots. With a spear-headed stick in one hand and a lantern in the other, we caught flounder swimming close to shore. Mom baked the flounder with a cornbread-style stuffing; sometimes she fried it.

Being the first grandchild in my family molded my character and also ushered me into a career as a chef. This is where I developed my entrepreneurial spirit. After high school, I took the first job that allowed me to travel and see the world. I trained to be a military cook and specialist in culinary logistics and was later stationed in Louisiana and Hawaii. With a real passion for food, I enrolled at the Culinary Institute of America in Hyde Park, New York, and graduated in 1994. I apprenticed in France and became a head chef in Chicago and Washington, D.C. After many years of travel, I settled down in North Carolina and moved to the Raleigh-Durham area.

In 2012, I opened my own restaurant in Durham, the Saltbox Seafood Joint. The concept for Saltbox was inspired by North Carolina's classic fish camps and coastal seafood shacks. I consider myself a local seafood evangelist, or, I guess you could say, an "evangelfish." I believe in honestly made, high-quality food, traditionally cooked and prepared with creativity and intelligence. Quality is far more important than quantity. I interpret classical, regional, and global methods of cooking. My motto at Saltbox is "Seasonal Seafood, Freshly Cooked. Good Fish, That's the Hook."

The backbone of my business—North Carolina fish and seafood—is sourced from local fishermen and women. Most people are familiar

Ricky Moore, downtown New Bern, North Carolina

Fried sugar toads, fried oyster roll, day boat shrimp, spiced griddled sheepshead, hush honeys, slaw, crispy seasoned sliced potatoes, Saltbox Seafood Joint, Durham, North Carolina; *background*: Along the Neuse River in New Bern

with flounder, whiting, catfish, and trout, but we serve less familiar varieties, including a few folks don't recognize. We love to introduce our customers to North Carolina fish such as sugar toads (a.k.a. pufferfish), dogfish, sheepshead, triggerfish, lionfish, triple tail, ribbonfish, and shellfish such as conch. Securing a sustainable supply is challenging, but I partner with innovative companies such as Locals Seafood in Raleigh, Salty Catch Seafood in Beaufort, and Nixon Fishery at the Outer Banks. What affects the fisherman affects me. Commercial fishermen follow regulations that specify which fish can be harvested at what times of year to prevent overfishing of one species. Volatile and severe weather affects seafood inventory. Climate change and coastal erosion have tested fishermen because the fish are not coming at the same time every year due to the change in habitat. Many of the coastal towns have become tourist destinations where development alters the working coastline and increases property taxes for local businesses and residents.

Since Saltbox Seafood Joint opened, the restaurant has become a teaching place as much as an eating place. Each day we share information with our guests about native seafood—the many delicious, local, and seasonal varieties of fish available from the North Carolina coast. I have two menu boards at Saltbox, one for more commonly known seafood and the other labeled, "Trust Me." This includes native fish like mullet, bluefish, and sugar toads, long enjoyed by past generations of North Carolinians and fished by both commercial and independent fishermen. I urge our guests to try these delicious varieties. At Saltbox, we cook fish in a variety of ways. Mullet is prepared with a deviled, spiced marinade and grilled over charcoal. Sugar toads—the chicken wings of the sea—are fried in a wet batter and seasoned with signature Saltbox spices, which bring out the flavor of the tender meat under the skin. We serve the sugar toads with fried broccoli, coleslaw, or, when in season, charred asparagus. Even some professional chefs are not always familiar with our North Carolina fish and how to best prepare them. The native species on my menu are found off our coast where southern, warmer waters meet northern, colder waters, the perfect breeding grounds for fish.

One of the most important issues related to maintaining North Carolina's local fish resources is sustainability. Today about 90 percent of the fish eaten in this country is imported from abroad and undergoes little to no inspection. I support local saltwater seafood from the North Carolina coast as my fish of choice because I know and trust my fishermen and suppliers. Their industry is strongly regulated to prevent overfishing, and for many it is becoming harder and harder to survive due to the competition from imported seafood and recreational fishermen, as well as the impact of climate change and environmental contamination.

Many North Carolina fishermen use paddle nets, a more sustainable method than trawling and gillnets, which can trap unwanted bycatch, such as marine turtles or juvenile fish.

There is a great deal of farm-raised fish or aquaculture in our region, too, which can also be done sustainably. Whatever fish you choose, you must be a knowledgeable consumer and eater.

"I can taste the North Carolina fish. It's cooked the way I like it cooked, but also the fish is a product from our area, straight out of our waters."

—JULIUS TILLERY, describing Saltbox Seafood Joint; founder, Black Cotton, Garysburg, North Carolina, June 3, 2019

Much like local farm produce, seafood is seasonal. When you go to the farmers' market certain products are in season, and the same goes for our coastal resources. Particular seafood tastes better during certain seasons, such as the succulent oysters of wintertime, flounder in autumn, or shrimp in summer. Buying seasonally is usually more economical, too, and from a fisherman's perspective, seasonal fish is easier to catch because it is abundant. North Carolina Catch, a local group that supports and educates consumers about our state's seafood, maintains a helpful list of what is in season. I believe that local, seasonal fish tastes superior, offers more diversity, and, most important, supports North Carolina fisherfolk.

My guests at Saltbox want to know where to purchase their seafood. My advice is to go to your local fish market. At your neighborhood restaurants, do they serve regional fish? Where do they source their fish? Do not assume that all North Carolina restaurants get their seafood from our coast. Ask questions. What part of the North Carolina coast does the seafood come from? Is the fish in season? How do they acquire their seafood, where and when and from whom? My guests also want to know how fish should smell. If it smells fishy or rotten, it is old or has been handled incorrectly. Fresh seafood should have no smell at all or only the icy, fresh whiff of the ocean.

The flavor profile of our native fish can be divided into two main categories, mild versus full-flavored or fatty. Flounder is an example of a mild-flavored fish, as is red drum, our state fish, also known as puppy fish. Swordfish, tuna, dogfish, and mahi are denser in texture—almost steaklike—and have a mild flavor profile. Full-flavored fish like mullet and bluefish are similar to thicker species like salmon. Spanish mackerel and king mackerel are thinner fish, yet also full of flavor. My mother used these two varieties to make the fishcakes I loved as a child, which I now offer my guests. Mom prepared the savory fishcakes for any meal. She made them by combining mackerel and boiled potatoes, mixed with cooked onions, green peppers, salt and pepper, and eggs. The fishcakes were then dredged in flour and pan fried. At breakfast time, my mom served them with grits and gravy, and she saved the leftovers for sandwiches.

Today many North Carolinians feel a little unsure about how to cook seafood. It is my mission to change this forever. My first rule of thumb: always purchase the freshest seafood you can find. Second rule: keep it simple. Fish can be fried, grilled, broiled, poached, smoked, cured, roasted, baked, braised, stewed, or preserved by pickling and salting. Add your favorite seasonings and a drizzle of lemon. Red drum is great in a tomato-based veggie and fish stew. Mullet is delicious smoked over wood chips and eaten in a salad with pickles and crackers, like a can of tasty sardines. Trout is excellent when baked with potatoes, cabbage, Dijon mustard, and bay leaves. Shrimp can be prepared many ways but is wonderful sautéed shell-on with a spicy, vinegar-based barbecue sauce. Once you develop a little confidence about your fish-cooking abilities, this diverse and easy meal will become a regular feature of your weekly menu. You can find my favorite recipes and easy preparations for cooking fish and seafood in *The Saltbox Seafood Joint Cookbook*.

Aside from my professional advocacy of North Carolina seafood, I also practice what I preach at home. We integrate seafood at least two to three times a week into our family meals. When we want good fish sandwiches we eat flounder and fried trout, served with lemon pepper broccoli. These are also good sautéed with olive oil, lemon, white wine, salt and pepper, and served with a fresh salad. We sauté shrimp with butter and olive oil, salt, and pepper and serve it with a side of pasta olio (spaghetti with garlic, olive oil, and crushed red pepper, topped with parmesan cheese). In the summer, when crabs are available, we boil them in beer and then sprinkle on Old Bay Seasoning. The cooked crabs are dipped in vinegar and hot sauce with salt and pepper. My daughter, Hunter, is an adventurous eater just like me. She is open to trying any food, from foie gras to chitterlings, and she loves raw oysters and duck confit. My son, Greyson, is not quite as daring, but he does enjoy salmon, shrimp, and bonefish. He loves flavorful croakers served whole, and mostly fried hard, so that he can eat the fins and tail like bacon. My wife, Norma, appreciates and understands the history of our coastline the way I do. She grew up in a fishing family in Virginia's Northern Neck, in Westmoreland County. After retiring from his position as supervisor in the building industry in Washington, D.C., Norma's grandfather, Charlie Jones Sr., fished and crabbed well into his eighties. He provided seafood to many restaurants in the area. I prepare our fish at home by smoking, grilling, and broiling, but one of our favorite meals is just how I ate it growing up—fried hard with hot sauce and a side of soft, white bread.

Regardless of where I have lived and traveled, eastern North Carolina is my home and my place of comfort. Although I have experienced cuisines from around the world, my palate and culinary DNA were formed in New Bern. The fisherfolk who tend our coastline are the backbone of the Saltbox Seafood Joint and the heart of my preaching. Our state's rich seafood culture has fed my family for many generations, and I will always advocate for our native seafood and the fishermen and women who bring it to our tables. I hope I can spread the joy, flavor, good health, and sense of community seafood has brought me from my earliest years in New Bern to all North Carolinians for generations to come.

Potted Crab with Herbs and Salted Butter, Oriental, N.C. RICKY MOORE

Makes 6 servings

11 ounces fresh backfin crabmeat
4 tablespoons crème fraîche
1 tablespoon fresh lemon juice
1 tablespoon finely chopped shallots
1 tablespoon finely chopped tarragon
1 tablespoon finely chopped flat-leaf parsley
½ teaspoon ground cayenne pepper
½ cup (1 stick) salted butter, melted, divided
Pinch of fresh mace (or nutmeg)
Salt and pepper to taste
Finely chopped tarragon and parsley for sprinkling

In a large bowl, mix together the crabmeat, crème fraîche, lemon juice, shallots, tarragon, parsley, cayenne pepper, and ¼ cup of the melted butter. Then add the mace and season with salt and pepper. Mix well to combine.

Divide the crab mixture among six 4-ounce crocks or clamp-style Mason jars, then top each with a thin layer of the remaining melted butter. Sprinkle with salt, pepper, and fresh herbs. Transfer the crocks to a refrigerator to set for at least an hour.

Remove the crocks from the refrigerator about 15 minutes before serving. Serve with thinly sliced toasted bread, crackers, or eastern North Carolina–style "country" flat cornbread.

MALINDA MAYNOR LOWERY

To Be a Lumbee Is to Cook, Sing, and Gather

The Lumbee Indians are one of North Carolina's eight state or federally recognized American Indian nations. Lumbees are also the largest tribe east of the Mississippi, headquartered in Robeson County along the border with South Carolina. There are at least 55,000 enrolled members, but we don't all live in that territory—we are everywhere, all over the world. Accordingly, Lumbee foodways are present wherever Lumbees reside. I was born in Robeson County and raised two hours away, in Durham. Yet my parents, Waltz and Louise Maynor, both Lumbees, taught me to think of Robeson County as my eternal home, no matter where I lived. My twelve-year-old daughter, Lydia, was also born in Robeson County and has been raised in Durham and Atlanta, Georgia. She has her own perspective on Lumbee foodways, people, and places.

Lumbee geographies contradict our expectations about the importance of place to Native people, to North Carolinians, and to southerners. Place is not contained within borders indicated by terms like "Indian country," "the Old North State," or "below the Mason-Dixon line." Place is not about unique geographical or built features of the landscape, like cotton fields, columned plantation homes, or Confederate statues. For me, as a Lumbee, a southerner, and a North Carolinian, the South is many, not one. The idea of a "solid South," a unified region, has dispossessed us, has taken away our political power to determine our futures, our foodways, and our own definitions of who we are. Instead, this region of subregions can liberate us as we move through and with places and the people who live in relationship to them. This is not a linear memory, nor is it always sweet—it is often bitter. We circulate, wander, die, reinvent, lose, compromise, sustain, and revitalize; our conscious efforts to rethink tradition are our source of survival. Our foodways offer a path to return but also a source of reckoning.

Southern food is Lumbee food because we express it and enjoy it among our own people, nurtured by centuries of attachment to one another and to place and, in particular, by a determination to survive the invisibility imposed by inaccurate notions of southern food. Presentations of southern food, whether in print, media, or dining venues, have long ignored the transformative role of Indigenous people in shaping regional foodways. Southern food is Indigenous food. Separating the story of food, no matter what kind of food it is, from its people and their specific place is part of an insidious process to deny a people's existence. When Lumbees talk about food, we honor places and the people who belong to them.

> *"The Cummings [family] . . . I'm a lot Cummings. Mom can see the Cummings in my face."—Lydia Lowery*

My mother, Louise Cummings Maynor, is a leader of her family, in her workplace, and in our communities, both in Durham and in Robeson County. I like to think of her as a Lumbee combination of Jane Fonda and Jackie O. During her thirty-five-year career, she was a professional, an English professor waging a battle against institutional racism and sexism and the bystanders who perpetuate both. My whole life I have known her as a devoted churchgoer, volunteer, and unpaid community organizer. She coordinates book club and carpool, as well as meals and housekeeping for elderly neighbors. She has a green thumb and keeps a spotless house—she literally believes that cleanliness is next to godliness. Mom later told me cleaning was the only way she could get any alone time when we were kids.

"I can't really remember a time not being aware of how my family ate a little differently."

—MALINDA MAYNOR LOWERY, University of North Carolina at Chapel Hill, January 21, 2019

Before I went to college, she provided for my father, my younger brother, and me on a daily basis with an unfailing moral compass and a deep well of patience that I took for granted at the time. She was kind but suffered no fools and seized every opportunity to instruct us in how to achieve the high expectations she and my father had set.

Those expectations included knowing how to interact with both our Lumbee family and our mostly non-Lumbee friends and acquaintances. Food was an entry point to both worlds, though my mother's tacit instruction included a slight prejudice in favor of Lumbee ways of doing things. We often visited our large extended family, especially when my brother and I were younger. We went to Pembroke for Sunday dinner at my grandparents' or aunt's home on the Cummings side, and sometimes we spent the weekend with other aunts and great-aunts on the Maynor side. I remember watching my grandmother mix flour and Crisco when I was young and wondering what it would become—biscuits, of course. I snuck up behind my aunts as they scooped cornbread batter into the frying pan, singing a hymn a cappella in three-part harmony. In the summertime, the dining table held multiple vegetable side dishes—raw cucumbers with vinegar, greens (collards, cabbage, turnips), corn, butter beans or field peas, and squash—served alongside a couple of meats, such as stew beef with new potatoes and baked or fried chicken.

Between June and January, Mom brought back vegetables from her mother's and sister's gardens. Starting in June, corn, cucumbers, summer squash, zucchini, and field peas or butter beans (if she could get them shelled); then, through fall and winter, more corn, collards, cabbage, sweet potatoes, and turnips. Mostly she and her sister picked them straight from the field and put them in the trunk of the car, just shaking off the loose dirt before the two-hour ride to Durham. They still smelled like sun-warmed soil when they arrived in our kitchen. Cooking and eating from the family's gardens were connections to home. My mother had no need to display her identity by making something unfamiliar to her neighbors; instead, cooking Lumbee ingredients—even if sautéed quickly in butter or olive oil rather than fried in fatback or simmered slowly—was just for her. She cooked collards strictly according to what I knew as the Lumbee way, cut into ribbons and stir-fried to maintain their dark green color, taste, and crisp texture. She hated excess grease in her kitchen, so we never had anything deep-fried, but she made pan-fried cornbread, as Lumbees do. She cooked to satisfy her own soul, not to assert her difference.

Growing up, I knew nothing of rural North Carolina except Robeson County, so it didn't occur to me that anyone else ate the way Lumbees did. I didn't think of it as Lumbee food; it was just country food. And when I thought of the country, only Robeson County and Lumbees came to mind. As an adult, especially when I worked with Cynthia Hill's and Vivian Howard's documentary television series *A Chef's Life*, I began to meet people from all over eastern North Carolina. I realized that many people fry cornbread or cook collards like my mother, grandmother, and aunts. I do it the same way, and I hope Lydia will, too. Cooking this way doesn't depend on what kind of North Carolinian you are. It depends on where in North Carolina you're from and who your people are.

> *"A country dish is black-eyed peas, collards, cornbread—[but] we usually have a simple thing like pizza."—Lydia Lowery*

Mom also contended with the foodways of Durham, not so much its local ingredients but the circumstances of an urban working mother and the convenience she sought. We had brussels sprouts from the freezer section and sweet peas from the can when time was short and she needed an easy side dish for supper. Baked cornbread rather than the traditional Lumbee fried cornbread was fine when company came—they didn't know our fried cornbread. Like any kid, pizza was my favorite food. Lydia eats a lot of it, too.

In addition to the immediate family my mother governed, family and friends from home visited frequently. Our house was full of my parents' Lumbee contemporaries, professionals earning their graduate degrees and commuting from Pembroke in Robeson County. Many worked in government in Raleigh. My mother's brothers lived with us off and on, usually while they attended school or worked.

Sometimes folks would stay with us for weeks at a time, especially if they had family undergoing treatment at Duke University Hospital. These Lumbees were rarely blood kin. When the phone rang late at night, typically the caller wouldn't announce themselves. Instead, we overheard, "Do you know who this is?" in that unique Lumbee dialect. A story ensued until my parents guessed the caller's identity. That familiar telephone ring was our sign that company from home was coming and that my mother would soon be cooking. Chicken casserole with cornflake topping was my favorite. Her other standards were chicken salad and chicken and rice. People brought gifts of homemade chowchow (a salty, spicy, fermented combination of garden vegetables) or seasonal preserves. I was picky and now I regret not trying all of those gifts. I encourage Lydia to taste everything. If a family stayed with us long enough, a Lumbee woman might make us fried chicken or her particular specialty, such as chicken and pastry. Such food was labor intensive, and we didn't have it often in Durham. And even though it might be the same familiar dishes we could eat at a local meat-and-three café, it wasn't the same food; those ladies made us Lumbee food because Lumbees cooked it and we ate it.

"It was something about knowing that it was a Lumbee cook that made it feel like Lumbee food."

—MALINDA MAYNOR LOWERY, University of North Carolina at Chapel Hill, January 21, 2019

> *"Around the table the [Cummings] kids are hanging out, playing on the trampoline, and me, I might be a little shy at first. When I walk toward the treehouse someone might say, 'Hi, Lydia.' I think when we have that family time it's pretty much a lifetime full of memories. When we eat, it's fried chicken, pork, beans, and maybe like a big hog, right, Mommy? My aunt Sally—she makes this delicious, really good creamy corn. I've always loved that since I was little. The corn comes from the farms, the fields, the corn patches. She makes really good pastry—chicken and pastry—and lemonade. Thin pieces of chicken, shredded up in a really creamy sauce. The actual pastry is not really like noodles, it's squares. My aunt Sally's fried chicken is good, but I'm not a huge fan of fried chicken."—Lydia Lowery*

At Lumbee Homecoming in 2019, I first realized that my Cummings family's food traditions might be in peril. This didn't unfold in Durham, where you might expect food traditions to unravel, but rather in

Malinda Maynor Lowery and daughter Lydia Lowery, Durham, North Carolina; *background*, fried cornbread

Robeson County, at the annual Lumbee Homecoming. This yearly renewal of our community draws our far-flung population home. I have attended almost every Lumbee Homecoming since I was born in the early 1970s, the only exception being a few occasions in the 1990s when I lived in California and the Northeast. In 2019, though, I worried if we would ever come together again and eat as a family.

My mother's parents, Foy and Bloss Cummings, died in 1997 and 1998, and we have held gatherings in their honor every year since then. Sometimes we meet several times a year. With over thirty grandchildren, they left a great legacy. Their oldest son Donald's children have taken on the responsibility for our family feast; several of them lived with my grandparents when they were growing up. The passing of beloved, aged elders can come with a solid dose of acceptance, but for this side of my family, my grandparents' deaths were a deep rupture we still feel. Gathering every year is a way to cope with their loss.

For the past ten years, Donald's children have organized a week's worth of meals at Lumbee Homecoming. As generations of family members have moved farther away, it is difficult to celebrate birthdays and holidays throughout the year. We remember those special events at Lumbee Homecoming. The point is the gathering, less so the food itself, but the food is still special because it is cooked by special people. We eat dishes we know well, the same as those from my childhood, but our younger generation seldom prepares them because they require more time than most of us have and use techniques we don't always know.

The most important quality of these gatherings is that everyone is welcome, whether you bring a dish or not. No one checks genealogies at the door—we all know one another and who belongs. Many of the meals open with a ceremonial welcome, introducing the people who came the farthest, the descendants of Foy and Bloss who are there for the first time, or those who have not visited since childhood. In addition to the living children and grandchildren, most attendees are great-grandchildren and great-great grandchildren, a legion of descendants gathering together in a powerful space and time.

My cousin Raymond, Donald's second oldest son, and his wife, Betsy, often host the meals in their garage turned rec room, which has a tiny kitchen. My mother and aunt and uncle host other meals. Donald's youngest daughter, Brenda, who lived with my grandparents the longest, communicates with far-flung family members (these days on a twenty-plus person text chain that keeps growing), raises the funds, handles the schedule, books the water slide for the children, and keeps everybody in line.

In the summer of 2019, Raymond and Brenda's eldest brother, Ronald, tragically died of cancer in his early sixties, following a rapid decline many of us were unaware of due to our distance from home. In those same weeks, Raymond was also hospitalized at Duke. By the time of Lumbee Homecoming the week of July 4, I was sick, too, having contracted walking pneumonia. My family gathered at Ronald's house to sing to the dying. Raymond, much of the time unconscious in intensive care, was not permitted visitors. We could not gather at the hospital to sing to him.

Two desperately ill brothers, especially within a tight-knit family still grieving our grandparents twenty years after their death, prompts more than sadness. We dreaded the struggle that our relatives would endure. Ronald's death was hard enough. The fact that Raymond was cut off from the healing powers of song threatened to tear our family apart. To be a Lumbee is to cook, sing, and gather; to be a Lumbee is also to hold closely the pain of your family.

And this was hardly the first wave of such pain; it is decades, generations old. We internalize the pain of our ancestors. The land where my grandparents lived, where my mother was raised, where my cousins live now, was my great-grandfather James's land—only twenty-two acres, but enough to farm so that Foy, Bloss, and their children and grandchildren didn't have to move each year to sharecrop land owned by others.

That patch of land became a bond after a rupture none of us remembers but all of us feel. In 1927, my twenty-year-old grandfather Foy and his older brother Leslie were falsely accused in a hit-and-run accident that killed a white man in Robeson County. The two brothers were tried for the murder, but neither had a hand in it. Leslie and Foy had driven the car to a box supper at the Indian Normal School (now UNC-Pembroke), where someone stole the vehicle and later killed the victim. Yet the police never pursued the thief, content to prosecute the owners of the car. The only incriminating evidence was their race. White attorneys, police officers, jury members, and a judge tried and sentenced the brothers to two years in prison.

My great-grandfather James encouraged Leslie to leave the county after the trial and never come back. Apparently, Foy served time for them both. He told my mother a little bit about this story, but mostly he talked about his prison time and working as a cook in the county home across from the prison camp.

Leslie moved to Detroit, married, and raised his family there. He told no one except his wife that he was Lumbee, and she did not reveal it to their children until after his death. Leslie never returned home again. But his grandchildren and great-grandchildren, none of whom were born in Robeson County or ever lived there, now come for Lumbee Homecoming.

That difficult summer of 2019 I was unable to go to Ronald's house for the singing, so I remained at home in Pembroke, ready to visit with anyone who dropped by. When Uncle Leslie's family came, we talked in the kitchen together, and the injustice of the 1928 trial was at the heart of our conversation. "It's shameful," said my mom. "Of course, there's nothing we can do about it now. I reckon Daddy just wanted to keep it behind him." She paused. "But it changed the family forever. Uncle Leslie had to leave and never came back. And we are only now getting to know his children and grandchildren." Generations later, we still recognize and seek to heal the trauma of separation.

Because of the many tragedies that summer, our family meals were not possible. We could not make plans amid such uncertainty. I wondered whether our family would be changed forever, as when Uncle Leslie left in 1928. Yet after Ronald's funeral, we gathered together to eat at the church. The table in the fellowship hall was not as abundant as a Cummings gathering, but the ladies of the church set out pizza, fast-food chicken, store-bought cakes, and precious pots of pastry, along with peas and corn. I was late getting in the food line, and those country dishes had already disappeared by the time I got to the table.

Yet as Lydia reminds me each day, despair, not change, is the real challenge we face. We will always be of our places, beyond our region, so long as we are here, so long as we maintain dynamic relationships to places. Lumbee foodways show us that tradition is that which those who were here first choose to take forward; origins are largely irrelevant. Instead, respectful exchange matters. Also, instead of doing things the "original" way, Indigenous people do things the appropriate way, which is to say, we share, we remember, we retain our dignity. We don't forget, even though others have largely forgotten the crucial creativity, voice, and labor of Indian people in creating what we now know as southern food.

> *"But I've been thinking lately am I country, because I heard this song on the radio, what makes you country, and I asked my grandma, and she said, no, you're pretty much a city girl, but I was like, no, I was born from the fields, and born from southern cooking."—Lydia Lowery*

Collard Sandwich

Collard Sandwich **MALINDA MAYNOR LOWERY**

Makes 2 big or 4 small sandwiches

FOR THE COLLARDS
1 bunch collards, stemmed
2 tablespoons oil or fat (traditionally the fat rendered from frying fatback; bacon can be substituted, though it will alter the taste)
2 teaspoons sugar
Salt and pepper to taste

FOR THE CORNBREAD
¼ cup vegetable oil or shortening
1 cup yellow cornmeal
¼ teaspoon salt
¾ cup water or milk

Rinse the collards and place them in a plastic shopping bag, gently bouncing the greens to shake off the water. Hang the bag from a cabinet pull or door knob for a few minutes (the plastic bag wicks away just the right amount of moisture from the collards).

Remove the collards, then stack them on top of each other and roll tightly, starting from the longest edge. Using a sharp knife, slice the tightly rolled collards into super-thin ribbons. Set aside.

Set a large skillet over medium-high heat and add the oil. Add the collards all at once, gently tossing to fry. Cook until they are bright green and just barely wilted. Sprinkle with the sugar and toss again to combine. Season with salt and pepper.

To make the cornbread, set a cast-iron skillet over medium-high heat and add the oil.

In a medium bowl, combine the cornmeal and salt. Add the water or milk a little at a time until the mixture reaches the consistency of pancake batter (fluid but not too runny). When the oil shimmers, add a heaping spoonful of batter and gently spread it out with the back of a spoon until it's about the width of a softball. Cook for 1–2 minutes, gently flip with a spatula, and cook for another 1–2 minutes until the cornbread is cooked through and the edges are browned. Remove and drain. Repeat with the remaining batter until you have 2 pieces of cornbread per sandwich.

To assemble each sandwich, place a piece of cornbread on a plate, heap with a generous portion of collards, and then top with a second piece of cornbread. Serve with any or all of the following: bacon, fatback, chowchow, and hot sauce.

Black and Country

An Origin Story

My relationship to the land is personal. One of my most vivid childhood memories is my cousins, my sister, and me singing Phil Collins's 1982 revival of the Supremes' hit "You Can't Hurry Love" to a sold-out crowd of cornstalks in an eastern North Carolina field. We imagined a sea of adoring fans, screaming and cheering as we concluded the soulful tune. Afterward, we ran down the rows high-fiving each eager stalk. In the open fields, the outstretched stalks reaching back made me feel both humble and proud. In the late summer and fall my uncles spent long hours in those fields high atop combines and harvesters. My shared relationship to food, storytelling, activism, and advocacy in North Carolina begins here.

I grew up Black and Country, and honestly, I have never had a strong desire to be anything else. I am from Mount Olive, North Carolina, "Pickle Country." I often speak in a collective voice because my story is a story of "us." I am the result of an undeniable lineage. When folks see me, they recognize my Ammons eyes and Hamilton skin. My hands have toiled the same soil as my grammas Lillie and Adell. I am a product of Langston Hughes's "dream deferred"—sugared over and "syrupy sweet," while sagging "like a heavy load."[1]

There is a familiar narrative prescribed to Black Country people in the American South, many of whom grew up in tenant or sharecropping farming families like mine in North Carolina. It is often assumed that Black people despise farming and have no constructive relationship with the land. One cannot dispute this logic. Five hundred years of enslaved labor and subsequent Jim Crow–era crimes led to the systemic loss of millions of acres of Black land and generations of psychological trauma. The Emergency Land Fund, a southern-based nonprofit organization whose mission is to fight Black land dispossession, estimates that "6 million acres [were] lost by Black farmers from 1950 to 1969. That's an average of 820 acres a day—an area the size of New York's Central Park erased with each sunset."[2] It is presumed that this history leads *only* to hatred for the land.

I have worked with young people, mostly Black, who are offended by the notion of working the land and argue that it is akin to slave labor. They compare their experience of working in community- and church-sponsored gardens to that of enslaved Africans who stewarded and farmed land for their white enslavers without the slightest possibility of autonomy, ownership, or simple agency. I have also worked alongside Black elders insulted by outsiders who call their homeplaces "food swamps" and "food deserts," derogatory terms that ignore the rich cultural heritage that lies deep in their bones and the soil. How ironic it must seem to describe what was once a bountiful farming landscape that fed countless urban and rural families as now barren, a mirage, as useless terrain. These juxtapositions represent two profound truths among Black Country people. With every justifiable comparison to enslaved labor that farming brings forth, there are untold accounts of Black resilience, celebration, and resistance within southern agriculture at large and in North Carolina, my home.

"The stigma with Black people and fields runs deep. Cook, clean, pick. My grandmother, who was born in the thirties, she's gone now, but her mother taught her, 'These are skills you will need to survive.'"

—**SUBRINA COLLIER, co-owner, Leah & Louise, Charlotte, North Carolina, April 22, 2019**

Throughout the American South, farming and land stewardship has historically been a Black thing, innate to the historical Black experience. The word "steward" implies love, care, and an ethic that goes beyond maintenance. The term is both a verb and a noun, an action and an actor. In the American South, the legacy of Black farming and land stewardship has been essential to our emotional, psychological, and economic survival. Food and land are a place of rescue and healing in times of grief, a place for celebration in better times. Food and land represent freedom and fellowship, reparation and remedy.

I have fond memories of Easter Sunday sunrise services in Mount Olive. My enthusiasm was not about the awkward pastel dresses that my twin sister and I grudgingly donned. It was the joyous music and post-service spread of food I loved—bacon from Deacon Charlie Lofton's smokehouse, fresh eggs from a congregant's chicken coop, fried chicken from birds whose necks were wrung and feathers plucked only days earlier, and flaky pies filled with succulent sweet potatoes.

Today in Conetone (pronounced "Kuh-Nee-tuh"), the Reverend Richard Joyner and his Edgecombe County congregation enjoy fresh vegetables grown on church land for repast after funerals. The parishioners bring healthy dishes made from ingredients grown by church youth. These bowls and platters of food enliven the community rather than the nutritionally vacant fast food and gallons of Bojangles sweet tea that have long diminished southern and Black health throughout the region. Youth learn how to monitor their blood pressure and to cook meals for themselves and their families using the produce they've grown themselves. It is no irony that a significant amount of Black-owned land

Shorlette Ammons, Durham, North Carolina; *background*, Ammons's homeplace, Beautancus, North Carolina

in the United States today is held by Black churches.[3] Food and faith are inextricably linked. Most growing seasons on Black-owned land in eastern North Carolina begin with a prayer for abundance, just as each family and church meal begins with saying grace to offer gratitude for the bounty as well as those who grew and prepared the food.

At the 2018 Black Farmers and Urban Gardeners Conference, sponsored by the New York–based organization Black Urban Growers (BUGs), like-minded contemporary Black agrarians generated a buzz of energy and possibility. Exclusively Black and People of Color–centered gatherings, like this conference, are vital to keeping the contribution and methodologies of Black agrarianism relevant and visible, in spite of the painful history of our farming forebears. This annual conference is one of many platforms where old narratives of racial division regarding Black involvement in agriculture are no longer tolerated, such as those between prominent early twentieth-century Black educator and reformer Booker T. Washington, a proponent of farming and racial accommodation, and intellectual and political strategist W. E. B. Du Bois, who argued for higher education and political action. Those earlier divisive attitudes toward Black farming are today seen as a means of perpetuating white supremacy by reinforcing competition and isolation between Black intellectualism and agrarianism, both of which remain needful contributions to Black culture.

My food and farming experiences are wrapped in a mindset that is not about farming alone. Over the years I have dedicated a notebook to random thoughts, doodles, and lightbulb moments sparked at conferences and lectures. At the conference, I scribbled a question posed by a presenter, "Have we collapsed our liberatory visions into *just* growing food?" This important query transforms the act of growing food into a larger, collective purpose. A system of growing local, seasonal food that is healthy and accessible to all people is a mandatory component of a comprehensive, justice-centered movement that cultivates self-determination and self-sufficiency. Black Country and rural people have lived this vision of food for generations in North Carolina.

Our story encapsulates a racialized legacy of an American farming culture that required much of Black agrarians but returned little to them and their families. My granddaddy Rasper Ammons raised hogs at Route 1, Box 80, in Mount Olive, just up from Tram Road. He supplemented that profession by working at the local poultry processing plant and selling Nabs, the North Carolina–created peanut butter snack cracker that has sustained generations of working-class people. Granddaddy Rasper's hog farming operation fed thirteen or more mouths but could not insure his family's financial stability. That unease kept him a chain-smoker who made and sold stumphole (moonshine)—called this for its hiding place, nestled in the hole of a tree stump. He ultimately damaged his heart tending the land he loved but never owned outright. When he died of heart disease, so did our hog farming operation. This loss is familiar in Black Country families, whether the loss of land is due to heirs' property disputes (legal ties to the land by multiple family members) or the eroding physical and emotional health of our Black farming elders. I was only four years old when Granddaddy Rasper died. But the lessons he conjures, and my memories of his joyous presence, remain constant.

Hog killing time was typically in cold weather so the meat would cure and last through the winter into the warmer months. We also had a hog killing right before the July Fourth holiday. Those animals were slaughtered and processed mostly to sell. The Fourth of July was our biggest family holiday next to Christmas. My family didn't care about Independence Day. July 4 was the one day everyone had off in the summer at the poultry plant. Granddaddy and our uncles killed the hog—a single shot to the head followed by a quick bop to the forehead with a heavy board. Our role as young'uns—me, my twin sister, and my cousins—was to help dress the hog after killing. The deceased hog was placed in a huge tub of hot water. We used the lid from a Duke's Mayonnaise jar to scrape the hair off the hog. We each had our own lid. Our role in hog killing time made us feel important and special. I remember laughter yet focus; the feeling of unconditional peace and joy in the midst of this animal's end; a debt well paid and utterly appreciated.

"'Country.' I take comfort from it. Meant down to earth. Opposite of citified. Definitely rural. Poor folk. Black or white."

—RANDALL KENAN, University of North Carolina at Chapel Hill, January 30, 2019

People, places, and experiences are deeply embedded in my identity as a Black Country girl born, raised, and still making a living in North Carolina. My daddy's side of the family, the Hamiltons, are from a small town farther east in Duplin County, a place known for having more pigs than people. Hog farming put food on our table growing up and still does for many families Down East.

However, the environmental costs of industrial hog farming are high: excrement-filled lagoons, unsanitary, inhumane confinement of animals, dangerous work conditions for laborers, and exposure of people who live nearby contaminated water, soil, and air. Rural people attempting to make a living are often pitted against ecological justice, labor, and animal welfare advocates rightfully prioritizing the long-term health and well-being of workers, animals, and residents. The conflict only adds to the complexity, as there is little common ground and no room for compromise where climate and health are the main concerns. I think of my aunts, who are over sixty years old and continue to work at the local poultry plant during the COVID-19 pandemic. They have no other

Gramma Adell's Tea Cakes;
***background*, Ammons's cornfield**

options but to work. The number of Black southerners who are disproportionately contracting and dying from the coronavirus is staggering. This is a contemporary manifestation of racial exploitation that has long affected the lives of essential Black food workers and farmers nationally.

Even efforts at rectifying past injustices, such as *Pigford v. Glickman*, one of the largest civil rights financial settlements in American history, could not save thousands of Black farmers from the economic, physical, and emotional realities of systemic poverty, poor health, and residual stress. In 1997, North Carolina farmer Timothy Pigford was joined by 400 Black farmers from around the country in a class action lawsuit that cited discriminatory lending practices by the United States Department of Agriculture (USDA). The few hundred farmers who subsequently filed were a fraction of the more than 2,000 growers who had formal discrimination claims. Countless others, like my daddy, didn't have the capacity or resources to take legal action. Settlement funds could not possibly reconcile generations of land loss and legacy. Furthermore, the gerrymandering of these settlements contradicted the collective culture of Black farming represented by Fannie Lou Hamer's Freedom Farm Cooperative in the Mississippi Delta (1967), which later sparked the founding of the Federation of Southern Cooperatives. Many farmers who had experienced discrimination lacked the necessary paperwork for a claim or filed too late, after the imposed deadline. Although Pigford and the subsequent settlement in Pigford II benefited hundreds of farmers, they did little to force institutional change. In 2009 a newly established USDA Civil Rights Task Force released an action plan with ninety-two recommendations to address racial bias but included no solid mechanisms of accountability.

I moved from eastern North Carolina to the big city of Durham in 2014. It's a food town. I live down the street from several high-end restaurants and around the corner from a McDonald's where protesters staged a boycott in favor of a fifteen-dollar minimum wage. I eat in Durham's Beard-nominated restaurants that feature overpriced Black Country staples like deviled eggs, chicken liver, and fancied-up pig parts. In these places I find an uneasy comfort, yet I learn to celebrate the gifts that Black Country culture affords the South through its food cultures. Black people seldom own these places. In Durham, I live amid the American ideals of individual ownership rather than the collective culture that sustained the Black Country community of my childhood.

Durham is also a town of activism. From the front stoop of my home, you can practically see the empty space in front of the county courthouse where a Confederate statue once stood. It was toppled by a group of activists in August 2017. I recognized many of their faces. Even though my life in Durham is up the road a ways from the rural crossroads linking the towns of Beautancus, Calypso, Faison, and Mount Olive, where I grew up, I am never far removed from those worlds. A rural sensibility follows me wherever I find myself, whether it be the vibrant clay fields of Cuba or the lively streets of the Bull City. I am forever drawn to people and landscapes that remind me of those Black Country connections.

Inasmuch as white supremacy cannot be dismantled by the toppling of statues alone, neither will we have a more just and equitable food system in North Carolina if we do little to change old institutional structures of oppression. Symbolic exchanges between our privileged land-grant campuses as part of outreach initiatives to impoverished communities provide nominal grant dollars, rather than engaging in the hard work of social transformation, democratization, and self-determination. We continue to sacrifice the health and dignity of marginalized people of color.

The history of the racially divided land-grant universities in our state and throughout the South is rooted in Jim Crow era separate but equal policies that institutionalized segregation after the Civil War. These structures fertilized the racial hierarchy that permeates our food and agriculture systems today. Historically Black colleges and universities (HBCUs) in the South were born out of the racial exclusion of Blacks in the establishment of the land-grant system.[4] Yet African American knowledge and leadership within these institutions fostered progressive agricultural reforms to stabilize Black family farming legacies by educating the next generation, building on their ingenuity and encouraging them to work the land. Solutions were sought to lessen the drudgery of agricultural labor and to embolden Black excellence. At Tuskegee University in Alabama in the early 1900s, agricultural scientist George Washington Carver conducted trailblazing research that legitimized and elevated the work of Black farmers. Carver's mule-drawn Jesup Agricultural Wagon brought instructional materials, soil samples, equipment, plants, and recipes to area Black farmers through the university's Movable School Program—just one of many projects that led to the modern cooperative extension programs at HBCUs and predominantly white land-grant institutions.

To work effectively within institutions that historically perpetuated racial injustice requires a fair amount of soul-searching. I ponder how organizations like North Carolina's historic land-grant universities can give racial equity practitioners like myself a mandate of racial justice to empower marginalized people and places. How do we remain in service first and foremost to people rather than institutions? Solutions exist in genuine relationships with Black Country people and rural communities. Cooperative land ownership and stewardship has the power to shape consequences. The collective resilience spearheaded by Black farmers and cultivated by such organizations as Durham's Land Loss Prevention Project remind us what land represents.

The food and farming paradox led many of us away from the land, but a yearning for that land also pushed us toward agricultural institutions, such as North Carolina State University and North Carolina A&T State University, first as students and later as educators, writers, and researchers. As we consider our relationship to the land, those of us who work in these institutions increasingly see our role as resisters. In her work *Freedom Farmers*, sociologist Dr. Monica White examines the experience of Black farmers of the civil rights era, the "rural resisters" who fought repressive conditions using land as a strategy toward freedom.[5] The more I reflect, the more I realize that my life echoes the rural resisters who came before me: a series of experiences that reverberate, coming back at me with added memories, lessons, depth, and dimension. The older I get, the closer I feel to the ways and experiences of home that led me to my work in the food systems of North Carolina. Despite this state's difficult histories that I confront daily, I recognize the significance that land, food, and farming have for my future and the people I love.

My connection to the land comes from Gramma and Grandaddy, Mama and Daddy, uncles and aunts, and their deep roots to the farming and food communities of eastern North Carolina. The many faith-filled leaps we have made as Black Country people were catapulted by a shared understanding of our origins, courage, risk, and resistance. Food, farming, family, freedom—and the audacity to confront the contradictions they muster—are inherent to our history. These stories are weighted by ancestry and remembrance, like the heaviness of wet tobacco leaves.

Gramma Adell's Tea Cakes SHORLETTE AMMONS

Makes 9–12 palm-sized cakes

3 cups self-rising flour
1 cup sugar
1 cup lard (or 2 sticks butter), plus more for greasing the baking sheet
2 eggs
1 capful vanilla flavoring

Adapted from Phoebe Exum's "Ole Timey Teacakes."

Sift the flour into a large bowl. Clear out a hole in the center of the flour and add the remaining ingredients. Mix everything together with your hands, gently rubbing the fat with your fingertips, until a nice, cohesive dough forms.

Set the oven to 350° and lightly grease a baking sheet (you can do this with your hands or with a paper towel).

Flour your hands (so the dough won't stick to 'em) and transfer the dough to the baking sheet. Using your fingers, gently pat the dough into a large, ½-inch-thick rectangle. Transfer to the oven and bake until the cake is golden brown on the edges (and slightly raised in the middle) and you can stick a toothpick in the middle and it comes out clean, about 20–25 minutes. Allow the cake to cool for a minute, and then, using a sharp knife, carefully cut it into large squares—about the size of your palm. Cool the tea cakes completely before serving with coffee and fresh berries or enjoying them by themselves.

NOTES

1. Langston Hughes, *The Collected Poems of Langston Hughes*, ed. Arnold Rampersad and David Roessel (New York: Alfred A. Knopf, 1994).

2. Vann R. Newkirk II, "The Great Land Robbery," *Atlantic*, September 2019.

3. Carey Biron, "With Land to Spare, US Churches Turn to Farming," *Christian Science Monitor*, September 19, 2018.

4. J. M. Lee and S. W. Keys, *Land-Grant but Unequal: State One-to-One Match Funding for 1890 Land-Grant Universities* (Washington, D.C.: Association of Public and Land-Grant Universities, 2013).

5. Monica M. White, *Freedom Farmers: Agricultural Resistance and the Black Freedom Movement* (Chapel Hill: University of North Carolina Press, 2019), i–iv.

The Pig Math of Pasture-Raised Pork

It's just past the main lunch hour at Buxton Hall Barbecue, but the bar seats are still full and people are sipping Cheerwine slushies and vodka tonics as they wait for an open table.

Pam McCurry, fifty-two, of Greenville, South Carolina, is visiting Asheville for a Valentine's Day getaway. McCurry and her boyfriend had enjoyed a progressive dinner at a series of Asheville restaurants the night before. Today they are exploring Asheville's South Slope, the downtown brewery district with eight breweries within walking distance and where Buxton Hall Barbecue is located. When McCurry sat down at the bar and looked at the menu, she knew what she had to order: "I love hash. Hash and rice is one of my favorite things."

Hash is not well known outside of South Carolina's barbecue tradition. In fact, the server questioned McCurry when she placed her order for the fourteen-dollar hash plate: "The bartender warned me: Do you know what our hash is? It's meat gravy, a little spicy."

So, what exactly is hash? It is made from the pig parts leftover from cooking barbecue, usually with some added pig liver, water, and seasonings, stewed a long time and served over rice. Historian Robert Moss dates the culinary tradition to enslaved Black cooks before the Civil War along the Savannah River in South Carolina and Georgia. But hash hasn't migrated very far from there—except to Asheville.

Buxton Hall Barbecue chef and co-owner Elliott Moss made sure to include it on his menu. Hash isn't just a tribute to a barbecue staple that Moss grew up eating in Florence, South Carolina. It's a key part of the equation that makes Buxton Hall Barbecue one of only a handful of barbecue restaurants in North Carolina that can afford to serve pasture-raised pork.

"If we didn't make hash, I couldn't make it work," Moss says.

Pasture-raised meat is central to the local food movement, which began to take hold in North Carolina in the late 1970s. That's when the Carrboro Farmers' Market started; the state's first farmer-run market required what was sold there to be grown or raised within a certain distance. Farmers at those local markets often adhere to sustainable, organic practices even if they don't seek certification. In the next three decades, as consumers began asking more questions about where their food came from, North Carolina's barbecue restaurants seemed separate and apart from that conversation.

The state's barbecue restaurants fit a particular mold: barbecue was either pulled pork from shoulders or chopped from whole hogs and purchased mainly from the state's booming commodity pork industry. The restaurants were not fancy. They served 'cue, a handful of sides, and sweet tea. In season, local cabbage may be used to make the coleslaw or North Carolina sweet potatoes may star in the pie. For the most part, local pork or vegetables were too expensive or required too much labor to migrate onto those menus. Plus, consumers' expectation at these beloved institutions was that a barbecue sandwich or meal cost about the same as fast food.

"Barbecue took off after World War II. People were really used to buying it fairly cheap. It was in the same category as hot dogs and hamburgers," says Bob Garner, author of *Bob Garner's Book of Barbecue.* (Garner was also the longtime correspondent on UNC-TV's *North Carolina Weekend* who regularly profiled restaurants and was known for his "mmmm-good" reactions to the food.)

But Garner saw all of that change when the Pit opened in 2008 in Raleigh. The Pit was the work of Raleigh developer Greg Hatem, who grew up in Roanoke Rapids, and pit master Ed Mitchell of Wilson, an early proponent of pasture-raised whole hog barbecue because it reminded him of the barbecue from his childhood. Mitchell says, "I liked the quality of the product, which enabled me to produce an end result in barbecue closest to what I remember."

With the Pit, barbecue restaurants in North Carolina began to change. They had full menus with appetizers and desserts, table service, cloth napkins, a full bar, and even valet parking. "They found that a new generation would eat barbecue and collards when it was presented in a milieu that they were familiar with—and they could order craft beer," said Garner, who helped organize special events at the Pit after Mitchell left in 2011 to open his own restaurant.

"A lot of people didn't think we could pull it off," says Hatem, who also owns other area restaurants—the Raleigh Times, the Morning Times, Sitti, and Gravy—all in Raleigh, and another Pit location in Durham. Hatem said the Pit recruited farmers to raise hogs to supply the restaurant and now they have a network of them. "One of the things I'm most proud about," he says, "is we helped build the market for that."

The Pit was based in the state's capital city, where diners were willing to pay more for a dining experience. It had a full bar serving not just beer and wine but liquor, which was verboten at most old-school barbecue restaurants. They also don't let anything go to waste. Leftover barbecue is stuffed inside fried egg rolls for an appetizer at the Pit and sent over to the Raleigh Times to top nachos.

"If we ever had to start doing commodity hog, I'd rather close down."

—ELLIOTT MOSS, chef/partner, Buxton Hall, Asheville, North Carolina, September 24, 2019

Beyond the Pit, only a handful of barbecue restaurants in the state serve pasture-raised pork, but how each restaurateur makes it work to incorporate this higher-priced product is unique.

At Buxton Hall, Moss buys whole hogs from Vandele Farms in Rutherford County. That's possible, in part, because hash is on the menu. In his South Carolina childhood, Moss grew up steeped in a world of whole hog barbecue, eating it regularly from local restaurants and enjoying his family's barbecue feasts around the holidays. His grandfather, Bob Moss, owned a welding business and made barbecue pits. In fact, his father, Terrell Moss, also a welder who still lives in Florence, South Carolina, built the Texas-style offset smoker at the Asheville restaurant. This self-taught chef opened the Admiral, a much-lauded Asheville gastropub, in 2007 before opening Buxton Hall in 2015. He's twice been named a semifinalist for a James Beard award for Best Chef: Southeast.

On that same Valentine's Day weekend, Moss demonstrates how they make their hash at Buxton Hall. It starts by rendering the back fat pulled off the whole hogs; the rendered fat is siphoned off for use in the fryers, and the meaty bits that remain are the foundation of hash. Moss combines those meaty bits with pieces of rendered hog jowls in a hog stock. The stock is made from bones pulled off whole hogs before they are chopped into barbecue. The hash stews up to ten hours before Moss adds ground pork liver for an umami bite and other seasonings. It is pureed with an immersion blender before being served over rice. "I buy pasture-raised pork," Moss says. "I can't justify throwing this stuff away."

Here's how the hash math works: Moss pays about $2.50 a pound for whole hogs, so a 200-pound hog costs him about $500. One batch of hash made from what would normally be thrown away from a week's worth of about a dozen whole hogs will make twenty-two quarts. "We can turn that into $1,500 from that waste," said Moss. One dish pays for about three of those whole hogs each week.

Hash is only part of the financial equation at Buxton Hall, which has a great location in a busy tourist town and where Moss acknowledges

FACING PAGE: ***Top left***, **Elliott Moss, Buxton Hall Barbecue, Asheville, North Carolina;** ***top right***, **whole hog pulled pork and hash with collard greens, Cheerwine slushie, Buxton Hall Barbecue, Asheville, North Carolina;** ***bottom left***, **potato salad, cornbread, fried chicken, mac and cheese, pulled pork, coleslaw, baked beans, fried okra, Picnic's barbecue sauce, Picnic, Durham, North Carolina;** ***bottom right***, **Sam Jones, Deep Run, North Carolina**

COCO

they have a special clientele. Many of their diners are farmers' market–shopping, local food–supporting consumers. Plus, Moss notes, they sell a lot of T-shirts, those Cheerwine bourbon slushies, and former pastry chef Ashley Capps's desserts, especially her well-known banana pudding pie. Still, Moss says, it's a challenge. He buys up to fourteen hogs to serve between 3,000 and 6,000 customers during lunch and dinner seven days a week.

Moss's commitment to pasture-raised pork would not be possible if diners weren't spending money on other things at the restaurant. He explains: "If we didn't have that bar. If we didn't have that Cheerwine [bourbon] slushie. If we didn't have T-shirts. If we didn't have the desserts."

Over in Chapel Hill, Sam Suchoff, chef and owner of the Pig, can serve pasture-raised pork at his restaurant because he created a role for himself: pork distributor. Suchoff is a former mathematics major who fled his office job for restaurant kitchens. He worked at Lantern and Neal's Deli, two Orange County restaurants known for their commitment to local food. He ended up at the Barbecue Joint, which closed abruptly due to financial difficulties. Suchoff bought the equipment and opened the Pig in the same space in 2010.

Suchoff buys about thirty-two whole hogs a week from the North Carolina Natural Hog Growers Association, a group of nineteen farmers who have secured Animal Welfare Approved (AWA) certification. AWA is an independent, nonprofit farm certification program that audits farms' production, transport, and slaughter practices to ensure that animals are raised outdoors on pasture or range for their entire lives.

At the Pig, Suchoff cooks only the shoulders for his barbecue, and that leaves a lot of other pig parts. He sells loins, Boston butts, pork bellies, and ribs to high-end restaurants, such as Lantern in Chapel Hill and Stanbury in Raleigh. He started making hot dogs to sell at the Carrboro Farmers' Market, which led to a partnership with Weaver Street Market. Now he uses the food co-op's commercial kitchen to make his hot dogs, as well as pork loins and other home cook–friendly cuts that Weaver Street sells in its meat case. An excess of hams led Suchoff to make country hams, which ultimately became his own line of Lady Edison products, including all kinds of charcuterie. Suchoff's Lady Edison hams appear on restaurant menus alongside Italian prosciutto and Spanish serrano hams at Mateo in Durham, Roberta's in Brooklyn, and Momofuku in New York City. Figuring out other uses and buyers for parts of the pig, Suchoff says, "allowed me to move more animals and get more meat for barbecue."

In Durham, pit master Wyatt Dickson partnered with farmer Ryan

FACING PAGE: ***Top*****, Skylight Inn hogs, Ayden, North Carolina;** ***bottom left*****, Sam Suchoff holding a long-aged country ham, Chapel Hill, North Carolina;** ***bottom right*****, Ryan Butler, Green Button Farm, Bahama, North Carolina**

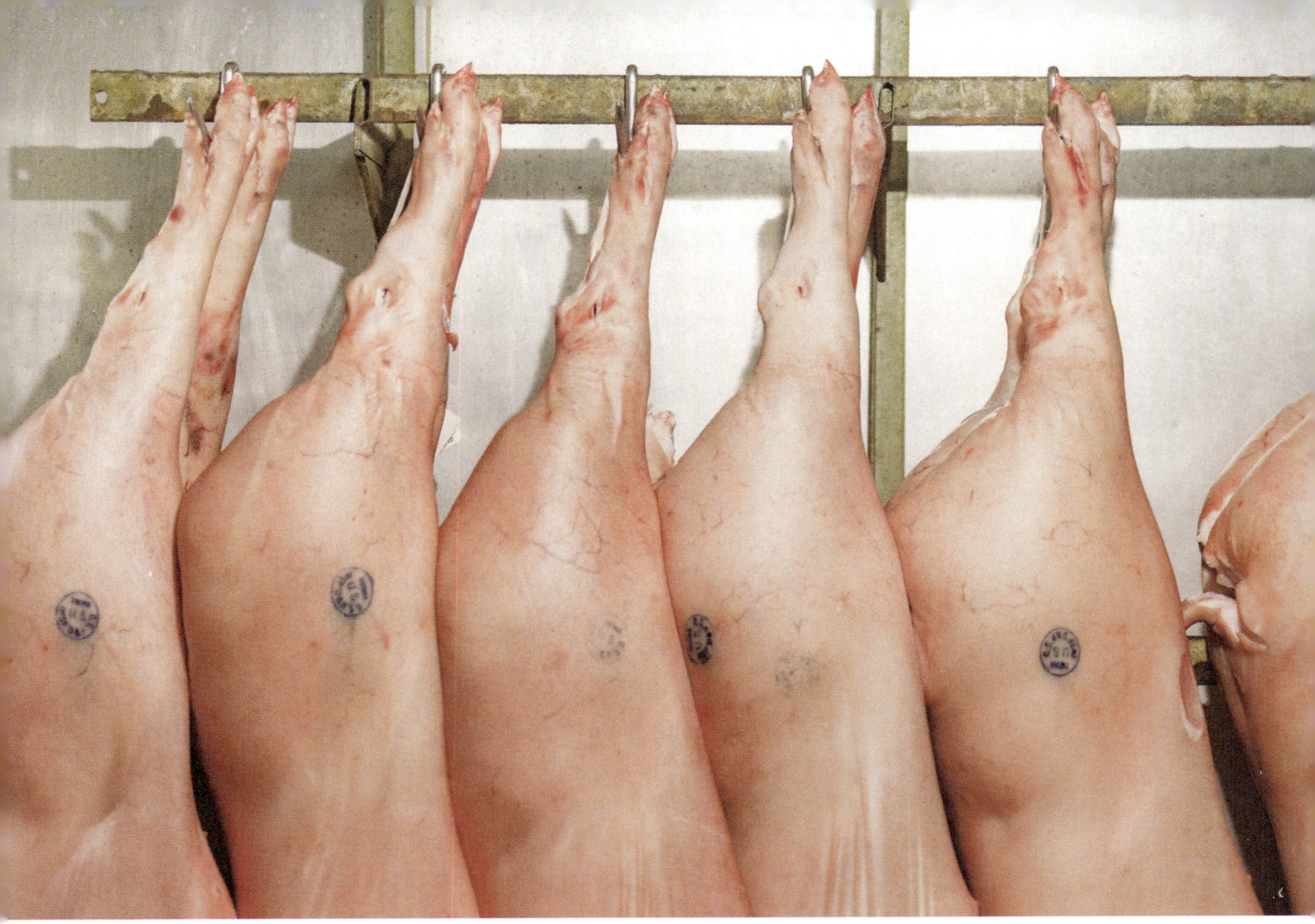

Butler of Green Button Farm. The pair and chef Ben Adams opened Picnic in early 2016, making whole hog barbecue only from pigs raised on Butler's northern Durham County farm. When Dickson and Butler first met in the late 2000s, Butler was working full time as a financial planner and trying to make a go of his farm. He sold pork to Dickson, who worked as a caterer specializing in pasture-raised pork and whole hog barbecue. They often met in the parking lot of the financial planning office on Shannon Road where Butler worked. "I had a van with a cooler full of pig parts," he explains.

As a farmer, Butler sold pork to twenty to thirty fine-dining restaurants in the Triangle. He soon realized that selling whole animals was better than selling the pieces and parts. But many restaurant chefs didn't know how to break down a whole pig, and so Butler trained them. That in part made him the perfect partner for Dickson and Adams when they wanted to open Picnic.

"It's been a challenge," says Dickson, who says they have to predict how much barbecue they will need nine months ahead of time and make sure they have enough for the peak barbecue seasons of spring and fall. "It was helpful that we lashed to the mast together to get through that storm."

Adams has since left the business, and Dickson and Butler are now co-owners. Butler left his job as a financial planner in February 2019 to focus full time on the farm and the restaurant. "Ryan's first restaurant job was as an owner," quips Dickson.

Like Moss and Suchoff, the key to Picnic's ability to use pasture-raised pork is using every part of the pig. On a recent weekday morning, Butler broke down a 222-pound whole hog, which is a bit too big for whole hog barbecue, so he carved it for weekend specials and other dishes. The hams and shoulders became barbecue along with the whole hogs. The tenderloin was smoked and then fried for pork chop biscuits on the Sunday brunch menu. The pork shank was brined, braised, and flash fried for a thirteen-dollar weekday special. The feet were smoked for seasoning meat in collards or beans. The rib rack and belly were cured to make bacon and seasoning meat. Any leftover trimmed meat was used in Picnic's homemade sausage or added to the restaurant's burger mix.

The cut that really makes the math work for Butler's pigs is the rib loin roast. Off this pig, Butler gets twenty-two pork chops, which become a smoked pork chop served with wild rice and creamed collards for twenty-five dollars as a weekend special. "We'll pay for the whole hog with that dish," Butler says. "The rest is house money."

The only parts of that pig going into the trash are the connective tissue and a few dried scraps.

At Picnic, even the skin from cooked whole hogs doesn't go to waste: it is cut into squares, deep fried, and sold as dog treats for six dollars a bag. "That's basically trash that we convert into cash," Dickson says. "It allows us to keep a barbecue sandwich from being too expensive."

That doesn't mean they don't occasionally get pushback on their prices on their ten-dollar barbecue sandwich. "In North Carolina, barbecue is the state cuisine," Dickson says. "For a lot of people, a cheap barbecue sandwich is a God-given birthright. If you're charging a lot, they think you are putting on airs."

"We've developed systems to have not just pasture-raised, local, animal welfare-approved, non-GMO pork, but really *good quality pork that people want to eat—because it has to taste good at the end of the day."*

—JENNIFER CURTIS, cofounder/co-CEO, Firsthand Foods, Durham, North Carolina, March 13, 2019

Dickson adds: "What I tell people is the first thing I go to is taste. I'm hip to all of the other things, but taste won me over."

As many ways as there are to cook barbecue, there are arguments about which method is best. Not all pit masters agree that the added expense of pasture-raised pork makes a better barbecue sandwich.

Sam Jones is a fourth-generation barbecue man in Ayden, North Carolina. His grandfather, Pete Jones, opened Skylight Inn in 1947, an hour's detour off Interstate 95. It soon became a barbecue destination. Skylight Inn is eastern North Carolina old school: a huge woodpile out back, wood paneling and terrazzo floors inside, limited menu (you order pork as small, medium, or large or as a sandwich), and cash only. The Jones men are definitely salesmen; Pete Jones added a replica of the U.S. Capitol Building dome to the top of the restaurant—a fitting crown for what he declared was "The Bar-B-Q Capital of the World."

Sam Jones helps run the Skylight Inn for his father and uncle but has also opened his own restaurant, Sam Jones Barbecue, now with locations in Winterville and Raleigh. Jones's place is in that vein of upscale barbecue restaurants offering chopped whole hog 'cue cooked over wood with cornbread and coleslaw but also flat-screen televisions, craft beers, and house salads topped with your choice of smoked meat.

Jones buys about fifty-five to seventy pigs a week from a hog processor in Ayden for both restaurants. He buys all the "dirt-raised sows" that he can get from that processor, but it's not enough to supply the restaurants. Jones has cooked a lot of hogs in eastern North Carolina and all over the country, including with the FatBack Collective, a group of chefs and pit masters who support the work of small hog farmers in the South.

"I don't think it's fair to say it's better," Jones said. "I've cooked all different breeds, all over the country from $1 a pound to $4.50 a pound. There's not a lot of difference when you're cooking a whole animal and blending it together." Jones has even cooked Mangalitsa hogs, a Hungarian breed of pig renowned for its fat level and often called the "Kobe beef of pork."

His conclusion: "The good Lord didn't intend for all hogs to be made into whole hog barbecue."

Barbecue is a tough business, and Jones doesn't have a large, metropolitan area from which to pull customers who are willing to pay more. Jones's clientele expect a $5 barbecue sandwich. (He hears complaints from customers because his namesake restaurant charges $6.49.) Jones once had a truck driver walk out of Skylight Inn upon learning that prices had gone up 50 cents. And while Jones remembers a man who flew a helicopter from west of Raleigh and landed it in the woodpile yard to get a Skylight Inn barbecue sandwich, he knows that customer cannot sustain his restaurant in eastern North Carolina.

One thing Jones has always loved about his family's barbecue restaurant is seeing the customers lined up to order food at the counter. There can be a farmer, a sanitation worker, and a physician. If they only serve pasture-raised pork, they would have to raise prices significantly.

"That physician is unaffected," Jones notes, "but that sanitation worker is priced out."

Barbecue Hash ELLIOTT MOSS *with* ANDREA WEIGL

Makes about 6 servings

1 pound leftover pulled pork or whole-hog barbecue (can use pulled chicken)
½ pound chicken liver, finely chopped or ground
1 yellow medium onion, finely diced or ground
1 or 2 cloves garlic, finely diced
1 tablespoon kosher salt
1 tablespoon freshly ground black pepper
½ tablespoon onion powder
½ tablespoon garlic powder
2 cups red barbecue sauce (store bought is fine)
1 cup mustard sauce (a common South Carolina-style sauce, store bought is fine)
8 cups water, divided
¼ cup Worcestershire sauce
2 tablespoons Texas Pete hot sauce
1 cup cooked white rice
Additional hot white rice, for serving

In a large pot set over medium heat, add the pork, chicken liver, onion, and garlic. Season the mixture with the salt, pepper, onion, and garlic powder. Cook until the meat is slightly browned. Add both barbecue sauces, 5 cups of water, Worcestershire sauce, Texas Pete, and 1 cup cooked rice. Bring the hash to a boil, then reduce the heat to low so that the mixture is at a simmer.

Cook at a simmer for about 1½ hours, uncovered, stirring frequently to avoid sticking. Add about 2 cups of water and continue to cook and stir for another 1½ hours. Add a final cup of water and cook for 45 minutes or until the water has reduced to leave you with a loose, meaty, gravy-like consistency. Serve over hot white rice. Garnish with additional hot sauce and soda crackers.

Bringing Food Back Home

The View from Warren County

To find us, take I-85 to Warren County, then get off at the Manson exit and head north. We are at the end of a long dirt drive that winds past oaks and pines, shaggy fields, and tobacco barns. This is Carla's family's farm. It is a beautiful, peaceful place: if you saw where we live, we believe you would understand why we and our three children live here.

How to live here, however, is harder to figure out. Fifty years ago, Carla's family was actively farming this land, growing food and tobacco. The same thing was happening on small farms across Warren County and across the state. Agriculture and food was central to the function of this farm and this community. But nowadays we, our family members who also live here, and most of our neighbors leave daily to work somewhere else. Many of the bonds that connected people here to the land and each other have weakened or broken. Most of our food is now shipped in from distant states or nations. Today Warren County's economy and food system (the processes and infrastructure that connect farms to plates) are dislocated—quite literally out of place. All the cues from the modern world seem to say: leave this place behind; go to a city with high-paying jobs, where you can shop at upscale supermarkets and eat in trendsetting restaurants.

But we, and many others, want to live in our rural place, where we see the stars each night and our children ramble freely. So how? For us, the answer involves working to relocate our food economy back home by creating value that is rooted in this place. We begin by drawing connections between three periods of Warren County's history: the not-so-distant agrarian past (fifty to one hundred years ago), the largely dislocated present, and a not-so-distant possible future, in which more of the food system—through necessity, conviction, and strategic collaboration—will return to our county and region. The past fifty years have seen drastic changes in how we produce and consume food; we argue that the next fifty years will require equally drastic changes if we are to survive and thrive.

Dislocation: The Past Fifty Years

Fifty to one hundred years ago, Warren County was part of a working landscape encompassing farmland, small towns, and nearby cities, with the prosperity of each linked to the others. Farm products, such as tobacco and food crops from cantaloupes to cucumbers to cows, were grown on family farms, aggregated and processed in small towns, and then either consumed locally or delivered to cities for further processing and sale. Today these elements have been disarticulated from each other. The success of North Carolina's thriving urban centers is less connected to their surrounding rural regions, and agricultural supply chains largely bypass small towns. These changes have had devastating consequences for rural areas.

The older members of our community can recall when almost every family in Warren County was involved in farming. Small towns were centers for the aggregation, processing, and transaction of these local harvests. In downtown Warrenton one hundred years ago, food was sold by four grocery stores, including a wholesale grocer and a meat market, while seven facilities handled tobacco and two processed cotton. The remainder of the storefronts offered a full complement of goods and services—in short, a diversified local economy. There was even an opera house! More recently, within the memory of many Warren County natives, Warrenton's Main Street was still bustling.

"The reality of the food scene is that people will eat what they can afford. It doesn't matter if it's good for them or not, if it's available and it's something they need, they're going to eat what they can afford."

—**GRACE SUMMERS, small farms consultant, Guilford County, North Carolina, October 7, 2019**

Today some of the county's land is still farmed, but the number of farms has decreased by 90 percent. The landscape is dotted with abandoned barns and country stores that recall the earlier agrarian economy. Our small towns, meanwhile, have lost the businesses that transacted and processed local crops and livestock, including warehouses, slaughterhouses, cotton gins and textile mills, the feed and seed store, and locally owned grocery stores. The crops that are still raised in the county—the largest of which by acreage is now soybeans—leave upon harvest. Delinked from the farm economy and agricultural employers, Main Streets face decreased customer traffic, which makes business survival harder. These changes have also decreased the community's ability to provide food for itself; the vast majority of food in today's stores comes from distant corporate farms and food conglomerates, often in highly processed form. As full-service groceries have closed, low-income consumers are doing more of their shopping at increasingly ubiquitous dollar stores; therefore, the limited selection of food available at such stores has become an important factor in community health outcomes.

Warren County now faces the predicament of being almost entirely dependent on yet simultaneously marginalized by the larger economy.

Local jobs are in short supply; the poverty rate is high; household income is less than half what it is in nearby Raleigh. Most of the county's workforce departs daily for jobs elsewhere. When it comes to food and nutrition, a similarly dismal story emerges. Food access is inadequate and getting worse. The number of grocery stores has dropped from four to two in recent years, and healthy, local food is largely absent from places where people eat daily, such as school cafeterias, childcare centers, and fast food restaurants. Our county is among the state's lowest ranked in terms of health outcomes; the obesity rate is high. The fact that 23 percent of county residents are food insecure (lacking consistent, sufficient access to food) while living in an agricultural landscape epitomizes how the dislocation of the economy has affected our modern food system.

The trajectory of Carla's family place, the Spain-Norwood Farm, mirrors the changes in our community's agricultural economy. Carla's great-grandfather was the last family member to farm full-time, raising tobacco until 1967. Pigs roamed the oak forest; a stable housed cows and a mule; there was a small orchard and a large, diversified garden. The next generation, Carla's grandparents, worked off the farm but maintained the garden and canned enough vegetables to last through the winter. The next two generations, Carla's parents' generation and our own, still live here but have little time to keep up the garden. A neighboring farmer has rented the fields for soybeans. As each successive generation has led an increasingly sedentary lifestyle, with processed foods gradually displacing farm harvests in their diets, health has declined. Carla's great-grandmother lived to be ninety-nine and never needed any medication; her grandmother lived to eighty-six; her mother, seventy-two. And so, we ask ourselves: Are we better off than Carla's great-grandparents?

Relocation: The Next Fifty Years?

Warren County's past, riven by racial and economic divisions, was certainly no idyll. At the same time, the dislocation of our food system from our landscape over the past fifty years has been disastrous for the health and prosperity of our rural community. What would it take to relocate the system over the next fifty years, in a way that learns from the past but does not replicate it?

Upon closer examination, examples of what a relocated food system could look like are not hard to find in Warren County. After all, our local food economy never completely disappeared, and lately it has been growing. If you want to get farm-fresh food in season, you can visit one of the farm stands along Highway 1 or, on Saturdays, browse the

Sweet Potato Pie

Growers Association Farmers Market in Warrenton. Multigenerational farmers have now been joined by those who have moved to the county specifically to farm. These racially diverse growers produce delicious food that ranges from Ridgeway cantaloupes to pasture-raised pork, from free-range eggs to heirloom apples, from shiitake mushrooms to heritage-breed turkeys. Recently, new businesses on Warrenton's Main Street, including an ice cream parlor and a distillery, have begun sourcing ingredients from local farms.

At Working Landscapes, the nonprofit rural development organization we founded in 2010, we are trying to help relocate the Warren County food system. We have established a food hub aimed at connecting diverse local farmers and food entrepreneurs to new markets. Consistent with the idea of relocation, we have repurposed vacant buildings in downtown Warrenton. One, the site of a former cotton gin and flour mill, has become a value-added processing facility where we dice locally grown collards, cabbage, kale, and sweet potatoes for use in school lunchrooms and other cafeterias. The other, a former bank, now houses a commercial kitchen and café.

We are not alone: people across North Carolina are returning to the land, starting Main Street food ventures, and launching food hubs. When we talk to food system entrepreneurs from other parts of the state, we find that their motivations align with ours. They, too, are using food to rebuild the economic and social infrastructure of their communities. Yet they face serious challenges. Many who are making tangible investments in farms and food businesses are shouldering an enormous amount of risk with little ongoing financial and organizational support. As a result, they frequently struggle and fail. When local food ventures do not thrive, skeptics argue that such ventures were never needed or wanted. We view this struggle differently. We see good, important work that is never given a fair chance to succeed because of inadequate support from the community and the state.

Currently, projects that attempt to relocate the food system within communities are being approached by project personnel, policy makers, and funders as isolated endeavors. Essentially, they are regarded as beneficial but discretionary projects. Instead, we believe that they should be considered as part of the essential infrastructure linking farmers to consumers. If this food system infrastructure is understood to be as vital as other kinds of infrastructure—roads, the power grid, water systems—then its development cannot be pursued haphazardly. Imagine a road system being built simultaneously by dozens of small organizations that shared no plan and did not speak to one another; this is essentially the state of our food system. Broad food highways connect us to distant growing regions, feedlots, factory farms, and processing facilities, but the linkages that could move food efficiently within and among our local communities are stunted and fragmented.

Rather than a constellation of discrete projects across the state and region, food system initiatives must be a coordinated effort. Today local food suppliers must collaborate to grow the pie—the market for local products—they all share rather than fight for the biggest slice of the current paltry pie. This involves recognizing and addressing entrenched racial and class divides that have undermined solidarity and pursuit of common purpose. We must map a detailed path to a relocated food system with advance commitments from major buyers of food that will drive supply chain investments. For example, if North Carolina's grocery chains, school systems, university systems, or health care systems would make firm commitments to buy certain amounts of local food, assuming that the products met their requirements, this would give nearby growers and intermediaries the confidence to invest in collectively producing food for those markets. Policy makers and funders have crucial roles to play in supporting this transformation, which would yield meaningful benefits for producers and consumers of food in Warren County and communities across North Carolina. A relocated food system must be appropriately scaled and resilient; we discuss each of these aspects below.

"If we can build and construct healthy regional and local food systems, then we're addressing issues of equity, issues of race discrimination, issues of gender discrimination, and issues of education discrimination."

—LINDEN THAYER, cofounder, FIG (Food Insight Group), Chapel Hill, North Carolina, December 3, 2019

Food Economies of an Appropriate Scale: Toward Food Regions

Warren County's agricultural/food economy was more localized in the past than it is today, but that does not mean it was isolated from the surrounding region. Indeed, regional trade has been an important part of the economy here for thousands of years. A vital part of relocating the food system, then, is not only reintegrating food ventures into our communities but reintegrating our communities into food regions.

Our work has led us to see the city-region composed of an urban center and sufficient surrounding rural lands to supply it with food as the most promising scale at which to build a resilient food system. When it comes to food, North Carolina's populous cities and farmland-rich rural areas need each other. Hundreds of thousands of hungry urban eaters can provide the markets that anchor food infrastructure development in the surrounding region. Like other supposedly new food systems ideas, linking a city to its surrounding region through agriculture is an ancient model, and it was the prevalent American model before the

Top, Gabe Cumming and Carla Norwood, ByWay Foods Hub, Working Landscapes, Warrenton, North Carolina; *bottom*, Ethel Fogg and Gabe Cumming, Warrenton, North Carolina

past half century. In a city-region food system, crops from farms in Warren and other rural counties could once again be aggregated and processed in small towns like Warrenton. A portion of these harvests would then be delivered to Raleigh-Durham or Richmond, Virginia, while the remainder would feed people within our own rural communities.

City-regions face the challenge that their geographic scope is unclear. For this reason, most North Carolina food system initiatives have aligned themselves with more clearly defined geographies: individual counties or the state as a whole. For long-term resilience, we see the former as too small and the latter as too large. Counties acting alone mostly lack the capacity (land, people, institutions) to build their own food systems, and such narrow, county-focused efforts can impede collaboration across broader geographies. North Carolina, meanwhile, is a 500-mile-long landmass that makes no sense as the basis for an efficient food distribution network. However, city-regions are now gaining more prominence in food system planning. Feast Down East in Wilmington began connecting small rural farms to urban restaurants and institutions years ago, and regional food system initiatives are now underway in the greater Triangle and Triad regions. These efforts are important steps in the right direction.

Resilience: Preparing for the Coming Storm

Ultimately, the most compelling reason to relocate our food system—reconnecting people to place and communities to regions—will be nothing less than survival itself. The current dislocated food economy is not only relatively new but also destined to be short-lived. Reliance on long-distance, fossil fuel–intensive, and highly concentrated supply chains for most of our food is not only environmentally costly but extremely risky because these chains are highly vulnerable to disruption.

To preview the impact of disrupting concentrated supply chains, consider the effects of Hurricane Florence, which struck North Carolina in September 2018. The hurricane caused flooding that directly compromised food and water supplies. However, the effects of the storm were not limited to storm-damaged parts of the state: our immediate vicinity avoided severe weather, but when Gabe went to the grocery store a few days after the hurricane had passed, he found almost all of the perishable products—produce, meats, dairy—gone. Store personnel explained that even though the local store itself was not affected by the storm, the supply chain had been.

So, in the wake of a single weather event, it took less than a week for an unaffected community to lose fresh food access. It is not hard to imagine how much worse it would get if the disruption was not an isolated storm but prolonged climatic, geopolitical, or fossil fuel infrastructure upheaval. This is no longer the stuff of apocalyptic-themed movies. Florence is only one of the multiple hurricanes that have devastated North Carolina's coastal plain and the Outer Banks in recent years. It is only a question of time before such upheavals make a sustained impact on our food supply. What will happen then? After the fresh foods run out, the shelf-stable and generally less nutritious boxes of grains and frozen entrees would last a while longer—but not that long. Quite quickly, being able to grow one's own food or knowing people who do would become much more important.

Supply chain disruptions cast the issue of food insecurity in a harsh new light. Most of us who are fortunate enough to have consistent access to food, even if we are very concerned about food insecurity and work professionally to address it, implicitly approach it as an issue that affects "others." But the lesson of the hurricane is this: in the current food system, confronted with the climate crisis that increases severe weather events, we are all less than a week away from being food insecure. This recognition gives greater weight to the project of developing food regions. It is reasonable to expect that, in the not-too-distant future, our own region will need to meet most of its own food needs again.

How do we build regional food systems that are more resilient than the current system? To a certain extent, the American agrarian past provides a template. Probably, a much larger proportion of our population will need to be involved, once again, in growing and preparing food, not just consuming it. Food infrastructure will need to be distributed, rather than concentrated. A dense network consisting of thousands of small farms and food facilities spread across the landscape will be much more resilient than a handful of massive consolidated supply chains.

In important ways, however, the resilient food system of the future will also need to depart from the past. Climate change will transform farming itself; for example, much food production will have to move under cover of greenhouses or hoop houses to survive increasingly hostile and unpredictable growing conditions. And control of food system assets must change in our region. Since the era of plantation agriculture, the means of production have been controlled by a few—an American model of capitalism first fueled by enslaved labor. In a truly resilient system for North Carolina, a diverse array of food enterprises will be led by an equally diverse array of community residents. Cooperatives, community land trusts, and social enterprises can help create and ensure access to land and food in durable ways that benefit communities and people across the state. Regional food systems should be designed to generate more nourishment for people and the soil and less extractive profit.

Reconnection

Just as our organization seeks to help relocate our food system within our community and region, we, too, are trying to relocate our lives to the family farm. Doing so has not been straightforward. Over the past fifty years, Carla's family's lives became disconnected from this place; we envision a process of reconnection over the next fifty. Though we have lived here full-time since 2012, our lives are not yet in sync with the rhythms of this land. While we leave daily to work on food systems issues more broadly, our own fields do not grow food for ourselves or our community.

We struggle with the dissonance between our commitment to our homeplace and the demands and patterns of modern life—two jobs, busy schedules, far-flung obligations. How to navigate this is far from obvious, but it is our task for the next half-century. In the end, achieving resilience in our personal lives and our food system will require a renewed recognition of the value of small and humble places, connected to other nearby places, each stewarded by the people who love them. Collectively, we are going to need our farm, our neighbors' farms, and our small towns to be viable, productive, and sustainable contributors to a food economy that can provide both the food we eat each day and fundamental food security for everyone. We are going to need each other.

Addendum: Looking Forward from the Pandemic

This essay was written just prior to the COVID-19 pandemic. Although we did not anticipate that a virus would jeopardize the conventional food system, the coronavirus pandemic is providing an all-too-real illustration of that system's fragility, as discussed here. Some steps in our nation's corporate-controlled, consolidated food supply chains, such as the mass processing of factory-farmed livestock, have teetered on the brink of collapse. These disruptions have awakened many people to the importance of more localized food sources, including both nearby family farms and home gardening. The local food system in our area, having atrophied over decades of agricultural consolidation, is now struggling to adapt and meet the increasingly urgent food access needs of our population.

However, just as it has exposed the radical dislocation of our food system, the pandemic has also provided something of a blueprint for relocating it. Quite simply, it has strengthened the bonds that we and others around us feel to our home terrain. Here at the farm, we've planted blueberry bushes in what was most recently a soybean field and rows of vegetables in the dormant garden that fed my family for generations. Without being forced to stay home, who knows if we would have found the time for these things. In a way, this crisis has helped us pause and recognize that all the world of human design can be designed differently. We do not want to go back. More than ever, we want to go forward, building a more sane, just, ecologically healthy, and place-based life.

Sweet Potato Pie CARLA NORWOOD & GABRIEL CUMMING

Makes two 9-inch pies (one for now, one to freeze for later)

FOR THE CRUST:
1 cup (2 sticks) unsalted butter
2½ cups all-purpose flour
1 tablespoon sugar
1 teaspoon salt
Ice water

FOR THE FILLING:
2 pounds North Carolina sweet potatoes
¾ cup (1½ sticks) unsalted butter, at room temperature
1½ cups sugar
1 cup milk
4 eggs, at room temperature
1 teaspoon ground nutmeg
1 teaspoon ground cinnamon
2 teaspoons vanilla extract
Pinch of ground cardamom

Based on a Warren County recipe from Bev Wilson's family.

To make the crust, dice the butter and chill it in the freezer for a few minutes. In a food processor fitted with a dough blade, add the flour, sugar, and salt. Pulse a few times to mix. Add the chilled butter and process about 10–20 seconds until the mixture is uniform and no large chunks of butter remain. With the food processor running, add 3 tablespoons of ice water. The flour mixture should start to form into a ball. Add water, a little at a time, as needed until the dough comes together but is not sticky.

Remove the dough from the food processor and divide it into 2 disks. Immediately roll out the disks into large circles and gently press each one into a pie pan. Trim and crimp the edges and set aside.

To make the filling, set the oven to 425° and bake the sweet potatoes on a baking sheet until they are soft all the way through, about 45–50 minutes. Remove from the oven and cool.

Once the sweet potatoes are cool enough to handle, peel them and transfer them to a large bowl. Add the butter and mash until smooth. Add the remaining ingredients and stir to combine. (For a smoother filling, pour the potato mixture into a blender and pulse for a few seconds.)

Divide the filling between the 2 pie crusts. At this point, you can wrap the pies in plastic wrap and freeze them for baking later. Otherwise, bake the pies at 350° until the center is set and the top just begins to brown, about 1 hour. Allow the pies to cool completely before slicing.

SANDRA A. GUTIERREZ

Pulling Up a Chair at the New Southern Latino Table

Food is the bridge that spans a divide between my two beloved cultures of Latin America and the Nuevo South. When people migrate from one place to another, they bring recipes, ingredients, and traditions with them. I did the same. Food is a witness to our histories. Long before immigrants like me are accepted, our food is embraced. However, true assimilation can only occur when a country, a place, and a region are open to diversity and equality. We need more chairs pulled around the American table instead of walls built to divide us.

I was destined to live between two worlds. Born in the United States, I was raised by Guatemalan parents in Latin America, where I graduated from an American school that celebrated two cultures, two languages, and two culinary traditions. After attending Smith College in Massachusetts, I arrived in North Carolina, a young bride, in the early 1980s. The South I encountered was not unlike that depicted in vintage Hollywood movies: a place solely of Black and white southerners, where no one dared bring up race in polite conversation and where other people of color were a rarity. Stereotypes abounded. My husband, Luis, was a student at Duke University's Fuqua School of Business, where we temporarily found a small oasis—as was often the case at university campuses then—where otherness was not only acceptable but celebrated. That was not the case outside the university walls where we settled and started our family.

In America, first-generation immigrants learn to adapt, to adopt, or to succumb to the ways of their new country. Yet what first-generation immigrants will not tell you—even though some of us were born here—is that we are seldom offered a seat at the American table. That seat is earned by joining others at a table that we, too, create.

Having grown up in a country torn apart by political strife, I possessed a steely resilience for a young woman in her early twenties. I knew what it was like to be positioned politically between right-wing military dictators and Marxist guerrilla insurgents. By the time I moved to North Carolina, I had already lost many friends and acquaintances to violence: an innocent six-year-old boy who was forcibly removed from the school bus by armed leftist kidnappers while we children watched in horror; the parents of a dear friend who were gunned down in the street in a union dispute; a young high-school friend who was murdered by a politician involved in a weapons exchange. I knew real danger and therefore was unafraid in a South that expected me to submit to its racism. I was not willing to stand at the side of the table.

I had a clear advantage in that my bicultural upbringing allowed me to adapt and adopt with fierceness. It was the way I had always lived: taking a little bit of here and a little bit of there and making it my own without apology. In a land where all were created equal, I had arrived to claim my piece of equality.

My story is not that of the thousands of Hispanic migrant workers in our region, whose singular experiences of diaspora have been flattened to a dehumanizing stereotype by politicians and media. I am part of an invisible Latino generation who sought professional degrees in America and remained and others who arrived with educations and well-paid occupations in hand. But like the Hispanic migrant workers, these affluent Latinos also came to find a better life for their families, having escaped political insurrection, personal persecution, and failing economies that imperiled their children's futures.

When I speak at conferences, some attendees appear uncomfortable when they learn I am a published author, because what Latinx could possibly be *that*? How could an immigrant have an education or economic status comparable to theirs? Othering rejects equal opportunity and shared class status. In a story on my food writing, one reporter ignored that my mother was an economics professor in a leading university in Guatemala so that I better fit her preconceived notion of a Latina. America understands the Latinx migrant experience solely in a working-class frame—the janitor in a building, the dishwasher in a restaurant, the domestic worker in a suburban home. Yet our experience and identity is more complex. We are an economic and cultural force in the American South who stand in solidarity with a diverse Latinx population across this country.

"Right now what we're experiencing as a country, the fear of the 'other,' is one of the biggest challenges that we have. We're finding our own voice as New Southern Latinos. This is our new South. We're not only worth it, we're pivotal for the rest of the country."

—**SANDRA A. GUTIERREZ, Cary, North Carolina, February 4, 2019**

To understand the Nuevo South is to understand this: Latinx immigrants are not only Mexican; we come from a large territory home to twenty-one countries with diverse cultures and histories. In the industrial and agricultural South of the early twentieth century, Latinx immigrants journeyed to the region via the Southwest, seeking work and better situations for their families. In the 1990s, legal changes including enactment of the Temporary Protected Status designation (which precludes the deportation of immigrants back to their countries due to natural disasters or armed conflict) opened the way for the arrival of more Latinx residents. According to the U.S. Census Bureau, the number of Central American immigrants to the South grew ninefold between 1980 and 2013. Arriving contemporaneously were highly skilled South Americans and professionals from the Latin Caribbean. From 2000 to 2010, the Latinx population in the American South grew by almost 70 percent, and in North Carolina, since 1990, it has increased by 150 percent.[1] Data from the 2020 census shows continued growth, and Latinx now make up almost 11 percent of the population here.

Working-class Latinx seeking seasonal agricultural jobs and white-collar Latinx professionals were just starting to come to North Carolina when Luis and I arrived in 1985. Salsa had not yet become a part of the southern culinary lexicon; a decade later, it would outsell ketchup. When I arrived in Cary and became the first Latina food columnist for the local newspaper, the resistance to my voice was swift. I had been at the paper only a week when my editor heard from a disgruntled subscriber, upset that her beloved paper had chosen "a Mexican" as the writer for its food section. Had I capitulated to this racism I would not have witnessed the birth of a new culinary movement in the region. I embraced the culinary traditions of my southern white and Black readers but at the same time found my passion to introduce them to a global world of flavor.

One day I noticed chipotle peppers in barbecue sauce and hushpuppies speckled with chorizo. My readers filled tacos with leftover pulled pork and served them with chimichurri (a garlicky parsley sauce). My neighbors smothered their grandmothers' biscuits in dulce de leche (sweetened milk cooked down until it becomes a thick caramel) and doused pound cakes with rum. I was witnessing the beginnings of what I would later call the New Southern Latino food movement. If you had taste buds, it was impossible to ignore. White and Black southerners expanded their culinary roots by joining their food traditions with those of Latin American immigrants, exposing the new racial and sociopolitical realities of a region one dish at a time.

In my own home, I began to combine ingredients and foodways from both of my cultures—by necessity at first, when nostalgia for loroco buds (an edible wild flower) from my Guatemalan home inspired me to add collard greens to tamales, chicharrones (pork rinds) to my biscuits, sweet potato to enrich our pozole (soup with pork and hominy), and the creation of layered potato salads in the tradition of Peru. Surely, if I was doing this in my own kitchen, others were, too? I asked my readers what they were cooking at home and what my southern neighbors and new immigrants alike were cooking for dinner each day. Soon, a picture of blended culinary cultures began to emerge—one that expanded

Pecan Polvorones
with Coffee Granita

traditional notions of southern foodways and opened my eyes and palate to the birth of a new food movement in the American South.

The New Southern Latino food movement grew at a grassroots level throughout the region. I remember the surreal moment that the movement became real to me. I was invited to a party at an upscale golf course subdivision in Cary in 2002, where my southern white hosts served cabrito (goat) pit-roasted instead of barbequed pork, with sides of potato salad, coleslaw, and tostones (fried plantains). No one thought twice about this menu. The guests enjoyed the diverse buffet if not fully understanding the significant cultural changes it reflected in its embrace of Latinx dishes, ingredients, and flavors.

Latin American *tiendas* (stores) began to appear across the Raleigh metro region and the Triangle in the late 1990s—from tiny storefronts to enormous food chains bigger than most supermarkets. I could drive to a store owned by Central Americans in Cary to purchase my beloved loroco buds, trek to Main Street in Carrboro to find the long-leaf herb culantro for my Latin Caribbean–inspired dishes, or pop over to Apex to shop at the Galaxy Supermarket, now part of the extensive Compare Foods chain. There I bought fresh epazote (a bitter herb) and dried chiles of all kinds to make Mexican dishes, Ecuadorian chocho (lupini) beans for ceviche, Brazilian mandioca (cassava flour) for bread, Honduran crema (like crème fraîche) for topping beans, and Guatemalan pickled chiltepe chiles for adding heat to my dishes. Among the myriad Spanish-speaking customers, I always encountered non-Latinx southerners eager to ask how I use a certain ingredient or curious to learn about a particular cuisine and relieved that I spoke English. I also met with many African, African American, and Afro-Caribbean community members, who used many of the same ingredients of Latino community cooks.

Suddenly, I didn't have to describe what a pupusa (stuffed corn cake) tasted like to my children; I could cook as many as I wanted and serve them with authentic Salvadoran cabbage slaw (curtido). I began to introduce my family, my friends, and my readers to Colombian sancocho (hen stew), Cuban mojo (a citrus and garlic marinade), and Puerto Rican rice and peas (arroz con gandúles). My readers sent me leads for where I could find ingredients and shared new recipes and dishes they prepared at home. They stopped me in my local market to tell me about the coconut milk they added to their seafood chowders as is done in Belize, the bourbon that found its way into their Mexican mole, and the Brazilian malagueta peppers in their barbecue sauce. I visited the Carrboro Farmers' Market to buy goat from Cane Creek Farm to make Peruvian seco (a spicy stew), and I left with collard greens and garlic scapes, grown by my favorite farmers, but also chile varieties (such as ají dulce from South America) that I wouldn't have dreamed of finding in North Carolina a decade before.

The clear delineations that once separated the many cuisines of Latin Americans and southerners have blurred, creating a cornucopia of new dishes. In the kitchen, people of all races use similar basic ingredients. A tomato, an avocado, a portion of cornmeal, a pile of beans—these foods do not differentiate among races but simply reflect diverse interpretations, each equally delicious. The budding New Southern Latino food movement was not only Mexican driven, as it had been in Texas and California, once a part of Mexico. Ingredients, people, and food traditions from across the entire Latin American continent transformed southern food. Southerners were open to new flavors, if not as open to the people who brought these flavors with them. Change entered quietly yet forcefully through the kitchen door.

"No one complains about hot food, spicy food anymore. It's unheard of. When I first came to work at Crook's, everybody complained that the collards had too much cayenne in it. I haven't heard that in a hundred years."

—**BILL SMITH, chef, Chapel Hill, North Carolina, February 6, 2019**

In 2010, the Southern Foodways Alliance's annual symposium in Mississippi focused on the Global South. Sessions and speakers explored the merging of Latin American and other food cultures with those of African Americans in shaping the foodways of an evolving New South. I had just completed my book *The New Southern-Latino Table*. By the time my friend Chef Bill Smith of Chapel Hill's Crook's Corner had served sweet potato tamales at a benefit dinner in 2012, the Mexican cooks in his restaurant had inspired a menu featuring a green peach salad with chile powder and the Mexican-style cheese and green onions that topped its hoppin' John (a classic southern side of rice and black-eyed peas). Crook's Corner patrons loved these dishes. Bill explained, "We were trying to 'Southernize' tamales a little." As one of the first chefs to pull more chairs up to his southern table, Bill Smith created a space of equality, creativity, and agency for the skilled Latinx cooks in his community. Soon, the Carolina Inn at the University of North Carolina offered pulled pork tacos with chimichurri, and at the upscale North Carolina resort community of Southern Pines, tamales and grits were served with shrimp and pineapple salsa.

In 2013 Chef Oscar Diaz, an American of Mexican heritage born in Chicago, became chef at Raleigh's first New Southern Latino restaurant, Jose and Sons. Owners the Ibarra brothers, first-generation Mexican North Carolinians, opened this innovative restaurant to great acclaim. Jose and Sons represented a delicious blending of Mexican and southern cuisines, and although it did not reflect the totality of the New Southern Latino movement, it celebrated one of its strongest elements. The

Sandra A. Gutierrez,
Cary, North Carolina

restaurant earned a stellar review in the *New York Times* and a James Beard nomination for Diaz in 2019. The New Southern Latino movement that began in the homes of both immigrants and deeply rooted southerners in the 1990s had finally trickled upward into restaurants where customers willingly accepted higher prices in an immigrant-owned business. Throughout the South today it's not surprising to find menu items like pork tacos with pico de gallo.

In 2017, I was invited to speak at the Southern Foodways Alliance for a conference focused on the Nuevo South. I took the podium to represent a group of Latina women who, like myself, had long been ignored in the national conversation surrounding food, race, and gender. These women are editors, authors, journalists, chefs, social activists, and entrepreneurs—all Latinx, all doing important work connected to southern foodways. Women like Lis Hernandez, a Venezuelan immigrant and chef-owner of restaurant Arepa Mia in Atlanta; activist Renata Soto, a Costa Rican immigrant who founded Conexión Americas, a nonprofit that assists Latino immigrant families in Nashville, Tennessee; and Liz Balmaseda, a Pulitzer Prize–winning journalist of Cuban American descent who lives in Florida. It was my intent to make this invisible group to which I belong, the Mujeres del Sur, invisible no more. We are everywhere within your communities; you just have to open your eyes.

In 2016, my work on the food worlds of the Nuevo South was featured in the Smithsonian's *Gateway/Portales* exhibition, which explored how Latinos have made a home in four distinctive metro areas in the United States, including Charlotte and Raleigh-Durham in North Carolina. Later, my work became a part of the National Museum of American History's new permanent exhibit on food and the transformation of the American table, 1950–2000. Having my food story and those of Latinx women like me—our voices, our families, our rightful place at the table—acknowledged by the Smithsonian was one of the greatest honors of my life.

My loves of Latin America and the Nuevo South are grounded today in an unstoppable New Southern Latino culinary movement. As long as the tree that is southern foodways continues to grow in diversity, it will reinforce its roots and grow stronger branches and, in turn, create a greater canopy of inclusiveness over a racially divided South and nation. For this to happen, southerners must understand that the roots of their culinary tree are formed of three cultures: Native American, European, and African; that the trunk of the tree includes people of color who have been a part of the region since its earliest history; that the branches represent different culinary movements that speak of Africa, Appalachia,

Asia, Latin America, and more; and that the leaves are its many ingredients, flavors, foods, dishes, and recipes. This does not weaken the tree; rather, it makes its canopy larger and stronger. I envision an expansive welcome table beneath the tree of southern foodways, laden with food for all. Pull up a chair and join us.

Pecan Polvorones (Pecan Shortbread) with Coffee Granita SANDRA A. GUTIERREZ

Makes 2 dozen cookies | Makes 8 servings

FOR THE GRANITA

3 cups hot brewed coffee
¾ cups granulated sugar
1 tablespoon Kahlua (optional)
1 teaspoon vanilla extract

FOR THE COOKIES

2 cups all-purpose flour
1 cup finely chopped pecans
Pinch of salt
1 cup (2 sticks) unsalted butter, at room temperature
½ cup packed dark brown sugar
1 teaspoon vanilla extract
½ cup powdered sugar
1 envelope Vanilla Sugar by Oetker (optional)

Start the granita the night before you wish to serve it. In a large bowl, combine the hot coffee, sugar, liqueur, and vanilla and stir until the sugar has dissolved. Let the liquid sit at room temperature until cool, about 15 minutes. Transfer the mixture into a large metal pan (9 × 13-inch works well) and set it in the freezer for 1 hour.

Once the mixture is frozen, scrape it with a fork, forming crystals as you work, and then refreeze it. Repeat this process every 30 minutes, for a total of 8–10 times. The resulting granita should look like fluffy, loose ice crystals. Wrap the granita tightly and leave it in the freezer until you're ready to use it or overnight. To serve, simply scrape the granita one more time and use.

To make the cookies, in a medium bowl, combine the flour, chopped pecans, and salt and whisk until thoroughly mixed. In a separate bowl, cream together the butter and brown sugar until smooth. Stir in the vanilla and mix to combine. Add the dry ingredients to the wet ingredients. Using your hands, mix the ingredients until they come together into a ball. Wrap the dough and chill for at least 2 hours or overnight.

Set the oven to 350° and line 2 baking sheets with parchment paper. Measure 1 tablespoon of dough, roll it into a cylinder, and then gently bend and shape it into a crescent. Place the cookies 2 inches apart on the prepared baking sheets. Bake the cookies for 12–15 minutes or until the bottoms begin to turn a golden color. Remove from the oven and allow to cool for 1 minute.

In a small bowl, combine the powdered sugar with the vanilla sugar. Gently roll the cookies in the powdered sugar to coat. Let the cookies cool completely, and then roll them in the sugar again. Serve a few cookies with a portion of the coffee granita.

NOTES

1. Milton Ready, *The Tar Heel State: A New History of North Carolina* (Columbia: University of South Carolina Press, 2020), 375; National Research Council et al., *Statistics on U.S. Immigration: An Assessment of Data Needs for Future Research*, ed. Barry Edmonston (Washington, D.C.: National Academy Press, 1996); Hannah Gil, *North Carolina and the Latino Migration Experience: New Roots in the Old North State* (Chapel Hill: University of North Carolina Press, 2010).

Pandemic Reflections from a Musician-Organizer-Activist-Chef-Restaurateur

My husband, Paul, and I had flown to California to celebrate a friend's birthday. We were taking a much-needed break and hadn't traveled west in more than a decade since we became owner-operators of the three-story behemoth that is our triple-layered business in downtown Raleigh. At the heart of it all is Garland, our eighty-something-seat restaurant that has defined and dominated my life for the past seven years. Garland's menu is driven by in-season ingredients from our home in Raleigh, prepared with the flavors and techniques of Indian and Asian cuisine. Underneath Garland is the subterranean cocktail bar Neptunes Parlour, and resting on top of Garland is the music venue Kings. In its second incarnation and location now, Kings was born out of Paul's mission to create a venue that was music driven and musician run and a place for all the weirdos to call our own. When it opened, he and I were spending the majority of any given year in a van with our bandmates, touring across the country, Canada, and sometimes western Europe. Lifelong friendships with other bands dotted the map of our tour itineraries. On double-bill tours we shared stages night after night.

Eli was one of those band friendships that developed after spending many weeks touring together. In Berkeley, Paul and I met Eli and his wife, Rachel, for an early lunch at Chez Panisse. It was Friday, March 13, 2020. This was the last time I ate inside a restaurant. Over warmed goat cheese salad, the best marinated anchovies I've ever had, and indulgent lunchtime glasses of rosé, we reminisced about the old days, ex-bandmates, and tour stories and generally caught up on life since we had last seen one another. We speculated about the developing COVID-19 threat. Could it *possibly* destroy everything as we know it? The next week, we shut our businesses down.

Paul and I were scheduled to return to North Carolina on Monday, March 16. We had reluctantly left the businesses on March 11 stocked with bleach, rubbing alcohol, and aloe—everything our staff needed to make gallons of hand sanitizer. We wrote thorough safety protocols in an attempt to ensure the confidence of both our team and our guests. Our main concern that week was the many show cancellations at Kings, as well as the already declining reservations and sales at Garland and Neptunes. We were honestly just worried about getting through the month. The virus had not affected North Carolina significantly yet, but the empty tables at iconic San Francisco restaurants and our ease in snagging a reservation at Chez Panisse were foreboding signs of what we could soon expect in the eastern United States.

We read article after article trying to decipher the best pandemic-related science and counsel related to our businesses. Our level of anxiety was so high that we considered returning to North Carolina early each day of our short visit in California, and finally we changed our flight to come back on Sunday. Our manager at Garland said that Saturday night's service was busy but eerie, as though everyone was having one last hurrah before the world ended. The staff were scared and worried, their vulnerability focused on a serious threat that wasn't very well understood. Instructions to wash hands every fifteen minutes, "don't touch your face," and sanitize menus and check trays suddenly felt pathetically cursory and inadequate. The situation on the national and global levels was evolving at light speed as state after state began announcing shelter-in-place mandates. There was speculation about airports shutting down. On our flights home, we clicked link after link on our phones explaining COVID projections, theories of transmission, and best codes of conduct. "Don't wear masks—they should be reserved for doctors and nurses!" "Do wear a mask!" "Don't eat at restaurants—the virus can be transmitted through carry-out bags and containers." "Eat at restaurants, but only outside." The information was contradictory and confusing.

As soon as we arrived home in Raleigh, we started looking at our finances and projecting what payroll we could sustain for two to three weeks without income. A group of restaurant owners and chefs in downtown Raleigh began a text thread, frantically sharing advice, emergencies, and possible closing plans. Time moved slowly. The passing of every hour brought an entirely new scenario. Our reality shifted constantly. What was an innovative fundraising idea in the morning seemed trivial and dangerous by evening. Our collective guts were failing us. I was deeply conflicted. Do we try and work our way out of this? Do we keep at least some revenue coming in so we can pay our staff? Can we do that without endangering ourselves and our staff? If we stay open or do take-out, will we have any customers? Do we want customers? By Monday morning, it was clear that the only right answers were those that ensured the safety of our team and our loyal diners. No gamble was small. We could make payroll for a few weeks, but it would wipe us out. This virus was going to be with us for at least six weeks, so we thought. Of course, six weeks turned into months. On Monday, March 16, we informed our staff of our plan to close "until things cleared up." We committed to paying our managers a reduced salary so that they could earn more than was possible on unemployment. We promised a paycheck for our Latinx employees who could not or would not file for government assistance. We stopped paying ourselves.

The next morning, we wrote an official furlough letter for our employees, assembled each of their payroll statements, downloaded their W-2s, and began the grueling process of calling each one of the thirty-six people we had to lay off. It was hard to utter the words at first, "I'm so sorry, but so you have the best chance of getting unemployment benefits, and to ensure that you have a job to come back to, we have to temporarily furlough you starting today." By the fifteenth call, I struggled to not sound robotic, knowing that my words were equally scary for each person to hear. The calls took the better part of the day. By the time Governor Roy Cooper's orders to close restaurants and bars came on March 17, most of our people had the employment documents they needed in their inboxes.

We were dizzy managing what was required to shut down a business with so much perishable inventory. In the kitchen, coolers were still stocked with deli containers of sauces, garnishes, and mise en place from Saturday night's service. Confited young chickens sat ready to finish roasting, and whole snappers sat nestled in rapidly melting ice. We had prepared for unexpected shutdowns when a snowstorm or hurricane was heading our way, but we knew that this would be much longer. We itemized the most urgent tasks, made spreadsheets of food loss, stocked the freezers with what we could potentially save, and distributed the rest among our staff. We posted closures on social media, put signs on our doors, adjusted the thermostats, canceled reservations for the rest of the month, recorded outgoing voicemail messages. We checked and added to our lists at a frantic pace. We stocked our own pantry at home, realizing that we had nothing to eat or cook. It had been so long since I cooked for just Paul and me. I wanted comfort food—simple chicken curries, pots of beans, stews, quick stir-fried greens, and rice. I made masala for the freezer. We often grilled outside that spring and summer. Looming over everything was the frightening question, "What happens now?"

The first few weeks of the shutdown I spent a lot of time sitting at the kitchen table refreshing the state's infuriatingly broken Division of Employment Security website. Simultaneously I was on hold for hours,

Cheetie Kumar, Garland, Raleigh, North Carolina; *background*, Hot Hot Peanuts

seeking answers for why some of our folks had not received benefits weeks after filing. My phone was constantly buzzing with active text threads among local restaurateurs, food and beverage friends in other states, and my "Brown in the South" gang—a group of fellow southern chefs of Indian heritage who have forged a tight professional network and personal camaraderie in the past few years. All of us were cooking at home for a change, drinking a little too much, and reminding each other to get outside each day. I created a Zoom account and we started organizing.

"My grandparents were killed in the partition with Pakistan, so a painful history and oppression was a part of our family's food stories. Because of this, the painful history of southern food wasn't a barrier to me—this history is just a part of the story. The emergence of beautiful food and narrative in the face of unspeakable horror is transformational."

—**CHEETIE KUMAR, Raleigh, North Carolina, April 16, 2019**

As the days slipped into weeks, the rhythm we had fallen into of working, cooking, walking, and sleeping felt as though we were shirking our responsibilities. The open-ended nature of those early days was liberating in retrospect. No longer was I tethered to the rigorous schedule of packed days and nights of prep, service, constant new dish development, planning, prepping, and packing for festivals and distant events. I was used to fourteen-hour workdays, very little sleep, no sun, irregular meals, and no days off. Now, each day was just like the last. What were we accomplishing? COVID didn't appear to have an end, and we feared that New York's high infection numbers would soon be seen across the country.

The virus claimed the life of New York chef Floyd Cardoz soon after he returned from India in late March 2020. We had just visited his restaurants in Mumbai in February during an incredible trip to India with my friends Chefs Vishwesh Bhatt and Meherwan Irani. The loss of Chef Floyd sent a shockwave through the culinary industry. How many of our friends and colleagues would succumb before this was over? I imagined losing people I loved, and the fear suddenly felt insurmountable.

The sadness turned into hopelessness, which turned into anger. Why were we, as small restaurant operators, so alone in this fight? We were the first to help others and to raise funds for emergencies. We supported the local farm economy. We employed people in the community. We lived on as little as possible. Now we were free-falling with no parachute and no safety net in sight. Each appeal to local and state officials to establish relief packages met with resistance: "There is no money in the budget for specific sectors of small businesses." Restaurants collectively pay millions of dollars in food and beverage taxes. As we organized small groups of local restaurant operators to approach legislators collectively, the Independent Restaurant Coalition was established on a national level.

We spent the month of April frantically applying for grants and loans. I filled out applications daily while pushing city, county, and state officials to allocate funds for restaurant relief. I felt as if I'd taken a crash course in policy making. Once the federal unemployment benefits were released, the worry shifted from our staff to our business and future. Every restaurant owner we knew was in the same predicament. Whether you had to let go 20 or 200 employees, the stakes were equally devastating. Our profit and loss statements were similarly grim. How ironic it is that in these days of forced isolation we found ways to connect and initiate collective action. We were starting to feel like a cohesive industry—one that is flawed, yes, but we were finally working together, not against one another. We knew that our survival depended on much more than keeping the doors of our individual businesses open.

As spring bloomed around us, the bright, crisp air that normally inspired hope and optimism contrasted sharply with desolate streets, social isolation, and slowly simmering frustration. We kept in touch with our staff through a group app. There were messages of positivity and the deep affection our team members feel for one another. Those who had been furloughed had acquired their federal unemployment supplemental benefits. We finally received our PPP (Paycheck Protection Program) loan. We believed we could survive the summer and thought that there would be some return to normalcy in the fall. In early May, I received my first James Beard Award finalist nomination for Best Chef: Southeast, and though it was a moment of joy and gratitude, it felt like an echo in an empty room. It seemed so irrelevant. What was the value of these awards when there is so little security to show for our hard work? What once mattered to me now seemed ephemeral. We started a meal kit program at Garland to reengage with our diners slowly and safely, allowing them to heat and eat dishes at home. We prepared whole stuffed and spice-rubbed fish for the grill, lamb biryani in foil pans sealed with a dough lid, and a shrimp and chile stir fry, each meal accompanied with video links and step-by-step directions.

Things started to change as the pandemic underscored historic racial violence, inequality, resistance, and reckoning following the police murder of George Floyd in Minnesota on May 25. COVID-19, its economic impact, and Black Lives Matter revealed deep flaws in American society. Rage was directed at those with power—including employers and business owners—some of it very justified. The movement for racial justice was underscored by a demand for crucial social and economic reforms. As many workers across the country faced unemployment and others continued in low-wage jobs in often uncaring and unsafe environments, a breaking point was imminent. The nation exploded in a ferocious roar.

Downtown Raleigh was the site of multiple protests, the first resulting in sidewalks covered in broken glass and shattered storefronts. That night with two of our friends, we stood outside Garland and pleaded with guys about to toss a scooter or newspaper stand through our window. We luckily had little damage to our business, although we did lose a window after we left to go home at 1:15 A.M. We shut down again. The streets were barricaded for two weeks and a curfew was imposed. We never quite regained the energy of those first few weeks of the meal kit program. Everything felt simultaneously heavy and shallow. Downtown was boarded up and even more desolate than before—like a surreal set for a dystopian movie.

"All businesses have responsibilities; we just have more—how we pay employees, what we are supporting when we source our ingredients, the economic power of that. I'm affecting economies that are three layers removed from me—a local farm, the community those farmers pay taxes in, the family they are trying to support, whether their kids will see that farming is a viable career, not just honorable."

—**CHEETIE KUMAR, Raleigh, North Carolina, April 16, 2019**

As I write this in mid-December 2020, I'm reflecting on the past: Garland turned seven years old today. It has also been exactly nine months since we returned from California, and we are back to conditions and anxiety much like we experienced in mid-April. We began outdoor sidewalk dining three months ago. Gone are the chef-y dishes that feature delicate plating and micro herbs and flowers, replaced by takeout-friendly fried fish, pickled shrimp, addictive spare ribs with a spicy, sweet Szechuan glaze, and the mainstays of our menu—a turmeric-marinated and flash-fried cauliflower and warm Moroccan whole-bean hummus. Right now we're serving "hoppin' Jaan" chaat with stewed black-eyed peas, rice pilaf, toasted peanuts, herbs, and chutneys. "Jaan" is the Hindi word for life force.

It's getting cold. COVID-19 spikes are worse than ever, with terrifying daily statistics of newly infected and escalating hospitalizations and fatalities in our county and state. Epidemiologists predict more than half a million dead in America before the pandemic ends. The first vaccines just shipped this morning, but it will be months before the general population has access. We look at our depleted bank account, desperate for a federal relief program to provide the needed bridge to survive the coming weeks. Instead, there is no action from our government. We hemorrhage money weekly. We built a complete dining space on the sidewalk and created a new platform of contactless ordering, service, and plating. Although we are grateful to hear the ticket printer chirping away in the kitchen, we are also tasked with obtaining weekly COVID tests for our staff. I never imagined training team members how to administer a nasal swab. We worry about a staff member getting sick, but we are afraid to stop operations. If we lay people off again, they face inadequate unemployment. No relief measures have been passed since the spring. I am back to fourteen hours on my feet, yet there is the constant worry of how we maintain a core staff as we again face the threat of imminent business closures.

The next months are likely to be the most challenging of this entire crisis. In my better moments, I am deeply committed to a healthy food system, a happy and nurturing workplace, finding time for personal creativity, and helping others find joy in the simple act of preparing and eating a meal. Often these feel like ideals from a life I once imagined. What I am sure about is that our food systems need to be dismantled and reassembled. For starters, instead of subsidizing industrial crops for industrial food products, farmworkers should be paid a living wage. There needs to be a systemic acknowledgment that fast food restaurants and independent restaurants are vastly different business models. Independent restaurants build local economies by sourcing food locally and paying their professional workers a decent wage. It begs the question, Why aren't we encouraging those independent restaurant owners who pay a realistic wage with beneficial federal and state payroll tax incentives? Food is falsely cheap in America, and operating a full-service restaurant is expensive. We must make more changes to stay afloat. Which begs another question: Will we cook only for the rich now? Not necessarily. During the pandemic we have seen successful restaurant partnerships with government-sponsored food relief programs. Restaurants can be efficient points of access for healthy, affordable food for communities in need. Many of us got a firsthand education in packaging food for assistance programs. We were able to help while getting a little assistance with our own bottom lines. We can extend this beyond the pandemic.

Like most restaurant owners, I no longer think of myself as just a proprietor or a chef or a creative individual. Of course, I can't wait to pick up my guitar again! But I have also honed my skills as an organizer and a navigator of our political system while keeping my spirit of activism fueled. I will keep pushing for a more just and equitable business landscape that recognizes the vital economic and cultural contributions of the food community and our talented, dedicated workers. The North Carolina ground remains unsteady under my feet, our future unsure. But I see that we have a better, more equitable and hopeful road ahead of us, and I will not compromise what feels like a promising tomorrow.

Hot Hot Peanuts CHEETIE KUMAR

Makes 2 cups

2½ tablespoons garam masala
2 teaspoons kosher salt
1 tablespoon granulated cane sugar
1 tablespoon amchur (dry raw mango powder; can be found at Indian markets)
½ teaspoon ground cayenne pepper
½ cup grapeseed or good-quality canola oil
2 cups North Carolina peanuts, shelled (try to find unroasted, unsalted peanuts, but salted ones will work in a pinch; simply adjust the added salt to taste)
Grated zest and juice of ½ lime

In a small bowl, combine the garam masala, salt, sugar, amchur, and cayenne pepper. Set aside.

In a wok or deep skillet, heat the oil until shimmering but not smoking. Add 1 cup of the peanuts and stir over medium heat until toasted and golden, about 5 minutes. Remove with a slotted spoon or mesh spider and transfer to a paper-towel-lined plate or cookie sheet. Repeat with the remaining peanuts.

In a large bowl, mix the hot peanuts with the spices, stirring to coat evenly. Taste for salt and add more if you like. Sprinkle on the lime zest and juice before serving. If you can't find amchur, increase the amount of lime juice and zest to your liking.

Preserving Community

I am face down in the covered bed of my beat-up truck, stretching to reach the cases of pickles I set aside for my pickle-obsessed physical therapist. (My failing shoulder joint has taken the brunt of eleven years of running my preserving business, Farmer's Daughter.) Stiff from extra layers of clothing on a cold, damp winter morning at the Carrboro Farmers' Market, I grab the pickles, roll off the tailgate, and just manage to right myself as I am greeted by an enthusiastic customer. "What amazing NEW thing did you bring today?" he beams. I hesitate and look down at the table covered with dozens of varieties of jams and pickles. It is late winter, the season to market and sell my reserve stock and, as my physical therapist advised me, a chance for my shoulder to heal before strawberries start rolling in come May. "Nothing *new* this week," I stammer, "but still lots of great stuff from the fall harvest." "Oh, that's too bad! Maybe next week then!" he says before heading to the next stand. That was the last year of my business.

"When people tell the story of North Carolina, they're generally not talking about the chains or the giant developers. They're talking about folks who put it on the line to invest in and love and believe in the place where they live."

—ASHLEY CHRISTENSEN, chef/owner, AC Restaurants, Raleigh, North Carolina, April 16, 2019

There was nothing unusual about this interaction or that morning at the farmers' market. I cannot shame this customer because, as a friend explained to me, I created him. My business would not have survived without customers who appreciated quality and innovation and were willing to pay a premium price for it. I have been this customer on occasion. But that morning something snapped. I was hurting—the shoulder, again—but this was a different sort of discomfort. How had my labor become a source of affluent entertainment, where I, the performer, was expected to provide new taste adventures each week? Catering to a privileged, largely white clientele was definitely not what motivated me to start Farmer's Daughter.

When I founded Farmer's Daughter in 2007, I believed that my small-batch, labor-intensive preserving business was an important statement of protest (and flavor) that countered the highly processed, mass-produced condiments created by industrial food manufacturers. I used traditional open-kettle methods to produce fig preserves packed with whole figs like my mother and grandmother made, not the corn syrup goo that passes as such at the supermarket. I wanted to bring traditional, unpasteurized, and barrel-fermented sauerkraut back to local markets. The scientific and medical community was finally beginning to recognize the health benefits of fermentation. In most grocery stores, old-school sauerkraut and pickles had been replaced with sterile, degraded versions designed for so-called shelf stability. I wanted to do all of that while building connection and resilience in our local economy and creating products that burst with pride of place. Yet over time that sense of mission faded as operating my business controlled my waking hours. I lost my sense of purpose. By 2018, as I witnessed the growing crisis of white supremacy and misogyny in America, my work suddenly felt trivial. I tried to remember the values that had once inspired me and the fire they lit inside me. Twenty years earlier I had turned away from a career as a geologist to dedicate my life to food. My circuitous journey to create a local, farm-driven food business tells a larger story of the challenges of centering community within the evolving local food economy of Chapel Hill and the North Carolina Piedmont. In this telling, I search once more for that fire that will fuel my work to build healthy, sustainable food landscapes in North Carolina and across our country.

In 2000, I was a farmer's daughter, sister, and granddaughter in geology graduate school at the University of North Carolina, some 700 miles from my Mississippi home. In my first semester, I reported on recent climate scholarship. The data was conclusive that the planet was warming at a faster rate due to human influence, though the term Anthropocene—the current geologic era in which humans have altered the environment—would not become common for another decade. That same semester, I studied stratigraphy, a branch of geology dedicated to the earth's layers. Our textbook was published by Exxon. I wanted to do environmental work, not Big Oil. America's military-industrial complex was about to start a war over oil. I was having a career crisis.

I met my first non-graduate-school friends at Internationalist Books, a radical bookstore in Chapel Hill. The mix of folks there surprised me—mechanics, carpenters, farmers, librarians, journalists, and public health professionals. Farmers were much respected in this community, where people understood the importance of knowing how to feed ourselves sustainably. An older generation of farmers provided tireless mentorship. Through Internationalist Books, I met a fiddle player named Kate McDonald, who worked on the late Bill Dow's farm in Chatham County. A Mississippi native, Bill was a former physician and activist who organized health clinics in rural Appalachia before he turned to farming in the North Carolina Piedmont. I was deeply inspired by his belief that organic food is the truest and best medicine. I began to understand that people here took food seriously.

I attended frequent skill-sharing exchanges that fostered a do-it-yourself approach from designing your own website to greening your city through guerrilla gardening, or gardening without legal permission, as when we grafted fruit-bearing pear tree varieties onto Chapel Hill's many ornamental Bradford pears. These values were affirming since I came from a tradition of scrabbling a living off the land. The spirit of shared resources and community reliance in my new home in North Carolina reminded me of the generous old ways of my family and their community. My people gave away the fish in their freezers, loaned their equipment and vehicles, made food for weddings and funerals, and freely shared their knowledge and resources.

The first time I visited the Carrboro Farmers' Market, I was there to see my friend Jay Hamm's produce stand. We met at a gathering of Food Not Bombs, an anarchist-organized, antihunger mutual aid program in Chapel Hill begun during the anti–nuclear war movement of the 1980s. Jay had found his way from Athens, Georgia, to Nancy and Harvey Harman's Sustenance Farm in Chatham County as a farm intern in the late 1990s. At his stand a sign read, "MORganic" in response to customers' constant question, "Is your produce organic?" Getting certified organic status was too costly for most small farmers. Regenerative small farms like Jay's recycle plant and animal wastes continuously, thereby forgoing the need for synthetic fertilizers. Cover crops are grown between food crops to prevent erosion, enrich the soil, and nurture soil microorganisms that pull carbon from the atmosphere and mitigate the effects of climate change over time. Regenerative farming methods draw heavily on Indigenous farming knowledge.

As a teenager I worked in the hot, dusty sweet potato fields of my Mississippi hometown of Vardaman. I did not romanticize farmwork. The kitchen, however, was my happy place. While I was still in graduate school, I took a job at the recently opened Lantern, a Chapel Hill restaurant influenced by Asian cuisine and North Carolina ingredients. Chef and owner Andrea Reusing strongly supported local farms. After two years struggling with theoretical physics and staring at seismographs for eight hours a day, my first night in Lantern's kitchen felt as if I had come home. If I could cook and support my local farming community, that was the work for me. At Lantern, I met wonderful farmers like John Soehner of Eco Farm, who tried to persuade us to take another couple of flats of strawberries during the seasonal glut. I encouraged John to make jam from his excess berries. "Who's got that kind of time?" he said, and "besides, I don't know how." I discovered my niche.

Meanwhile, back home in Mississippi, a crisis was brewing. Our family leases the hundreds of acres on which we grow sweet potatoes and other commodity crops. It is a high-debt, high-stress, competitive business that, unlike the pastoral farm most Americans imagine, feels

OVERLEAF, LEFT: Carrboro Farmers' Market members holding their wares. *Top, left to right*: cabbage, Perry-Winkle Farm; fennel bulbs, Perry-Winkle Farm; lettuce, Eco Farm; eggs, Cane Creek Farm. *Bottom, left to right*: cheeses, Chapel Hill Creamery; beets and water spinach, Mu Tar K'Paw Gardens, Transplanting Traditions Community Farm; onions, Mu Tar K'Paw Gardens, Transplanting Traditions Community Farm; baguettes, Chicken Bridge Bakery

OVERLEAF, RIGHT: Carrboro Farmers' Market members holding their wares, continued. *Top, left to right*: elephant garlic, Cates Corner Farm; strawberries, Lyon Farms; kohlrabi, Nourishing Acres; garlic scapes, Nourishing Acres. *Bottom, left to right*: beef, Baldwin Beef; sweet potato donut, Yee Haw Doughnuts; flowers, Mighty Tendril Farm; tamales, Soul Cocina

HOT!
Farmers Cheese

Soul
TAMALES
WHITE: SMOKY PINTO BEANS & PLANTAINS
RED: SRIRACHA BRAISED LENTILS
BROWN: ROASTED CHICKPEAS, RED BELL PEPPERS & EGGPLANT
GREEN: BLACK BEANS, SPINACH & OLIVES
@SOULCOCINATRIANGLE

more like a gambling addiction, continually betting that the next hand will be the winning one. With extensive economic risk, as well as unpredictable pests, weather, and commodity prices, the only guaranteed winner is the house, or, in the business of agriculture, the banks and chemical companies. In 2006, my father and his work partner had just purchased new equipment for harvesting their sweet potato crop. To pay for the equipment, they loaned it to other farmers and let their crop continue to grow for a few more weeks while they helped their neighbors. The rains came and did not stop until the first frost. My father's crop was a total failure. Insurance would not cover the loss. My father defaulted on his loan and lost his equipment and other assets to foreclosure.

Just before I opened Farmer's Daughter, my younger brother Preston dropped out of college to farm, lured by a guaranteed loan for first-time farmers. He bought his own equipment and took on a large amount of debt in his early twenties. After my father's financial disaster, there was no borrowing Daddy's equipment while he got on his feet. We had no land to pass on to the next generation. My brother needed to farm more acreage to make his payments. In Mississippi, he found little to no examples of farmers engaged in small-scale farming, yet he was deeply tied to place. There were also no established, local markets for his crop. I pleaded with Preston to consider an alternative to commodity crop farming. He came to visit me in North Carolina. As his big sister, I hoped to show my brother an alternative way of making a living off the land that was less stressful and financially risky. We toured local diversified farms with two young and charismatic farmer friends of mine: Sara Fuller was farm manager for her uncle Ken Dawson's farm, Maple Spring Gardens, where Sarah Blacklin was working that summer. Blacklin later became the general manager of the Carrboro Farmers' Market. Ken Dawson and his partner, Libby Outlaw, are veterans of sustainable agriculture in Orange County, where Ken had served on the board and as president of the Carrboro Farmers' Market for many years. For weeks Preston talked about "Sarah and Sara," but nothing came of it.

My North Carolina farming and food community became my new family. Just as I had once turned the buckets of garden produce my father dropped at our Mississippi back door into relishes and pickles, I did the same here. By early 2007, I was on my way, selling pastries and preserves packed with local fruit at the Carrboro Farmers' Market. That spring I sourced fresh strawberries from my market neighbors and featured them at the next market in rustic tarts and whole berry preserves with twice the fruit found in standard supermarket jams. I made a contribution to the local economy that I felt good about, including creating a new market for my farmer friends to sell their remaining seasonal produce. In the spirit of the antiglobalization protests of the 1990s, my market friends and I engaged in what my pal George O'Neal of Lil' Farm calls "friendly capitalism." We fought global warming by building topsoil, reclaiming the skills of our ancestors, reducing our carbon footprint, and shrinking the miles from farm to plate.

My preserving work also honored the labor of the women in my family and my hometown community. Local family jellies, preserves, relishes, and pickles were well known, carrying the name of the person who created them. We passed around Miss Glenda's crunchy icicle pickles, searched the refrigerator for the last of Aunt Pat's blueberry jelly, and lamented how our peas didn't taste the same without Country Mamaw's chili sauce. When I made preserves, I preserved the memories of women who raised me, too.

"When I was getting started, I was very interested in the more obscure food traditions that we are leaving behind. That doesn't really adapt very well to capitalism because capitalism says we're supposed to find the thing that most people like and make a lot of it."

—**APRIL MCGREGER, Philadelphia, Pennsylvania, January 27, 2019**

Some of the best market days were my earliest at the Wednesday Carrboro Farmers' Market. Midweek sales at the market were generally low, but camaraderie was high. I always came home with boxes of beautiful bundles of collard greens, Easter egg radishes, and wonderfully misfit heirloom tomatoes, traded with market colleagues for my leftover sweet potato–ginger scones and crispy collard flatbread. My production volume was so small at the time that I could just buy produce farmers had not sold that day and turn it into delicious jams and relishes to sell the following week. As my business grew, I quickly needed more produce and bigger suppliers. Although I continued to buy North Carolina–grown organic produce, I could rarely buy enough from my neighbors. Things gradually grew less intimate.

In 2008, the recession led to a boom in artisan food businesses and small farming ventures. The Carrboro Farmers' Market had been my only sales outlet, but increased competition meant that I needed to cast a wider net for customers. A website with an online store and national recognition for Farmer's Daughter followed. I joined a second farmers' market. When my son was young and I needed a break from the all-night baking session before Saturday market day, I started a community-supported preservery. My customers signed up for a seasonal subscription of preserves or barrel-fermented pickles and krauts. Many young farmers and food artisans I knew were now working a half-dozen farmers' markets where our mentors had worked only one back in the day. As my friends' farms grew, they outgrew the small plots rented or borrowed from farmer mentors. They scattered far enough away from Chapel Hill and Durham prices to find land of their own to buy or lease. Some quit farming because there was no affordable land, others because they had broken-down bodies and no health insurance. For those of us without nearby parents to help raise our children and the essential labor to help work our farm stands and assist with production, it was nearly impossible. Our community suffered.

I began to realize I was still part of the same restrictive agricultural economy my family operated under in Mississippi. My market colleagues and I competed for a shrinking piece of the pie as new farmers' markets drew on the same customer base. Long hours damaged our health and stressed our relationships, while we remained stubbornly committed to the Good Food movement—the building of local and regional sustainable food systems that nourish both people and the planet. Through individual responsibility and strategic choices, I had believed we could create solutions through alternative markets. Farm-to-table activists Alice Waters and Michael Pollan told us that *eating is a political act*. If we support the right farmers and buy the right food, we can make a difference, right? We just needed to vote with our pocketbooks. But what difference were we really making? I had vastly overestimated my ability to bring about change in my own local food economy. Farmers' markets ballooned in number, but market shoppers made up only slightly more than 10 percent of consumers.

The industrial food system continued to grow and consolidate across the country while local food economies and their farmers and entrepreneurs struggled to survive. Healthy, locally grown food was largely accessible only to white consumers who could afford it. Meanwhile, the farmers, producers, and restaurant employees I worked alongside, and even those employed in my own kitchen, more often than not lacked basic health care and often even citizenship. Farming increasingly represented an experience of privilege as land prices rose. I searched for solutions to address many of these issues, but my frustration level grew. I realized that small tweaks to business models could never repair the larger structural problems within sustainable agriculture and the food industry. I paid my team a living wage, but I could not afford their health insurance. I was continuing to fail at making my own workload sustainable. So I quit.

After shutting down Farmer's Daughter, I hoped to use my twenty-plus years of experience in the food industry, as well as my family's farming history, to find a better path forward. Although our ties to North Carolina remain strong and we already dream of returning, my husband, Phil, and I moved north to live near his family in Philadelphia. Living in the nation's largest poor city has been an education. One train ride through the city, and it is obvious that our economic system serves few at the expense of many, a truth that is easy to ignore in the Triangle's bubble of affluence. I've learned we can't have a food movement without a *just* economy, rooted in democracy and shared resources, where the least among us has a chance to thrive. Without economic justice, the majority of Americans cannot afford local, seasonal eating.

I continue to wrestle with the current state of sustainable agriculture and small-scale, local food systems, what has worked and what has failed. We have created extraordinary food, farmers, and community while keeping traditional knowledge alive. Yet we are exceptions as the nation undergoes land loss, farm consolidation, and the corporatization of the American food system. Meanwhile, the Good Food movement's focus on consumer choice and personal responsibility is tinged with classism and racism as we shame fast food and demand that people pay more for their food. It is time for bold new ideas.

Twenty years ago, renouncing the industrial food system and opting out of it was my resistance. In a world of shared global crises like climate change and pandemics, there is no more opting out. We are in this together. What was once a niche issue of the counterculture has become a central focus in this era of food justice and climate action. While the world feels increasingly precarious, there is also a new feeling of possibility and the political will to create structural change. To do that, we must build alliances. North Carolina's patchwork of interconnected small cities and farmland is unique, and farmers' markets are ground zero for this rural-urban intersection. At member-owned farmers' markets in Carrboro and Durham, we saw how young punks and old-time farmers worked together to create something against all odds, and even shared some laughs while doing it. Could we collaborate across these boundaries and beyond to build a movement for progressive agricultural and food policies like a Green New Deal?

As we work for transformation, we need to make good food more accessible for everyone. During the COVID-19 crisis organizations like Durham Free Lunch set up in temporarily shuttered restaurants in downtown Durham to feed those in need. On their GoFundMe campaign, they write, "Solidarity not charity," to distinguish themselves from top-down, philanthropic-driven charity.

Restaurants reeling from the economic impact of the pandemic provide another opportunity to build a better system. How will the food industry of the Triangle restructure to better serve a broader portion of the population while supporting their own? Universal health care is essential for food workers, especially as servers and kitchen staff risk their lives for customers and employers. What if instead of *performing* hospitality in food service, we instead cultivated real conviviality and egalitarian connection in those spaces?

We need cross-industry collaborations and community visioning to develop new solutions. RAFI-USA, a farm advocacy nonprofit in

Pittsboro, North Carolina, sponsors "Come to the Table" conferences and community conversations that bring together farmers and community stakeholders to increase food security. It is not surprising that Black churches are central to much of the work around hunger relief and food sovereignty projects, including community gardens. As well as providing food security, gardens are centers for spiritual connection, conviviality, knowledge production, and intergenerational exchange, yet we seldom hear these life-giving qualities discussed in analyses of our contemporary food system. Back home in Mississippi, my brother recently opened a sweet potato packing and distribution business to build his market and protect the farm's future. He partnered with a private investor to make that happen. A cooperative model, if one existed, would pool financial strength and help rebuild much of what's been lost in rural communities like ours—connection and mutual support. Farmer co-ops are not new, but the need for them, and the social change they create, has never been greater.

In a July 2019, op-ed in the *Independent Weekly*, Alexis Pauline Gumbs argued that a "Mother Plan" rather than a master plan, is needed in Durham—referencing Alice Walker's capitalist alternative of Motherism in addressing the city's future. Imagine if we recognized the responsibility to *mother*, to create communities in North Carolina that at their heart are life-giving. What sort of food system would we create then?

Strawberry Preserves APRIL MCGREGER

Makes about 2½ pints

4 pounds strawberries, tops removed and sliced in half
3 cups granulated sugar
⅓ cup fresh lemon juice

PRESERVING TIPS

Work in small batches.

Cook the preserves in your widest pot to increase the evaporation surface so that the jam thickens quickly.

The perfect strawberries for eating out of hand are not the perfect strawberries for preserving. You want firm, ripe berries, even those with a bit of white on the tip. Very ripe strawberries are low in acid and pectin, which is necessary for the preserve to set properly. Alternatively, you can boost the pectin from your soft, ripe berries naturally by adding a peeled and grated green apple to your batch of preserves.

These preserves can be stored in the refrigerator for several months or canned for shelf-stable storage.

Combine the berries with the sugar and lemon juice. Cover and macerate for 4 hours at room temperature or overnight in the refrigerator.

When you are ready to cook, prepare your storage containers. If canning, sterilize the jars and lids and keep them hot. Place a saucer and 4 metal spoons in the freezer: these will be used to test whether the jam is ready to set.

Stir the strawberries to distribute the sugar evenly and transfer them to a wide, nonreactive 6-to-8-quart pot. Place the pot over high heat and stir gently for about 5 minutes until the sugar has melted completely and the strawberries begin to foam. Skim and discard the foam.

Boil rapidly for 15–20 minutes (the time will vary according to the size of your pot and the strength of your burner, so watch it carefully and let your senses guide you), stirring and scraping the bottom of the pot with a silicone spatula to ensure that the jam is not sticking. You will need to stir and scrape more frequently as the jam begins to thicken. Watch the heat and lower it if necessary to prevent sticking and scorching.

When the mixture begins to thicken and look shiny, check to see if it is ready. Remove the pot from the heat and place a small amount of jam on one of the cold metal spoons from the freezer. Return the spoon of jam to the freezer for 3–4 minutes and then remove it along with the chilled saucer. Drop the cooled spoonful of jam onto the saucer. If it is thick enough to hold its shape and not run flat on the plate, it is finished. If it is not done, return the pot to the heat, bring it back to a boil, and cook for about 5 minutes before testing again. When the preserves are ready, skim carefully again to remove excess foam.

To can the preserves, ladle the hot preserves into hot, sterilized jars and top with hot, sterilized 2-piece lids.

Check that the lids are secure, then flip the jars upside down and leave for 1 minute to sterilize the lid and the top surface of the jam. Flip the jars right side up, set aside on a rack at least 1 inch apart, and leave, undisturbed, for 24 hours. After 24 hours, when the jars are completely cool, check the lids to see that they are sealed properly by pressing the button centered on the top of the jar. If the button pops back, the seal is NOT complete and the jar must be kept in the refrigerator to prevent spoilage. Alternatively, you can process the jars in a water bath canner according to the manufacturer's instructions.

BILL SMITH

They Are My Friends, They Are My Family

A Mexico and North Carolina Brotherhood of Food

I first became aware of Latino immigrants around Chapel Hill in the late 1980s. I was working in the kitchen of La Residence at the time. If we needed a substitute dishwasher on short notice the people at Crook's Corner, another restaurant down the street, had Mexican guys on staff who were often looking for extra work. There was almost always someone available. They showed right up, worked for cash, did a good job, and never said much. We particularly liked Angel Sanchez. In a circular turn of events, a few years later, I found myself working at Crook's Corner.

What I didn't realize at the time was that a fairly constant stream of men to Chapel Hill and Carrboro had begun, mostly from the town of Celaya in the Mexican state of Guanajuato. Our area was booming and there were never enough people to work here. Construction was taking workers away from restaurants and landscaping. Now there were suddenly eager, pleasant men for hire. I don't like generalities, but since this is complimentary, I'll use it. Everyone said the same thing, "They can read and they don't do drugs." It didn't matter that they couldn't always read English; they quickly learned new words and followed complex instructions. Within ten years anyone around here who was working a job that was dangerous, unpleasant, or low paying was probably from Mexico.

Initially, all of this was amiable. No one asked about immigration status as long as a Social Security number was produced. This was before 9/11, of course. The border was merely a nuisance, often an amusing one. Everyone had sneaking-across-the-border stories, and mostly they were funny. Guys would work here for a year or two, run back home for six months, and then come back again to work. This was generally the case throughout North Carolina, where there were nearly a half-million people from Mexico by the mid-2000s.

The effect Mexican immigrants had on the food that we eat was two-pronged. First of all, many were agricultural workers or were employed either in the meat processing industry or in the seafood plants down on the coast. Second, they began to work in our restaurant kitchens. Big corporate restaurants are always looking for the cheapest labor possible. Small independent places can only generate so much income, so sometimes they can't afford to pay higher salaries. The stage was set. Immigrants were actively involved in putting food on our tables.

"These guys came here for jobs. They aren't working in these restaurants because they're foodies. They may turn into them, but they actually think it's really silly. They've come from places often where they didn't have enough food. They see sometimes the things we do as wasteful—both money and ingredients."

—**BILL SMITH, Chapel Hill, North Carolina, February 6, 2019**

The food business is a transient one, especially in a university town. Student cooks came and went. Not so Mexican dishwashers. They watched as they washed, so when students moved on there was often someone who already knew what the vacant job required. Slowly but surely, our kitchens were staffed by skilled Latino workers. And they didn't move on. They stayed. As they eased the labor crunch, they also began to teach us about their cooking. More than once, I was blown away by a staff lunch prepared by men who had never cooked for themselves until they made their solitary journeys to the United States. We rarely actually sat down and ate a proper meal at a table, but cóctel de camaron (a Mexican-style shrimp cocktail with a gazpacho-style base) can be quite astonishing even when eaten leaning over the sink.

My investment in these guys became personal quickly. The bad Spanish–bad English thing was always fun. An incident involving the daughter of one of my cooks and the mix-up of the words *molleja* (gizzard) and *muñeca* (doll baby) comes to mind. I'm always ready for a night on the town, and my new buddies were far from home and eager for new playmates. The next thing I knew, half of my best friends were from south of the Rio Grande. These friendships have been among the most important rewards of my career. I'm sure they are the main reason that I was able to maintain the schedule I did for so long and at my age. I was scooped up into family after family without so much as a second thought, both here and when I was in Mexico. This continues today. I started visiting my friends there in 1998, and except when I got so busy professionally around 2015, I've been there at least once a year and sometimes more. They hardly notice me now. Any irritation they might have had with American policies—and people—has never been transferred to me. Mexicans have been observing us quietly for a long time. They like us, but they don't buy any of our hype. Their eyes glaze over as we prance around waving flags, chanting about how great we are. Yet they admire us when we do things well. By and large they see America as safer and more orderly than Mexico, and that makes it attractive. Especially if you have a family.

Restaurants are among the first places that immigrant people seek work. I've been saying for years that your dishwasher never speaks English. You can wash dishes in any language. In America, menial work is often seen as a sign of laziness or failure, but to immigrants it is a first step up. This is fortunate for us and for them. Four or five men can share an inexpensive apartment and cook big pots of shared food. Everyone works at least two jobs. They send most of their money home to families and plan to return there someday themselves. I have several friends who built houses for themselves or their parents back in Mexico while they worked in North Carolina. Once I visited a small town in the mountains of Oaxaca where there were many new one-story houses. Fittings were already in place for second stories to be built when the money came in. Their careful planning for the future was clearly incremental and long-term.

Perhaps the best thing these guys did for the restaurant business here was to bring a sensible attitude into a profession in danger of believing its own heady euphoria. I say this all the time. They were interested in doing a good job first, not in celebrity. They learned what I wanted done, and then I never worried about that task again. This attitude introduced a bit of level-headedness in a stressful environment. It was good to have at least one person in the kitchen who wasn't always about to have a stroke. While the chef was somewhere weeping over raspberries, the amigos just kept cooking the steaks.

Another thing they did was teach the rest of us to respect a utilitarian cuisine. By example, they reminded us that something simple can be elegant and delicious in its own way. Food they cooked for themselves was usually quite elemental but also as sophisticated as any I'd ever eaten. I've used their *salsa casera* (literally, "homemade sauce") at more than one fancy dinner party since. This lesson needs to be relearned over and over again. A last favor they did for us was to nudge the public toward spicier and more highly seasoned foods. This ripple was smaller, but ultimately its effects were more widespread. Everybody asks for hot sauce now. And you'd better have more than one kind.

The reception of Latino immigrants in North Carolina has been schizophrenic at best. They were encouraged to come at first, then the terrorist attacks of 2001 threw a switch and the attitude turned more and more antagonistic toward all foreigners. The financial collapse that began in 2007 made things worse. As travel back and forth became more difficult for these men, many decided to bring their families here. The sudden rise of drug violence in Mexico reinforced their decisions. One last risky, expensive crossing and that was enough of that. People who

Bill Smith, Chapel Hill, North Carolina; *background*, dried peppers

intended to work a while and then return home realized it would be better for their children if they stayed here.

The complete flip-flop in American attitudes about immigration doesn't make sense to the Latino guys I've worked with, and many view it simply as unleashed racism. This is true to some extent, but it is also more complicated. Life in this country had once seemed so steady, and now economic security suddenly vanished, making Americans less welcoming to newcomers who were increasingly viewed as competition. It also matters whether you see things as "we are the world" or "us and them." I've watched how this has affected my Mexican friends, and it hasn't been nice. That being said, they are here, and most are probably staying. Their children who were born here certainly will remain. I have helped twenty-seven of these children obtain U.S. passports. All this became politically fraught, despite my friends' and coworkers' desire to avoid hostility. In spite of all of the nastiness, many are putting down roots, laying low and hoping things blow over. Remarkably, they continue to believe in the American Dream.

Latino immigrants remain a significant part of the labor force in North Carolina's commercial agriculture despite the impossible morass of the temporary workers' programs and the risk involved in working when undocumented. Immigrant farmworkers are able to live marginally at best. Student Action with Farmworkers estimates that approximately 150,000 immigrant farmworkers and their dependents live in North Carolina. That makes our state sixth in the nation. Wages are low, conditions are hard, and sometimes children are put to work. The children who aren't working have high dropout rates from school. These families earn only $11,000–$16,000 annually. Poor living and working conditions are well documented. The incidence of preventable health problems is high. These facts are well known, yet the Trump administration proposed less and less regulation and inspection of these industries.

Immigrant workers have also been an important part of the crab industry in North Carolina. The H-2A visa program allowed a workforce of mostly Mexican women to fill most of those jobs. Changes in the program rules have since disrupted that industry, and higher prices and shortages are predicted. I was surprised to learn of the large Hispanic community in eastern North Carolina. Tiny Ocracoke Island holds a Mexican fiesta each fall now.

Immigrant influence over our food will continue no matter what. Taco trucks are ubiquitous. The shelves of our grocery stores have expanded with countless varieties of fresh chiles, hot sauces, and such foods as canned tuna with olive oil and jalapeños. Fancier and fancier Latino restaurants are popping up all the time. In my professional life, my Latin American friends have had a huge influence on how I eat and cook. As I've said, the general public's appetite for spicy foods has increased constantly over the past twenty-some years. So has their curiosity about the differences and nuances of flavors, encouraging us to explore as we worked in the kitchen.

Although Crook's Corner was a southern restaurant by definition, my infatuation with all things Mexican was well known around town. But I did have to present at least the illusion of restraint. The first new ingredient I added at Crook's was posole, or Mexican hominy. My *cocineros* (chefs) cooked with it when they made staff lunch. This was a revelation to me. My father loved hominy, fried alongside eggs, when I was little, but I never warmed to it. I remember it as bland and mushy. The Mexican version, on the other hand, is fragrant and crunchy. Tamales were next. The Mississippi Delta has a tradition of tamales. Its origins are vague. They probably came up from Mexico, but they are dissimilar from the ones found there now. No matter—the connection was close enough. Women around town made them in their homes and brought them to the back doors of restaurant kitchens and construction sites to sell to workers, so I was already a big fan. There are a million kinds. A friend gave me basic lessons, and in the years that followed, if you were anywhere nearby, my tamales were inescapable. I used both corn husks and banana leaves. I even learned to make a dessert version.

Probably the most dramatic Latino culinary innovation in southern food has been salsas. First of all, they are fairly easy to make, especially when you consider how fabulous they can be. They run the gamut from raw pico de gallo to salsa ranchero made from vegetables that are charred black. Most southerners already like a version of a timid hot sauce. Dried chiles were a revelation, as was scorching vegetables to cook them, and boiling pork in grease for hours to make the fork-tender carnitas that lie beneath salsas.

"I grew up in eastern North Carolina in the fifties, so I know racist crap when I see it. I wasn't raised to be hateful, but I was raised in the segregated South."

—**BILL SMITH, Chapel Hill, North Carolina, February 6, 2019**

The most valuable things that Latino immigrants have brought us are not edible. Their many examples of courage, persistence, and devotion to family are beyond price. Their indomitable work ethic is admirable. Their skill at dealing with bullying and belittling is really quite startling. I've always considered it a privilege to work among these people.

Logically, they should be welcome here, but logic is rare in our world today. Fear, prejudice, and this society's sadistic need to punish the poor all play a part here. Even as crops rot in the fields because there is no one to harvest them, backs stiffen and lips purse when sensible solutions are proposed. I usually suggest we begin by facing the facts as they are, rather than as things ought to be. Laws have been broken to be sure, but these crimes were all but victimless. What about sensible

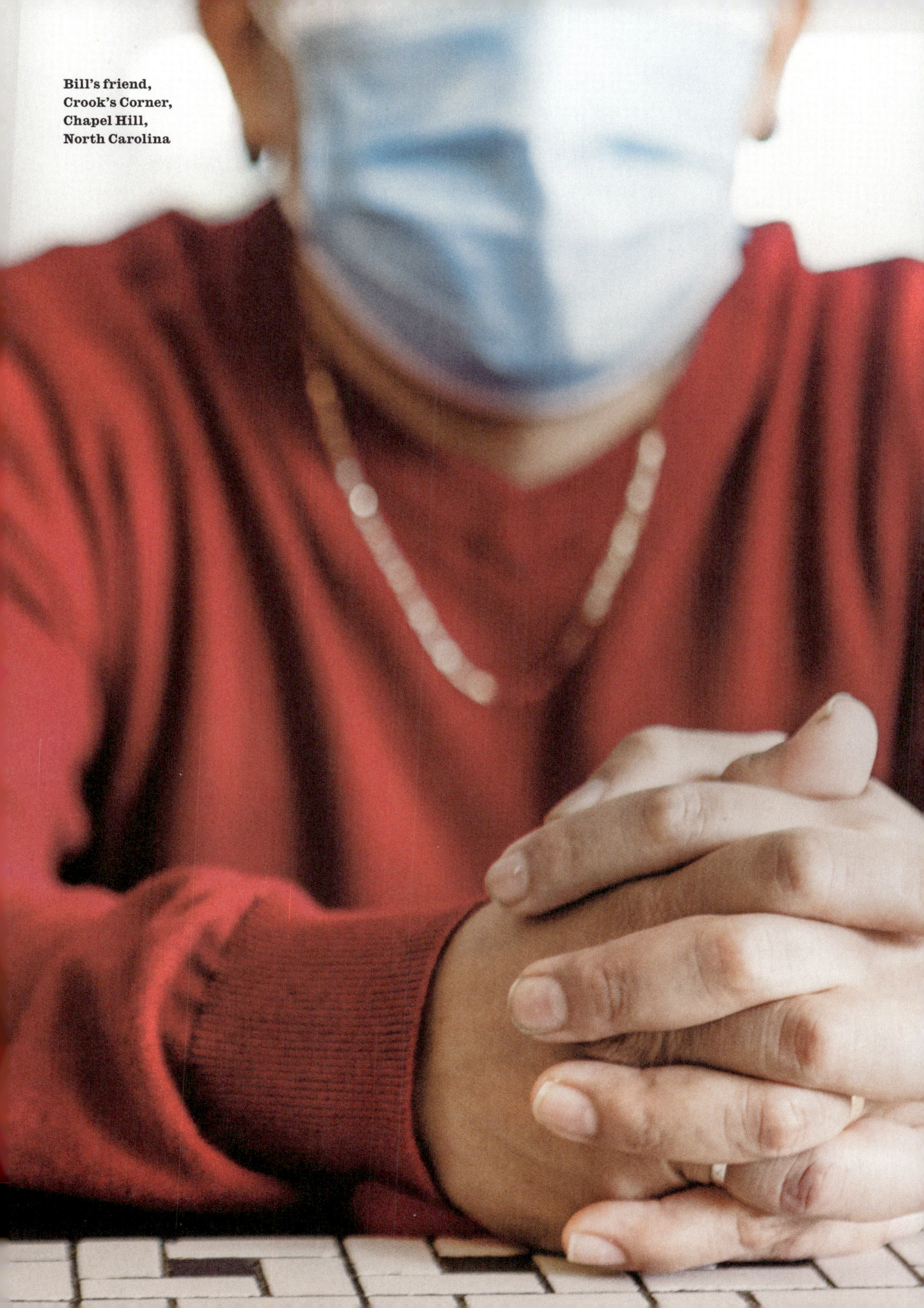

Bill's friend,
Crook's Corner,
Chapel Hill,
North Carolina

punishments—fines, probations, or forfeiture of money they have already paid into Social Security, for instance? Sneaking across the border to wash dishes is not terrorism, especially when dishwashers are needed here. We could have an orderly, sensible border policy if the powers that be wanted one. I often cause a ruckus by suggesting proportionality. Let's start with the people who all but brought down the financial system in our country, leading to the Great Recession of 2008. They cost tens of thousands of people their homes, savings, and retirements. Punishments should first be given to those folks, then we can work our way back down to the people gutting chickens in Chatham County. I rest my case.

With the arrival of the coronavirus pandemic in the spring of 2020, millions of people were thrown out of work, unemployment rolls were enormous, and the future of many businesses, especially small ones, was suddenly in doubt. As I have noted, the food industry is heavy in immigrant workers, and COVID-19-related consequences were all over the place. Meat processing facilities became hotspots for infection. They stayed open anyway. Restaurants and bars pretty much all closed, throwing untold numbers of people out of work. Because of documentation, many immigrant workers weren't entitled to unemployment compensation. Yet these immigrant workers will be needed again in America. Immigration reforms that must come were pushed back. It is likely that the nature of work has irreversibly changed. The present way of distributing health care is being proved unacceptable, and the days of routine social injustice need to end in North Carolina and everywhere else.

Sadly, the state of the nation has begun to erode the stamina of even my sturdiest Mexican friends. I sense this all the time now. Unlike their European predecessors, these Latino immigrants did not come here to colonize and push Indigenous people off their land. They came to pick tomatoes and clean hotel rooms. Mostly, this was done for the love of their own families, certainly not to impose villainy on the United States. The effect this constant hounding has on children especially is unpardonable. We've done this before in America, this singling out of innocent people for harassment. It's awful to watch as people's long-held dreams are summarily swept away. And most important, we need these people. They make our country, our region, and our state a better place. I know. They are my friends. They are my family.

Pork Shank Posole **BILL SMITH**

Makes 4–6 servings

2 tablespoons cooking oil
½ cup diced side meat (also known as lean bacon)
4 (13-ounce) pork shanks (cut as for osso buco)
½ cup all-purpose flour seasoned with salt and pepper for dredging
½ tablespoon chopped garlic
3 bay leaves
1 heaping tablespoon dried oregano
½ tablespoon freshly ground cumin seeds
5 tomatillos, husked, washed, trimmed of blemishes, and cut in half
2½ cups Mexican-style canned hominy, drained
3 ears of corn, cleaned and kernels cut from the cob
1½ tablespoons chopped pimento
Finely chopped cilantro and parsley and thinly sliced radishes for garnish

In a large heavy-bottomed pot set over medium-high heat, add the oil and render the side meat (side meat has a low smoking point and will sometimes get too brown before it has given up its grease; oil helps it along). Remove the side meat and set aside.

Dredge the shanks in the flour and add them to the pan in a single layer, browning the meat on all sides. Add more oil as necessary. Be sure to not crowd the meat; brown the shanks in batches if necessary. Add the garlic, stirring so it doesn't burn. Return the shanks to the pan and arrange in a single layer. Add enough water to come halfway up their sides. Add the bay, oregano, and cumin and bring to a hard boil. Reduce the heat to the lowest possible simmer, add the side meat, and cover the pot. Cook for about 3 hours or until the meat is fork-tender but isn't falling apart.

Carefully remove the shanks from the broth and set them aside. Bring the broth to a hard boil and add the tomatillos. Reduce the heat to medium and cook for about 15 minutes or until the tomatillos begin to break down and dissolve into the sauce (the skins may remain; they become tender once cooked). Add the hominy and corn, stirring to combine. Once the sauce has thickened slightly, add the meat and allow everything to warm through. Sprinkle in the pimento. To serve, place a shank in each of 4 bowls, ladle the broth over each shank, and sprinkle with the cilantro, parsley, and radishes.

Cooking Like We Mean It

Food for a Just North Carolina

"North Carolina—it's a patchwork of counties and towns with rural and agricultural land in proximity to eaters and consumers, with a historic farming infrastructure and a strong food heritage."

—JENNIFER CURTIS, cofounder/co-CEO, Firsthand Foods, Durham, North Carolina, March 13, 2019

Five months into the COVID pandemic, a high-profile food writer tweeted part of a letter he had received from a food colleague: "The nastiness that seems to permeate the national conversation in the U.S. has seeped into food as well. No longer is it a way to bring people together, but just another way to find fault with other people and to drive people away."[1] Before that moment, this statement would have drifted by unnoticed, but that day it was uniformly contested, and the writer doubled down: "For 200,000 years. It [food] did, does and will." The idea that food is an inherently unifying force that transcends systemic racism contradicts reality and contorts history. When I moved to North Carolina from New York in 1995, I also believed that food had the power to defy difference and bring people together. I had no understanding of my own role in the system of white supremacy on which our food choices depend. I naively believed that progressive policy and market-driven consumer choice could make radical change. I also had no idea that I was moving to one of the best places to cook and eat in the world.

The first time I went to the Carrboro Farmers' Market, it was still shaded by the remains of an old textile mill. The best eggs (and stewing hens) came from vegetarian farmer Cathy Jones and her stonemason partner, Mike Perry. His enormous wood-burning oven in their pasture was the center of an open-invitation Fourth of July picnic that hundreds attended. Stanley Hughes was growing vegetables and raising hogs, chickens, and organic tobacco on his third-generation, 100-year-old farm. He introduced me to okra so tender and juicy you could eat it raw. A former Long Island fisherman turned farmer, John Soehner, shared advice and gallows humor, along with free boxes of vegetables and flowers to cooks who passed by his stand. Across the street was Tom Robinson's seafood market, a pristine concrete shack, stamped with his own murals of shrimp and blue crab. There I bought the freshest fish I had ever cooked that Tom had picked up at the coast himself, making the long round-trip drive just the night before. Yankee snobbery told me that southern oysters were bland and flabby, but the ones from Stump Sound near Topsail Island, cultivated off a spit of deep, cold water, were a salty shock. In Chatham County, Andy Youngblood raised chickens and built a small processing plant on his own land. His birds—hatched, raised, and slaughtered on the farm—were slow-growing breeds who spent their days outdoors on pasture. It was the first time I tasted chicken that didn't taste like chicken, which is to say, chicken.

I started cooking early in college, first in a hot pot in my dorm room and then working as a line cook under women chefs in neighborhood restaurants in New York City's East Village. I loved it, but the relentless maleness, racism, and economic structure of even progressive restaurants made the idea of a kitchen career as appealing as working on the floor of an investment bank or a meatpacking plant.

But in North Carolina, what I was learning and eating confirmed to me that I wanted to work with food. By 2000, my brother Brendan and I were ready to open our own restaurant in Chapel Hill. Our budget was tight when we found a storefront with a tiny kitchen where we would do most of the construction with our family and friends. One of my earliest food memories from my New Jersey childhood was of my parents cooking together, preparing fried rice from Virginia Lee and Craig Claiborne's classic 1970s work, *The Chinese Cookbook*. Our favorite celebration meal was driving into the city for Peking duck. Paying homage to this food culture that we loved felt right. We imagined a place where regulars would eat a few times a week and where rowdy kids could share dumplings while their parents had a cocktail and a bowl of roasted pork and noodles.

We opened Lantern with $500 in the bank and only got there because of a hardcore group of friends and family. Silvia Pahola tore out the old drop-down ceiling while setting up the kitchen and hiring staff. Ric Palao constructed the bar while creating the bar menu and organizing our business logistics. Our father, Vince, painted the kitchen ceiling early on the morning of New Year's Eve and then helped us cook for a crazy late-night party that ended only when a security alarm went off at 3:00 A.M.

I didn't identify as a chef. The ubiquitous "Yes, chef!" shouted in all the kitchens I had worked was kitsch, deployed only ironically or savagely. Brendan and I established arbitrary, anti-1990s fusion rules to distance ourselves from chef culture and to avoid mucking up the foods we hoped to translate for our diners. No wasabi mashed potatoes, no ponzu beurre blanc.

After a few years of late nights shifted to early mornings, we had a bit more time to focus the menu on what ingredients were available and what local foods deserved to be enjoyed by many. Joe Hollis brought us

Flo Hawley and Portia McKnight, Chapel Hill Creamery, Chapel Hill, North Carolina; *background*, Chapel Hill Creamery pig

ramps, ginseng, fresh wasabi, and tender spicy leaves foraged from his land in Celo in western North Carolina. (His off-grid homestead also housed a large collection of rare psychotropic plants.) Backyard gardeners like Ron Goldstein opened his berry patches free to restaurant workers and shared family recipes for his persimmons and pears on the back of invoices handwritten on the margins of "Far Side" comics. Our friends were starting to raise shiitakes grown on real oak logs instead of sawdust as used in the commercial production of most mushrooms. Lee Calhoun's heirloom southern apples, many of which he had saved from extinction, were a gift and a history lesson.

We sourced as much local food as we could year-round and learned how to preserve fleeting southern fruit—strawberries, cherries, plums, peaches, muscadines, figs, maypops, and pawpaw. Citrus came to us from the L'Hoste family in Plaquemines Parish, Louisiana. Our sticky rice was grown by Chue Lee, a Hmong immigrant from Laos who farmed in Marion, near Asheville. We found fresh buckwheat for soba and dumplings. Illegal raw milk and cheese was acquired from friends I can't name.

We relied on Niman Ranch pork—a company founded by pioneer rancher Bill Niman to expand the availability of humanely raised animals, now owned by Perdue—until Carrboro butcher Cliff Collins taught us how to break down a whole hog in the back of a borrowed pickup in his parking lot. Soon we sourced whole hogs directly from Chapel Hill Creamery. As food producers, the creamery's founders, Flo Hawley and Portia McKnight, are a triple threat: cultivators of acres of grass, livestock managers who recognize each of their pasture-raised Jersey cows by their udders, and, when the chores are done, artisan cheese makers. Their primary concern is the health of their animals, and it shows in their award-winning cheeses and deep flavor of their whey-fed pork. Their pork is rightly twice as expensive as that of Niman Ranch and five times as expensive as commodity meat produced on an industrial scale. Together we navigated pricing that worked for all of us through years of open-book finance, friendship, and accountability.

Foodiest Place in America

North Carolina's forward-thinking small-farming community predates the contemporary food scene by fifty years and is the scaffold beneath our local food economy and restaurants. For the past twenty years I have hosted restaurant teams from every part of the country in North Carolina. When chefs visiting from Berkeley or Brooklyn taste Chapel Hill Creamery pork, wild North Carolina shrimp, or John Soehner's fava beans, they almost can't fathom the access that we have to incredible food. (Writer Andrew Knowlton designated Durham-Chapel Hill America's "foodiest small town" in a profile for *Bon Appétit* in 2008.) This is only possible due to decades of work by people like Bill Dow, a young doctor who helped found the Carrboro Farmers' Market after realizing that he could improve community health more effectively by farming rather than by practicing medicine. Historically, this is an agricultural state, but its unforgiving soil became fertile ground for equity and change only through the work of committed, collaborative leaders such as Savi Horne, Nancy Creamer, and Jennifer Curtis, who do the transformational behind-the-scenes work to help farmers revolutionize our food economy. Yet North Carolina has two food systems—one for the people who have the least resources, another for those who have the time and means to consider flavor, nutrition, seasonality, fair labor, environmental impact, and other ways food is socially ranked in American life.

North Carolina Food Inequality

North Carolina's divisions in its food systems are constructed and historic. Our food system is built on inequality and requires it to function. The components of this inequality—racism, lack of access to capital, exploitation, Black land loss, and nutritional and health disparities in communities of color—are tightly connected. In North Carolina as in the nation, the local organic food scene's glow distracts from how the production and processing of even the most pristine ingredients—from field or dock to slaughterhouse and restaurant or school cafeteria—is nearly always configured to rely on cheap labor. This work and the artificially inexpensive food it produces is cheap only because it is performed by people who are themselves poor and hungry. Food workers are members of both the largest and lowest-paid workforce in the United States, disproportionately female, of color, and food insecure. Even in ideal circumstances, the food industry is a complicated and difficult place to work. This is true in every part of the industry, from North Carolina apple orchards to shrimp boats, from slaughterhouses to every restaurant in the state, simple or fancy.

Since the 1970s, North Carolina has been the largest sweet potato–producing state in the country—2 billion were produced in 2019—and they are all harvested by hand. If you work on a sweet potato farm you must dig and haul two tons to make fifty dollars. The 150,000 farmworkers in our state who harvest sweet potatoes and most everything else we grow, from blueberries to commodity chicken, are nearly invisible. In North Carolina, as across the nation, many of these farmworkers are ten- and twelve-year-old children. And almost half of these workers and their families are food insecure.

Andrea Reusing, Lantern, Chapel Hill, North Carolina; *background*, Lantern's Chapel Hill Creamery pork and chive dumplings

At its inception, the cult of cheap food funded a growing wage gap and then fueled the current crisis of unprecedented wealth inequality. But cheap food exists only as long as it can externalize its real cost—spiking health care expenses tied to poverty-related illnesses, low-wage workers with no safety net, and worldwide environmental collapse. In 1960, an average American spent 17 percent of their income on food, nearly twice as much as we do today. The children of families who cannot afford the true cost of food (raw ingredients usually reflect these costs more than processed foods) will live shorter, less healthy lives than their parents. Any meaningful approach to food policy and confronting hunger and malnutrition must also focus on dismantling structural racial inequality.

The Problem with Chefs

Our thirty-year obsession with chefs and foodie-ism has neither expanded access to good food nor improved nutrition in low-resource neighborhoods. Before the pandemic, the demand for local food in North Carolina was at an all-time high, yet our state ranked tenth in national food insecurity. The image of affluent eaters and chefs shopping at farmers' markets is familiar today, but in the context of food sold in the United States, farm to table is pure spectacle and more like theater than an actual source of calories for the 99 percent. If we started from scratch to build the most efficient system of delivering good food, profitably grown, to the greatest number of people, we never would have the system we live with today. When you imagine a united food system based in equity, flavor, nutrition, and environmental regeneration, there is only one loser, extractive corporate agriculture.

The Movement

"I never saw this as a food movement here. I saw it as an agricultural movement."

—**ANDREA REUSING, Chapel Hill, North Carolina, January 30, 2019**

The local food economy has grown enormously in the past twenty-five years, but too few of us are making the profits we need to thrive and grow. Most important, this sacrifice is still not getting us where we want to be as a community. North Carolina may be the best place to cook and eat, but it's a dysfunctional place to work in pretty much every point in our state food chain. As recently as 1965, a typical dairy farm here was pasture-based, supplementing what animals ate from the pasture with hay and corn silage grown on farm. A sizable percentage of North Carolina milk is still produced on pasture, but much of it is dumped into the commodity market because we lack the infrastructure that once existed to make distribution of local milk feasible. Not all animal fat is created equal. Eggs from chickens raised outdoors on pasture and forage have many times more nutrients and flavor than their industrially raised counterparts. Milk and meat from cows that graze on green pasture are higher in omega-3s, or "good fats," than that from cows fed soy and corn.

One of our most urgent social and racial justice, environmental, and health issues in North Carolina today is confinement hog production, which didn't exist in North Carolina until the 1970s. At any given time, there are close to 10 million pigs in our state—more pigs than people. Until we again have diversified family farms, people who love BBQ will rely on the few huge, vertically integrated—many foreign-owned—companies that control almost all pork production to determine labor practices, animal welfare, and flavor.

Hundreds of small farms lie within thirty miles of Chapel Hill, and yet the amount of local food available in grocery stores is essentially the same as when I moved here twenty-five years ago. Although polls consistently show that most eaters will pay more for local and organic food, local food consumption in North Carolina has stubbornly held at 3–5 percent of total state food sales. The diverse community of Carrboro, next door to Chapel Hill, is home to one of the oldest and most successful farmers' markets in the United States, and yet the crowd there each Saturday morning remains uniformly white. We are told by ag forecasters that we are at peak farmers' market numbers, but the sustainable food economy is also incapable of meeting the demand from people with little or no access to high-quality food.

By 2020, I had lost confidence that Lantern could create real economic equity within our own four walls, much less continue to contribute meaningfully to broader food system change. After eighteen years, we were still one of the busiest restaurants in town, but we basically broke even after making our monthly debt payments. Emergencies like a sudden roof leak or an injury left us reeling, and we still couldn't afford to provide health benefits for most of our staff. Our hourly wages were high by community standards, but we paid less than fifteen dollars per hour to many on the kitchen team. Our food costs, like our labor expenses, were well above industry standards. We were effectively a nonprofit without nonprofit supports.

In mid-March 2020, as COVID-19 spread across the state and nation, we furloughed almost everyone on our thirty-five-person team who qualified for unemployment. As a business, we were lucky. Our landlord from whom we rent the majority of our space gave us a bit of breathing room. Our debt, including a mortgage on a small part of our space we own, was in a small-business loan that was deferred as part of the initial federal relief package.

A few weeks into our closure we had the opportunity to stop talking about injustice in our local food system and do something about it. As school lunchrooms closed, we used Lantern's kitchen, where our team prepared flavorful, nutritious meals for students no longer able to access the free breakfast and lunch programs schools had provided. Within a few weeks we stripped carpets from our dining rooms, lined the bar with shelving, and ordered pallets of industrial food. With U.S. Department of Agriculture reimbursement at around a dollar per student for breakfast and two dollars for lunch, we learned to cook in a new way. To break even and keep our kitchen team working, we braised local beef shanks and combined them with fifty-pound boxes of dried noodles and paired pristine spinach from a friend's farm with commodity chicken. We made meal kits of roasted local vegetables for the skeletal cooking crews at schools to add to their own commodity meats. We made breakfast cookies from nuts and seeds and spiked them with chunks of artisan chocolate from French Broad Chocolate in Asheville. We baked muffins with huge bags of commercial rolled oats and topped them with North Carolina–grown blueberries.

What began as a collaboration among Durham Public Schools, the county school foundation, and FIG (Food Insight Group—a women-led consultancy of food system researchers), local restaurants, and caterers turned into DURHAM FEAST. For four months, twenty-seven restaurants prepared 70,000 meals using fresh produce and shelf-stable ingredients delivered weekly by hundreds of volunteers to families in need. Costs were reimbursed by funding from the federal school meal program. When the state furlough for cooks in Durham schools ended in late July, the program evolved into EAT NC. By the end of 2020 we had served more than 1 million meals to students in our community.

Cooking Like We Mean It

North Carolina is a national leader in childhood hunger. One of every four children here is food insecure, yet the calories children consume in school come from processed foods, including commodity milk, applesauce made in China, and government cheese. After years of dedicated work by hundreds of activists and advocates, it is stunning to see the empty calories that continue to fuel this system. School food is a potential lever for change on every level in society. If we chose the best food for our schoolchildren rather than the worst, we would also create jobs, promote economic development, foster antiracism, alleviate a health crisis, protect the environment, and support sustainable agriculture policy reform.

As food businesses begin to crawl out of the chasm created by the pandemic, we must center our work on racial equity, economic justice, and food sovereignty. To support a local sustainable food supply, state and county governments should help subsidize the local food economy—our small-scale farmers, restaurateurs, and food entrepreneurs. (Think if government relief funds had paid food entrepreneurs to close during the months of COVID-19 surge in America.) By paying fair prices for good food grown in North Carolina we can create a new, just food system, transform the way we perceive the cost of food, and ensure that all North Carolinians have equal access to good food. We can keep money in our state while reviving economic opportunity in rural communities, protecting the environment, and preserving heritage and biodiversity. Supporting local food is one of the few daily, tangible choices that we as individuals can make to create positive change in the world. How we choose to produce and consume food in North Carolina and beyond is fundamental to also saving the flavor and culture of this place we call home. Imagine a small hog and vegetable farm next to every BBQ restaurant in the state. This could have many benefits: it would create small-scale, integrated farms and give us access to full-flavored, pasture-raised pork BBQ. It also might inspire thousands of these hipster North Carolina–style BBQ shacks all over the country to start taking some of these pigs off our hands and raising them for themselves.

Author and activist Arundhati Roy has called this pandemic "a portal, a gateway between one world and the next."[2] She says we have a choice—either to carry the heavy, broken past with us or to "walk through lightly . . . ready to imagine another world. And ready to fight for it." This portal is an opportunity to leave behind a food system that doesn't serve any of us. The process of growing, cooking, and eating food is our last tangible connection to the earth and the soil of North Carolina. It links us to people from all time and brings flavor, value, and meaning into our daily lives. Food here has the power to satisfy a deeper hunger—a hunger for connection, community, and taste that was suddenly so fragile during the pandemic. We have to fight for the world we want and it starts at our tables.

Charcoal-Grilled Pork Neck with Honey, Chiles, and Black Pepper ANDREA REUSING

Makes 4–6 servings

FOR THE PORK BRINE

1 cup kosher salt
½ cup granulated sugar
1½ teaspoons pink curing salt #1 (sometimes called Instacure or Prague Powder)
3 quarts cold water
1 quart ice
6 bay leaves, crumbled (fresh, if possible)
4 dried red chiles (such as arbol), crushed
4 cloves garlic, smashed
1 tablespoon whole black peppercorns
1 tablespoon whole fennel seeds, toasted
5 pounds bone-in pork necks
¼ cup olive oil

FOR THE GLAZE

2 cups honey
2 cups apple cider vinegar

FOR THE GARNISH

6–10 dried red chiles
1 medium head fresh green cabbage
2 small bunches of tender herbs, such as chives, scallions, mint, and parsley
Coarsely ground black pepper and sea salt to taste

To brine the pork, in a large container with a lid, add the kosher salt, sugar, curing salt, cold water, ice, bay leaves, red chiles, garlic cloves, peppercorns, and fennel seeds and stir to combine. Add the pork, cover, and chill in the refrigerator for at least 8 and no more than 12 hours.

Remove the pork from the brine and pat dry. Arrange the necks in a single layer on a sheet pan and drizzle with the olive oil. Before grilling, allow to come to room temperature, about 1–2 hours.

To make the glaze, in a nonreactive saucepan set over medium heat, combine the honey and vinegar and simmer until reduced by a third, about 15 minutes. Allow to cool and set aside.

To prepare the garnish, in a dry skillet set over medium-high heat, lightly toast the chiles, tossing frequently until fragrant but not browned. Allow the chiles to cool slightly before using sharp scissors or a knife to cut the dried peppers into slim rounds. If you want less spice, shake the chile rings and remove the seeds. Wash the cabbage, remove the core, cut into quarters, and chill in the refrigerator.

To prepare the grill, arrange most of the hot coals on one half and just a few on the other side. When the grill is very hot but the flame has died down and the coals are completely covered with ash, place the pieces of pork, largest flat sides down, on the hotter side of the grill. Watch closely for flare-ups, extinguishing them with a squirt bottle or teacup of water or by briefly covering the grill with its lid. Cook the meat for about 5 minutes, rearranging as needed to the cooler parts of the grill. Once each piece is golden brown and the fat is sizzling, flip it and do the same on the other sides. When the pork is browned on all sides, move each piece to the cool side of the grill and brush with the glaze (watch for flare-ups).

Continue glazing the meat on the cool side of the grill, turning as needed, until all sides have been glazed and begin to caramelize, about 7 minutes or when the temperature reaches 135° on an instant-read thermometer (pork should be cooked to 145° for safe consumption, but carryover will bring these to the correct temperature). Transfer the pork to a cutting board, cover loosely with aluminum foil, and set in a warm spot in the kitchen. Allow the pork to rest for 5 minutes.

While the pork is resting, arrange the cabbage and fresh herbs on a separate platter. Using a sharp knife, slice strips of the meat away from the bones and arrange it all (boney chunks included) on a second platter and drizzle with any remaining glaze. Sprinkle the meat with the dried chiles, sea salt, and freshly ground black pepper to taste.

To eat, use the cabbage leaves to make small cups and top with slices of pork garnished with herbs, chiles, and salt to taste.

NOTES

1. Michael Ruhlman (@ruhlman), "From sad email from highly respected food writer: 'The nastiness that seems to permeate the national conversation in the US has seeped into food as well. No longer is it a way to bring people together, but just another way to find fault with other people and to drive people away,'" Twitter, July 31, 2020, https://twitter.com/ruhlman/status/1289309299596959745.

2. Arundhati Roy, "The Pandemic Is a Portal," virtual conversation with Imani Perry, Haymarket Books, May 1, 2020, https://aas.princeton.edu/news/pandemic-portal.

VICTORIA BOULOUBASIS

From Restaurant Kids to Restaurateurs

First-Generation Southerners in the Triangle Culinary Scene

In the 1970s, my father, Gus, emigrated from Athens, Greece, to Astoria, Queens. Born at the tail end of a civil war, he left Greece during a military junta, following his cousins and a dream. At a Greek dance in Astoria, he met my Greek American mother, Lisa. When I was born in 1982, he had a union job working as a waiter in an upscale Manhattan hotel restaurant where he served celebrities like Johnny Cash and Diana Ross. Later, he managed Greek diners in New York and New Jersey, one of them owned by his father-in-law.

A call from friends in North Carolina, brothers whom he had known since birth in his Greek village, encouraged him to come south. My father, or baba, was presented with a business opportunity: a seafood restaurant, Captain's Galley, in the small western foothills town of Stony Point (nowhere near the coast). It was an opportunity to grow his own business and build a financial future for our family. Tobacco farmers and Democratic politicians, high school cheerleading squads and grandparents packed the restaurant's booths before football games. Couples celebrated important wedding anniversaries with mountains of fried seafood. Gus was on a first-name basis with everybody.

Baba's accented English mixed with the honeyed North Carolina twang of his restaurant family to sustain a thirty-year business in the rural Piedmont. It's where he learned to make foreign (to him) foods like popcorn shrimp, deviled crab, honey mustard dressing, and my favorite, cornmeal hushpuppies. My father served thousands of hushpuppies to his happy customers. I can't imagine anything more symbolic of southern hospitality. My southern experience is shaped by people like my baba, immigrants serving their neighbors and becoming a part of a place through their work.

Observing my father skillfully negotiate his immigrant identity at the restaurant shaped my work as a journalist. My ears became attuned to the lilts and disjointed phrases of English as a second language. Long before I studied it, I learned kitchen Spanish, which I still use every day in my reporting. The opportunities I had as a first-generation college student helped me create my own career path away from restaurants, but they were given to me due to my family's restaurants. I often joke that hushpuppies put me through college, but this classic southern food symbolizes my parents' sacrifice. My mother, Lisa, put her education on hold to start a family while still working at the family's Jersey diner and eventually running her own in North Carolina. She waited until I entered high school to enroll in community college and earn a degree. I carry that sacrifice with me as fuel.

First-generation Americans are often restaurant kids. Our parents arrived in the United States with an entrepreneurial hustle. We were children of immigrants whose parents worked over flat-top grills, deep fryers, and cash registers seven days a week.

Lisa's Diner, my mother's restaurant, served breakfast and lunch in an industrial pocket of Winston-Salem. During breaks from college, I worked a few shifts with my grandmother, Yiayia Eleni, serving her favorite mail carriers and car haulers, and counting out change at the cash-only register. Once, we took over the grill when a cook didn't show during a lunch rush, flipping burgers and fried eggs for hours while cursing and breaking into fits of laughter with Roberto, the restaurant's dishwasher.

When you say "restaurant kid" to a restaurant kid, it immediately resonates. We are quick on our feet, dexterous, and determined, cut from the same cloth sullied by grease and hope.

From Restaurant Kid to Restaurateur

In much of the United States, urban neighborhoods are strong ethnic enclaves—think Queens or L.A.'s Koreatown—where immigrant-owned restaurants are visible, integral parts of the community. But in the American South you don't stumble on these enclaves so easily; you've got to know where to find them. A persistent myth of the South is its cultural homogeneity, but there is no dearth of diversity in the South, and this dates from its earliest history. Foodways provide evidence of the complex relationships within a multiracial and multiethnic South. Today restaurant ownership among immigrants in North Carolina feels more recent not only because so-called ethnic food is trending but due to the rising movement for racial justice in this country for immigrants and especially people of color. Those of us who grew up here—and *in* these restaurants—know that our families have always been here, even if our menus did not reveal our stories.

A growing number of North Carolina's most celebrated restaurateurs

Lao Fog latte, mochi donut, Taiwanese fried chicken on garlic butter biscuit, iced matcha latte, braised pork (*thom kem* in Lao, *lo ba* in Taiwanese, *kakuni* in Japanese), Heirloom Brewshop, Raleigh, North Carolina

in the contemporary food scene began as immigrant restaurant kids. In the Triangle, these individuals are millennial or Gen Z. Their parents came to the American South from different corners of the world, seeking opportunity and, for some, safety from repressive regimes. Now, the next generation deftly navigates identity politics and business ownership doing things their way and on their own terms.

They express themselves through food and community. This is a luxury our parents didn't have, and it reframes how we view and understand immigrant-owned restaurants. Restaurant kids turned restaurateurs have gained cultural capital, wielding it to carve out their own niche in the region's culinary landscape.

Inside Heirloom Brewshop in downtown Raleigh, a soft rose hue contrasts with bright sunlight and the lush green leaves of giant birds of paradise. Sculptural wooden ceiling beams give the feeling that one has landed in the belly of a whale. Heirloom specializes in tea, sake, and coffee. Its food menu of small plates reflects Anna Phommavong and Chuan Tsay's upbringing as Asian Americans in the South with parents from Laos and Taiwan. The name, Heirloom, suggests that the shop is both an extension of their families and their personal vision. It's also their offering to the community. Raised in North Carolina, Phommavong and Tsay met in college and opened Heirloom in 2018.

Throughout her childhood, Phommavong's parents owned restaurants in High Point, North Carolina. "[In] a lot of Asian restaurants across the U.S. you'll always see that one child in the corner," she says. "And that was me in a hibachi restaurant, working or just hanging out after school." Phommavong notes, "My family opened up a hibachi restaurant, and that has nothing to do with their culture or our food." Food from their Lao culinary traditions remained off-menu. The purpose of the business was just that—to earn money and sustain a family. The Phommavongs began by serving pizza and sub sandwiches and often had Chinese dishes on the menu.

Tsay's family is Taiwanese. His father was a trained chef who came to the United States, where he worked at many Asian-style restaurants. Tsay remembers cookbooks arriving in the mail filled with recipes in Chinese that his father practiced to perfect. To Tsay, it presented a paradox. His parents taught him to speak Taiwanese and Japanese, which he calls a "language of controlled freedom," over Mandarin, "the language of oppression."

"So a family that's Laotian, [and] a family that's Taiwanese, both of them serving at one point in their lives Chinese food is, in my mind, very dehumanizing," says Tsay. "It takes away your individuality. It takes away your heritage and culture."

He describes "a repression of feelings or trauma." Tsay says their parents did not have the same platform that he and Phommavong do. Having been born in the United States, he says, makes them hyperaware of what their parents endured. "For us it is about identity and continuing that journey that they started."

To honor their parents' journeys and struggles, the pair celebrate the histories that brought them together through their combined cuisines. "This is a representation of our union. Coffee, tea, sake—those three do a good job representing us as a married couple. And the food and flavor profiles are about discovering what we enjoy eating."

The couple incorporates the lemongrass and coconut of Lao food and the mirin and five spice of Taiwanese food in both classic dishes from their childhood and modern riffs on rice and noodle bowls. They compromised on the pork belly dish (less sweet, more Taiwanese) and the rice porridge (leans Lao). Of course, as southerners, they felt that a new biscuit menu would be apt, presenting a choice of Taiwanese fried chicken or Lao sausage for their ideal breakfast sandwich. They source teas globally and coffee from another immigrant-owned business, Little Waves Coffee Roasters in Durham. Heirloom insists that you come in, pause, and listen.

Until recently, nuance in what is deemed ethnic cuisine was lost on most diners. Sociologist Krishnendu Ray explains that "the cuisine of two racially marked groups, Chinese and Mexicans—two of the oldest 'ethnic' groups in the USA—would both become ubiquitous and yet remain classified as permanently foreign foods."[1] Ubiquitous, and also cheap. In what Ray describes as a "global hierarchy of taste," the perceived value of "ethnic cuisine" was tied to the power a country wields. Besides a bargain price, consumers crave nostalgia and authenticity, even from a culture not their own. When we categorize food this way in the United States, based on capital, we treat it as a contribution to us, a commodity—along with the people and the culture who created it.

"Southern food was not available at my house. Golden Corral was the extent of my southern food knowledge."

—CHARLIE IBARRA, co-owner, Cortez Seafood & Cocktail, cocreator, Jose and Sons, Raleigh, North Carolina, June 2019

In the case of immigrant kids turned entrepreneurs, a layered personal nostalgia clashes with the consumer's expectation of authenticity. Oscar Diaz and I have had countless discussions about this.[2] A chef-owner at Cortez, Diaz is also a chef at Jose and Sons in Raleigh. Although he did not grow up in a restaurant family, his business partner, Charlie Ibarra, comes from Raleigh's El Rodeo family, Tex-Mex restaurants serving "ACP" (arroz con pollo) combo plates smothered in melted cheese. While Ibarra's family business may have encouraged customers to wear sombreros and pose for birthday photos, Ibarra and Diaz offer a deeper understanding of Mexican American cuisine inspired by Mexico's Pacific coast and Baja California.

Diaz jokes that his parents didn't leave the small town of Villa Hidalgo in Jalisco just so that their American-born middle son could sling tacos for a living. The culinary school dropout from Chicago set his creative ambitions on the big leagues with stints in Las Vegas and Los Angeles. Diaz didn't cook Mexican food until he arrived in North Carolina, where he answered Ibarra's Craigslist ad seeking a chef.

Tacos weren't trendy when Diaz was growing up, yet one of the most visible chefs was mega-restaurateur Rick Bayless, a white chef who built his career on bringing traditional Mexican food to North American palates.

Diaz's nostalgia is rooted in the first-generation experience. "It's nostalgic coming in here," Diaz said as we walked into Raleigh's El Taco Market, a former fast-food joint outfitted to be a taqueria, complete with a drive-through window. "But it's kind of funny," adds Diaz. "It's a Mexican American nostalgia."

Diaz is often asked where to get the best, most authentic tacos. It's not that he never offers a suggestion, but it makes him uneasy, this flattening of the iconic foods of his youth. This American obsession with tacos is symptomatic of a dissonance; the desire to master an exotic dish, to become the expert. "If someone else writes the history book about you, that's what is remembered," he says. "If we don't start controlling the narrative, someone else is. And then we become spectators of our own culture."

Diaz and Ibarra present dishes rooted in seasonality, a fusion of cultures, and what feels authentic to them as first-generation Americans obsessed with food. Oysters fresh from North Carolina's Crystal Coast round out happy hour. Heartier meals include guajillo pepper-marinated North Carolina swordfish, tuna al pastor tacos, and charred octopus nestled into butter beans. At Cortez, Diaz's working-class upbringing is apparent in a playful spin on classic fast food. The MexRib sandwich features North Carolina pork and a homemade sweet barbecue sauce vaguely reminiscent of the Golden Arches' version.

In Durham, the Palace International explores the subtleties of regional African cuisine in an extensive menu rooted in the Ochola family's Kenyan culinary repertoire. In the 1980s, downtown Durham was a desolate city. But on the corner of what is now the tallest skyscraper in the city was the first Palace International, a music venue and restaurant run by the late Maurice Ochola, who immigrated from Kenya to attend university in the United States. He opened the Palace to bring performers from Africa and the Caribbean for a growing African diaspora in Durham. Being in a college town, the venue attracted many former Peace Corps volunteers. Here, Maurice met his Kenyan wife, Caren, who had also immigrated to pursue her education. At the Palace, Caren cooked while Maurice deejayed and booked gigs at night. Today Caren oversees the kitchen while son Moses Ochola manages the restaurant and community space with assistance from his sister Susanna.

The Palace's curry goat resonates with most African and Caribbean people, but Ochola has pushed his mom to connect the menu more deeply to their home of western Kenya. This includes more fish dishes and dry-rubbed meats cooked on an open flame, as well as sautéed greens with ginger and spices. He organizes special dinners with a collective of local women chefs, including Samantha Kotey from Ghana and Adé Carrena of Benin.

"Legacy is really important for us. To try to grow from what our parents have started and make it our own."

—MOSES OCHOLA, chef/co-owner, the Palace International, Durham, North Carolina, January 2, 2020

Ochola says that his parents showcased Kenyan culture at a time when "it was unheard of in the South." He says he has a duty to continue that legacy. "The Palace was integral to raising my family. As a son of those immigrants, I make sure that story is kept alive."

Ochola acknowledges his dual identity as a first-generation southerner and Kenyan. "Oftentimes I don't distinguish southern culture and my culture, Kenyan culture," he says. "My friends laugh at me all the time, they say, 'Moses, you are so country!' But what I see in my [Kenyan] village are the same things I would see in Bahama [North Carolina]. Storytelling, politeness, southern hospitality: that all really speaks to me."

In March 2021, after fourteen years in business, the Palace International closed its Broad Street location when the landlord did not renew the Ocholas' lease. "This abrupt announcement is both disheartening and uncomfortable after working so hard and succeeding in staying open during COVID, paying bills, and supporting our staff through so many obstacles," Moses wrote on the Palace's Instagram page. But the community showed up, reflecting the southern hospitality so deeply ingrained in the restaurant's ethos. Donations poured in to help the Ochola family find their next location.

Ochola also leads the Black Farmers' Market project, which alternates between Durham and Raleigh, bolstering Black businesses and culture with fresh food from area Black farmers and chefs. His work caught the attention of James Beard award–winning Raleigh chef Ashley Christensen. She gave Ochola access to her Instagram page for a week in 2020 for him to promote the monthly market. Ochola uses food to promote equity in Black communities throughout the South and the region's African diaspora.

The restaurant landscape in North Carolina has changed tremendously in the past decade. Much of that growth is rooted in an immigrant workforce and the food inspired by the thriving multicultural community in the South. But the pandemic has revealed even more

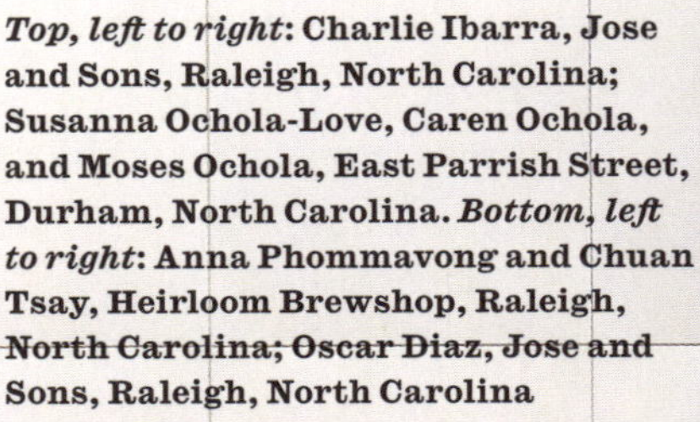

Top, left to right: Charlie Ibarra, Jose and Sons, Raleigh, North Carolina; Susanna Ochola-Love, Caren Ochola, and Moses Ochola, East Parrish Street, Durham, North Carolina. *Bottom, left to right*: Anna Phommavong and Chuan Tsay, Heirloom Brewshop, Raleigh, North Carolina; Oscar Diaz, Jose and Sons, Raleigh, North Carolina

massive change and a shifting foundation as we witness the instability—and unsustainability—of revenue in the restaurant industry. The pandemic was touted as unprecedented, even months into it. Lacking government protections, both owners and workers were left to fend for themselves. Functional government relief for small businesses was marginal or absent. As restaurants closed due to the coronavirus, service and food jobs were nearly wiped out. We are witnessing capitalism's facade crumbling into rubble.

"We need to speak out about who we're looking out for," says Diaz of the undocumented workforce left without relief, risking eviction and worse. "We can keep people anonymous to be safe. But we're humans, and we're Latinos. This is one of my concerns."

The restaurant's message is clear, as stated on the Cortezes' social media accounts during the pandemic: "We are driven by two things that have been on our minds daily: How do we act as responsibly as possible with our team and our offerings? How do we help those in the shadows and unable to receive benefits? We are all in this together . . . our minds are also heavy with concern for friends and folks not able to qualify for unemployment and other safety nets."

As North Carolina entered Phase Two of reopening during the pandemic, cases of police brutality against Black Americans erupted around the country. The murder of George Floyd, a Black man in Minneapolis, at the hands of the police launched a series of protests throughout the nation demanding justice and an end to police violence against Black people.

On Saturday, May 30, 2020, the first night of a peaceful protest in downtown Raleigh morphed into destruction and violence after police responded with tear gas and rubber bullets. Looters smashed windows of local businesses, including Heirloom and Garland, whose owners remain focused on the Black Lives Matter movement, not the looting.

On Heirloom's Instagram: "We started Heirloom with the vision of contributing to a better world around us. Having grown up as unwelcome members of the communities we were raised in, watching our parents endure torching and shootings, this nightmare is not over." Tsay is referring to a traumatic moment in his childhood—his father's car riddled with bullets outside their family restaurant in North Carolina, an attack that Tsay considered a hate crime. Heirloom's customers seek photogenic platters of authentic food, but those dishes never tell the full story.

I don't know if my family could have or would have chosen to speak up so openly in Stony Point. By cooking and serving working-class American food, my family's business model was not an artistic expression of their complex identities—a right now afforded young immigrant-owned restaurants today.

As a restaurant kid I see the glaring difference between today's idolized chefs and our apron-clad parents and grandparents who cooked and served plate after plate of fried seafood, pizza, and burritos. I also see contemporary immigrant entrepreneurs telling their truths and their stories. Tsay articulates it best: "I think restaurants and cooking and why Anna's parents got into the industry, and why mine got into the industry: food was how we spoke."

These new North Carolina chefs and restaurant owners—first-generation American millennials—are accessing a form of cultural capital that wasn't afforded to their parents and my parents. As they carve out their niche in a rapidly evolving restaurant world, they are turning the tide, creating a wave of change that ensures their voices are heard and recognized as Lao, Taiwanese, Mexican, Kenyan, and North Carolinian.

BrunsMex Stew **OSCAR DIAZ *with* VICTORIA BOULOUBASIS**

Makes 4–6 servings

FOR THE MEAT

4 pounds goat stew meat (can substitute lamb or beef stew meat)
Banana leaves or corn husks

FOR THE SALSA MOLCAJETE

7 Roma tomatoes
3 cloves garlic
5 serrano chiles

FOR THE STEW

1 cup canned or frozen butter beans, rinsed
1 cup corn
½ cup canned black beans, rinsed
1 cup diced yellow or white potato
½ cup diced carrot
½ cup diced white onion
6 ounces tomato paste
3 teaspoons white distilled vinegar
Salt and pepper to taste
Cilantro leaves, pickled onions, and thin fried tortilla strips for garnish

Season the meat with salt and pepper and rest it overnight in the refrigerator. Rinse the meat and wrap it in banana leaves. If you can't find banana leaves, corn husks soaked in warm water will work. Place the meat inside a steamer and cook over medium heat for 3 hours or until the meat falls apart. Alternatively, you can use a large stock pot fitted with a steamer basket or metal colander lined with the leaves and covered with a lid. Remove the meat, allow it to cool, and break it apart with a fork. Preserve the steaming liquid.

To make the salsa, set a cast-iron pan over high heat. Add the tomatoes, garlic, and chiles and char. Remove the garlic once it has dark brown spots on both sides. Remove the tomatoes and chiles when they are charred on the outside and soft throughout. Place all the ingredients in a blender and pulse until they form a thick, chunky salsa.

To make the stew, place a large pot over medium heat. Add the butter beans, corn, black beans, potatoes, carrots, onions, tomato paste, and vinegar, along with the steamed meat and salsa, and stir to combine. Add 1 cup of the steaming liquid and bring to a simmer. Season with salt and pepper. Let the stew simmer and reduce for 1 hour until it thickens. Add more steaming liquid if needed. Serve hot, garnished with the cilantro leaves, pickled onions, and thin fried tortilla strips.

NOTES

1. Krishnendu Ray, *The Ethnic Restaurateur* (London: Bloomsbury Academic, 2016), 105.

2. Victoria Bouloubasis, "Exploring the Downside of Food Culture's Authenticity Obsession with Jose and Sons' Oscar Diaz," *INDY Week*, August 17, 2016.

MICHELLE T. KING

North Carolina Chinese Restaurant Journeys

"I'm of Chinese descent, Indian by birth, American by choice, and southern by the grace of God," says Huan Hou (Phillip), chef of the China 10 restaurant in Greenville, North Carolina. Phillip, a second-generation Indian-born Chinese, immigrated to the United States, and specifically North Carolina, more than thirty years ago. The restaurant, which opened in 1998 and is owned by Phillip's wife, Lien, has become an established part of Greenville family traditions. Speaking of one of their regular customers, Phillip explains, "He used to come with his parents to eat. As he got older, he started bringing his dates to eat here. Then he went to Chapel Hill for school, but he came back and got married. Since then he brings his wife here to eat and his kids to eat." Phillip considers many of their customers as friends and is grateful for the opportunities this life has afforded him: "Doesn't everybody want to come to the United States? America is the greatest country on earth. We are a shining beacon to the whole world."

Jacky Zheng, a recent UNC–Chapel Hill graduate, has a decidedly different perspective on the life afforded by a North Carolina Chinese restaurant. "When I think of the South—and maybe this is just the climate I've grown up in—the biggest things that come to mind are white, straight, male, conservative. I think that definition rubs against everything that I am as a person . . . minority, immigrant, LGBT, poor. I think there is definitely a huge difference in my head between my image of southern and [my] identity." In contrast to Phillip Hou, Jacky was born in Wilmington and raised by his Fujianese immigrant parents in their restaurant, Chopstix. Starting at the age of thirteen and throughout high school, Jacky worked in the restaurant, but he always yearned for an ordinary American childhood. He resented the many hours his parents devoted to the restaurant, which was time they could not spare for him. At some point, his older sister pulled him aside to explain just how much their parents, neither of whom had graduated from high school in China and who spoke little English, had sacrificed in order to give their children the opportunities they never had. Looking back, Jacky sees his family's success as built on years of hard work and sacrifice—not freely

Crab Rangoon, imperial chicken, pan-fried dumplings, beef satay, shrimp and veggies with white sauce, China 10, Greenville, North Carolina

given, but painstakingly earned: "Symbolically, the restaurant represents how my family wrote our story in America and carved out a place for ourselves."

Both Phillip Hou and Jacky Zheng's stories are compelling visions of life as seen from the perspective of those who work in some of North Carolina's home-grown Chinese restaurants. These are not chains but independent *Mama*-and-*Baba* businesses, built on the grit and long labor of their owners-managers-sometime-chefs. And it is thanks to the intrepid work of students in my Chinese food history class that their unique Chinese American voices are now heard. Students in the course, including Danielle Kruchten (who wrote Phillip Hou's profile) and Peter Cohen (who wrote Jacky Zheng's profile), each interviewed a North Carolina Chinese restaurateur or someone who grew up in a North Carolina Chinese restaurant and then turned their interviews into a multimedia story.[1] The results of their collective labors over the past four years have astounded me, painting intimate portraits of Chinese immigrant lives in North Carolina.

It was actually Jacky's interview with his older sister in 2016 that inspired these student journeys into North Carolina's Chinese restaurants. That was the third time I had taught the course, and by then, I knew I didn't want my students to write traditional term papers—compositions they could churn out in their sleep, with little personal investment. That year, I asked the students instead to conduct oral history interviews with anyone involved with Chinese food, centered around topics we had addressed in class: notions of authenticity, Chinese restaurants as businesses, food as a form of identity, and more. Jacky's essay about his sister, who was fifteen years older and born in China, was filled with insights both tough and tender. Not only had their parents sacrificed, but Jacky's sister had not had the opportunities that would later be afforded Jacky, as both a favored son and a younger child, born after the family had gained some measure of financial stability through their restaurant. Jacky's essay was such a powerful narrative of his Chinese family's migration story that I started to imagine how other students might take this journey of discovery.

This germ of an idea became even more important to me in the wake of the 2016 presidential election. I was floored, utterly dejected and dispirited. The months that followed had moments of bittersweet solace, such as participating in the Women's March in Austin, Texas, with my seventy-seven-year-old mother and my five-year-old daughter, but these were too few and far between. I was determined to do something more, to take action, even in a small way.

Seeing Jacky's essay afresh in light of the election, I thought, surely there is not a corner of North Carolina that doesn't have a Chinese restaurant and locals who love to eat there, even in the most Trump-supporting counties of the state. Immigrants are not faceless outsiders or foreign others but people who live and work in your neighborhood—perhaps in the Chinese (or other cuisine) restaurant that you enjoy down the street. By collectively documenting the voices and experiences of Chinese restaurateurs in North Carolina, my students could vividly illustrate how Chinese restaurants—and the people who own and work in them—have become an integral part of the local fabric of so many North Carolina communities.

How did these migrants find themselves in towns and cities scattered around North Carolina, from Chocowinity in the coastal plain to Burnsville in the mountains? What have been their struggles and challenges, their passions and successes? What feelings and experiences does the journey from one side of the earth to the other in a single lifetime entail? What part does Chinese food play in these stories? How do some migrants end up calling North Carolina home?

So far, almost sixty students of mine have gone on their own journeys into the world of North Carolina's Chinese restaurants. Some returned to their hometowns to interview owners of Chinese restaurants they had frequented for years but knew nothing about. Others approached a restaurant they had never stepped foot in before and ended up with the personal history of a generous stranger. Some interviewed the second-generation children of Chinese restaurateurs in the state, who are now fellow students at Carolina. A few students, like Jacky, had grown up in their family's Chinese restaurant and interviewed a parent, hearing previously unspoken stories of hardship and struggle for the first time.

Many were surprised by the sheer diversity of the restaurateurs they encountered, reflecting the global nature of the Chinese diaspora. Several restaurateurs came directly from mainland China, but others hailed from Taiwan, Hong Kong, Singapore, Malaysia, and even India. In part, this diversity reflects three distinct waves of Chinese migration to the United States over the preceding two centuries. The first wave of Chinese migrants in the nineteenth century came primarily from Guangdong (Canton) Province. After an outright ban lasting more than sixty years on Chinese immigration under the Chinese Exclusion Act (1882–1943) and the opening of the United States to non-European immigrants with the Immigration and Nationality Act (1965), a second wave of Chinese migrants arrived from Taiwan and Hong Kong starting in the 1960s. My parents, who immigrated to the United States from Taiwan in the early 1960s, were part of this second wave. They eventually settled in Michigan, where they raised my two siblings and me.

Lien Hou, owner, and
Huan (Phillip) Hou, chef,
China 10, Greenville,
North Carolina

A third wave of Chinese migrants began arriving from mainland China after the People's Republic of China's (PRC) borders and economy opened in the 1980s. (Most of my students of Chinese descent are children of this third wave of mainland immigrants.) Perhaps most notable about this phenomenon is that most Chinese immigrants working in American restaurants today come, not just from the PRC, but by and large from the environs of one city in one province, Fuzhou, Fujian, on China's southeastern coast. All of my students who grew up in Chinese restaurant families are Fujianese, and most of the PRC restaurateurs interviewed come from Fujian. With limited English or little formal education, new arrivals have few other work options. Most have no previous culinary training but learn on the job after they arrive. Often they are drawn to settle in a particular place, such as North Carolina, because of connections to family, friends, or acquaintances already there.

Almost all of these portraits contain a single unifying refrain: the sheer hours of labor that immigrants put into their restaurants. Michael Lin interviewed his father, Ruishun Lin, who owns the Red Pepper in Sneads Ferry, near Camp Lejeune. "After a tireless twelve-hour shift, Mr. Lin returns home completely exhausted. His clothes are stained with grease and his face is covered with sweat. Mr. Lin grabs a beer, then heads to bed where he rests ahead of another busy day of work. This process is repeated every day for at least 350 days out of the year." Long hours with few days off are the norm for many of the Chinese restaurant owners my students interviewed. This devotion to keeping their restaurants open year-round has led to a tradition of many American Jewish families eating at Chinese restaurants on Christmas Day. Yet this same intense work ethic means that these Chinese restaurateurs rarely see their own families.

Many of the restaurateurs willingly concede that they are not particularly concerned with reproducing Chinese flavors—the restaurant is a labor of economic necessity, not epicurean delight. If customers don't order a dish and it doesn't sell, there is no point putting it on the menu; hence, the endless repetition of standard favorites from restaurant to restaurant, such as General Tso's chicken, beef and broccoli, and sesame noodles. Menus are often simply inherited from the previous owner because they are a known quantity that sells. Ping Lin, owner of Blue Asia in Wilmington, explained to Suhas Etigunta that he has occasionally added new items to the menu, but his efforts always fail: "In Wilmington, we are so close to the ocean, so sometimes when there are different seasons, there are different seafoods, and I try to put them on the menu, but people don't want to try it. . . . [American customers] can order the same thing years by years. If a customer is coming, I know their order, they don't even have to tell me what they like."

Of course, there are exceptions, particularly among more recently established regional Chinese restaurants in urban centers, which tend to have both more adventurous eaters and greater numbers of Asian customers looking for authentic tastes. Autumn Tucker interviewed John Yu at his Charlotte restaurant, Taste of SHU, which specializes in Sichuanese cuisine. When Autumn asked him to recommend a representative dish, he recommended their "spicy wok" dish (mala xiang guo), a numbingly spicy, stir-fried blend of various proteins and vegetables. The Taste of SHU version contains "fish fillet, squid roll, bovine stomach, pork intestines, shrimp, lotus root, and enoki mushrooms, among various other vegetables." As Yu explained to Autumn, "Around 70 percent of our customers are Chinese looking for traditional food, and 10 percent are other Asians. So, the majority of our customers are Asian and that's why we're here, for them. We could easily offer Americanized Chinese food, but we don't want to do that, what's the point?" Ironically, John Yu is not from landlocked Sichuan Province, known for its spicy cuisine: ever the enterprising restaurateur, he's from (you guessed it) Fujian Province on the southeastern coast, some 1,250 miles away.

"It may seem an improbable landing point for a woman who was once a twenty-one-year-old woman working in a shoe factory in Fuzhou. She spoke no English, had never been to the United States, and had no immediate family here. But nineteen years later, Minyu Zheng has an American husband, three children, and her own restaurant."

—**HOLT McKEITHAN, writing about Minyu Zheng, co-owner, China Bay Buffet, Chocowinity, North Carolina, spring 2019**

Yu's comments and the economic viability of his regional specialty restaurant—unimaginable here thirty years ago—attest to the rising numbers of Asians of all nationalities in the state, especially in urban North Carolina. Today more than 300,000 Asian Americans live in the state, making up 3 percent of its population. Most significantly, these numbers are rapidly rising: from 2000 to 2010, North Carolina's Asian population grew by 85 percent, making it one of the top three states with regard to Asian American demographic increase.[2]

For many of the Chinese migrants interviewed, the choice to remain in North Carolina was a matter of happenstance, but for others, the decision was a matter of fate. One of my favorite profiles is Holt McKeithan's interview with Minyu Zheng, who owns the China Bay Buffet in Chocowinity, a small town on the eastern coast, along the Pamlico River sound. At twenty-one, Zheng was working in a shoe factory in Fujian, but that year she made the leap and made it to New York. Eventually she arrived in North Carolina, working as a waitress in Fayetteville, where she met her future husband, a native Tar Heel. At first, she was reluctant to date him because of their cultural differences. "Then he kept on coming," she said, "every day for two whole years," eating his lunch quietly in the corner of the restaurant. He would always ask if he could help her in any way or give her a ride since she didn't have a car. He finally convinced Zheng that for him, as a Christian, a marriage vow was for a lifetime. Minyu Zheng married him, and they now have three children.

Most striking in the profile are the audio clips of Minyu Zheng narrating her own story: we hear very distinctly the southern lilt in her soft voice, layered over a Chinese accent. Zheng's warmth helps her connect with her customers and build community: "I like to sit down, talk to people, especially old people. They'll tell you their story, from when they are young and everything. That's what I like about the restaurant business. . . . When they come here [and say], 'Hi! How are you doing?' It just makes your day."

For a few months in spring 2020, it certainly seemed as if coronavirus and rising political tensions between the PRC and the United States would negatively affect Chinese restaurants. President Donald Trump's insistence on calling the coronavirus the "Chinese virus" or the even more childish taunt of "kung flu" seemed to have a chilling effect on Americans' eating habits, with 60 percent of Chinese restaurants in the United States closing their doors through April 2020. In a late March blog post for our course, one student, Alexis Cameron, wrote, "It especially pains me to look on social media and see people boycotting Chinese restaurants due to their fear. . . . Over the break [before quarantine rules were instated], I made sure to go to at least two Chinese restaurants and order as much food as I could possibly eat." Surprisingly, by the end of May 2020, Chinese restaurants had bounced back and reopened faster than any other category, making their open rate of 74 percent roughly equivalent to that of other types of restaurants.[3] This led some industry insiders to speculate that Chinese restaurateurs may have chosen to close temporarily due to fears of racist stigmatization or of bringing the virus home to elderly family members. As with the entire restaurant industry, it remains to be seen which Chinese restaurants will survive and which will fold in the course of this pandemic. The students from our disrupted spring 2020 class remain hopeful that all the business owners they spoke with will endure.

"We basically grew up in the restaurant. It was school, restaurant, doing our schoolwork at the restaurant while customers came in, and then we would go home. We spent more hours at the restaurant than our own house."

—HANNAH JIAN, daughter of Jian Xiaozhang, owner, Bamboo House, Greensboro, North Carolina, spring 2020

Yet the closure of Chinese restaurants is not entirely unwelcome on the part of some owners, at least as they near retirement. A *New York Times* article from December 2019 reported that the percentage of Chinese eateries of all restaurants in the twenty largest U.S. metropolitan areas had fallen in the past five years from 7.3 percent to 6.5 percent.[4] Many of those closures are likely due to second-generation mobility, as children such as Jacky and Michael are encouraged to excel in more lucrative, status-filled careers requiring a college education. As Hannah Jian, a first-generation college student at Carolina whose parents own Bamboo House in Greensboro, explained to Victoria Tran, "Owning a restaurant is the last resort. If you don't do well at school, you're going to be a restaurant owner, and you're going to do this for the rest of your life." This is why restaurant children like Emily Huang, whose parents own Great China in Wingate, go into STEM fields, as she told Aditi Adhikari: her family would rather that she choose an easier professional path than endure the hard work of restaurant ownership.

As any Asian American living in the South can tell you, living here often feels as if we are not part of the picture, which largely remains a portrait of fraught coexistence between Black and white. For many people in both dominant groups, Asians remain the ultimate outsiders, perpetual foreigners within the United States. Yet perhaps what is so compelling about the interviewees in this project is that they are not waiting for anyone else to determine whether they belong here: they are making their minds up for themselves. Phillip Hou concludes, "I've been living in North Carolina for over thirty years now. I guess that makes me a southerner, right?"

When I moved to North Carolina in 2007, I had no expectation that I would learn anything about Chinese food here. I had grown up eating the Chinese food my parents cooked for us every day, lived and worked after college in China, Hong Kong, and Taiwan, and spent many happy years in San Francisco for graduate school. I had enjoyed eating everything from an indescribably mouthwatering, multicourse banquet at a high-end restaurant in Shanghai to the most memorable bowl of noodles in my life at a small mountain farmstead in rural Hunan Province, with a range of delicious Chinese meals eaten in between. Yet it turns out that I had *a lot* to learn—namely, that it's not just about the food, it's about the people. By vicariously accompanying my students on their own North Carolina Chinese restaurant journeys, I have been alternately humbled and awed by the life experiences of the interviewees and the tenacity of my students in gathering their often unheard stories. One student, Beibei Du, explained it best: "It is never *only* a Chinese restaurant. It's choices of life that we are discovering from this."

Fried Rice with Anything **MICHELLE T. KING**

Makes 4 servings

2 tablespoons cooking oil, divided, plus more as needed
1½–2 cups chopped protein, such as cooked ham, tofu, or cooked chicken
8 eggs
Salt and pepper to taste
Several handfuls of vegetables, such as fresh or frozen chard, spinach, kale, bok choy, peas, corn, mushrooms, or chopped tomatoes
4–6 cups leftover cooked rice
Chopped green onions, sesame oil, and hot sauce for garnishes

Set a large sauté pan over high heat and add 1 tablespoon of oil. Add the cooked protein and stir to heat through and fry. Remove the protein and set aside.

Add oil to the pan if necessary, then add the eggs and stir to scramble. Season with salt and pepper. Do not overcook. Gently remove the eggs and set aside.

Add oil to the pan if necessary. Add the vegetables and stir gently to fry. Season with salt and pepper. Remove the vegetables while they are still firm and set aside.

Add 1 tablespoon of oil to the pan. Aiming for a mix of half rice and half other ingredients, add the cooked rice, breaking up any lumps. Fry until heated through.

Return all the cooked ingredients to the pan, tossing to combine. Season with salt and pepper. Fry until heated through. If you prefer crunchy rice on the bottom, brown the rice on low heat for a few minutes.

Serve in a bowl, topped with chopped green onions, sesame oil, and/or hot sauce.

NOTES

1. See class portfolios at http://mtking.myportfolio.com and http://chinese restaurantsnc.web.unc.edu/.

2. Allie Yee, "Asian Americans in North Carolina," North Carolina Asian Americans Together, March 2016, http://ncaatogether.org/wp-content/uploads /2016/08/Asian-Americans-in-NC-2016-final-03-10-0936.pdf.

3. Peter Romeo, "Chinese Restaurants Shift from Most-Closed to Fastest Reopeners," *Restaurant Business*, May 26, 2020, https://www.restaurantbusiness online.com/operations/chinese-restaurants-shift-most-closed-fastest-reopeners.

4. Amelia Nierenberg and Quoctrung Bui, "Chinese Restaurants Are Closing; That's a Good Thing, the Owners Say," *New York Times*, December 24, 2019.

KATHLEEN PURVIS

Charlotte, Where the Working Class Defines the Food

The best burger in Charlotte isn't one of the many decked-out versions available at gastropubs and high-end sports bars, with patties made from pedigreed cows and a tab that tips past fifteen dollars. The best burger in Charlotte costs four dollars with chili, mustard, and onions. Throw in another twenty-five cents if you want cheese. The best burger in Charlotte is at Brooks' Sandwich House, a cinderblock hut barely big enough to hold a constantly sizzling griddle. Outside, hungry office workers stand next to construction workers in neon yellow vests at a rough plywood table. The Brooks burger wins the prize, not just for the satisfaction of a good chili cheeseburger, but for what that burger represents: nothing less than the heart and soul of Charlotte.

When Calvin "C. T." Brooks Jr. opened his business in 1973 on North Brevard Street, the area around nearby North Davidson Street wasn't NoDa, as it's called today, a creative arts district crammed with loft apartments, craft breweries, and galleries in refurbished warehouses. It was North Charlotte, a mill village where textile workers needed lunch that was fast and cheap.

Brooks' holds its place in Charlotte's soul for being more about connection than just a place for an early morning breakfast sandwich or a cheap burger for lunch. In June 2019, twin brothers Scott and David Brooks, the sons of the late C. T. Brooks and co-owners of Brooks', decided someone ought to do something about the lack of affordable housing that dogs Charlotte's working class. They donated just over two acres of undeveloped land their father had bought as an investment in the 1950s, a $75,000 gift to their city. As a gentrifying neighborhood, NoDa occupies a place of pride in Charlotte, where defiantly creative urban pioneers share streets with low-income residents who have lived in the area for decades.

Six months later, on December 9, 2019, tragedy struck. Scott Brooks arrived at work at 5:00 A.M. on a chilly Monday to start the day's batch of chili when he was shot and killed in an apparent robbery. By December 2020, two men had been arrested and were awaiting trial for Brooks's death. The night after Brooks's death, hundreds of people—all ages, genders, races, and nationalities, from families pushing baby carriages to a Korean War vet in a wheelchair—gathered in the gravel and dirt parking lot at Brooks' Sandwich House. Struggling to keep candles lit in rain, wind, and winter bluster, people lined up to hug David Brooks until it seemed his neck would break from the love of his city. NoDa street artists hung banners with Scott's picture from streetlamps and painted a tribute on the side of the building.

Charlotte's modern skyline may punch like fists above the horizon, packed with promise and prosperity. But it's in the shadow of those gleaming office towers where you find the real Charlotte, a factory town fed by Greek diners, country-style meat-and-threes, and Black-owned cafés tagged with the northern moniker of soul food. The taste of Charlotte is baked macaroni and cheese, pita gyros, meat loaf specials, and chili dogs. It's inexpensive and filling food, the kind of home cooking that comforts people in the middle of the day when home may be hours and miles away. It's a city food scene built from Charlotte's proud working-class history, and it's easy to assume that history is slipping away if you don't know where to look for it.

Stitching a City Together

To understand the forces behind the working food of Charlotte, it helps to look back at the work that made modern Charlotte. City historians agree Charlotte's future was shaped by the railroad. As a city surrounded by cotton fields, Charlotte was where farmers brought their bales to sell. In the 1850s, rail lines connected Charlotte with Columbia, South Carolina, to the south and Raleigh to the east. More railways came after the Civil War, including the Southern Railway, known as the Main Street of the South, which joined Atlanta, Georgia, to Washington, D.C., and went right through Charlotte. Here lie the roots of the modern "Charlanta" corridor that ties Atlanta, Greenville, South Carolina, and Charlotte into a sprawling region of commerce today.

It wasn't long before actual manufacturing of textiles focused on the North Carolina Piedmont, with Charlotte right at its center. The first mill, Charlotte Cotton Mill, opened in 1880, with three more added by 1889, bringing workers in from the countryside and beginning the city's divide into mill districts that circled the city, with small houses surrounding each factory.

Manufacturing in turn drew financial institutions, the beginnings of the banking empire that cemented Charlotte's reputation in the American scene and laid the foundation for the region's blue-collar and white-collar jobs. Today, even within Charlotte's center city, you can still see

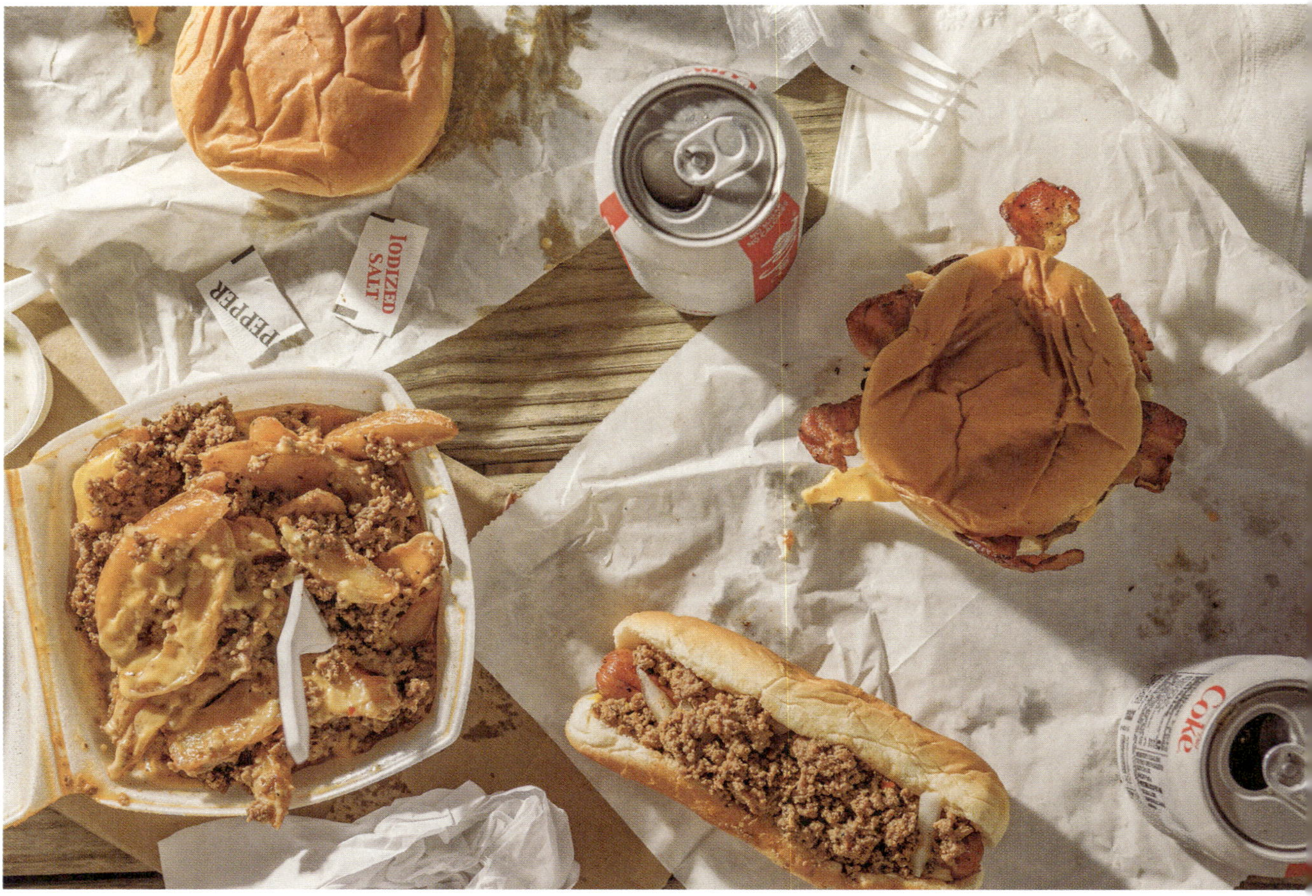
IODIZED SALT
PEPPER
Coke

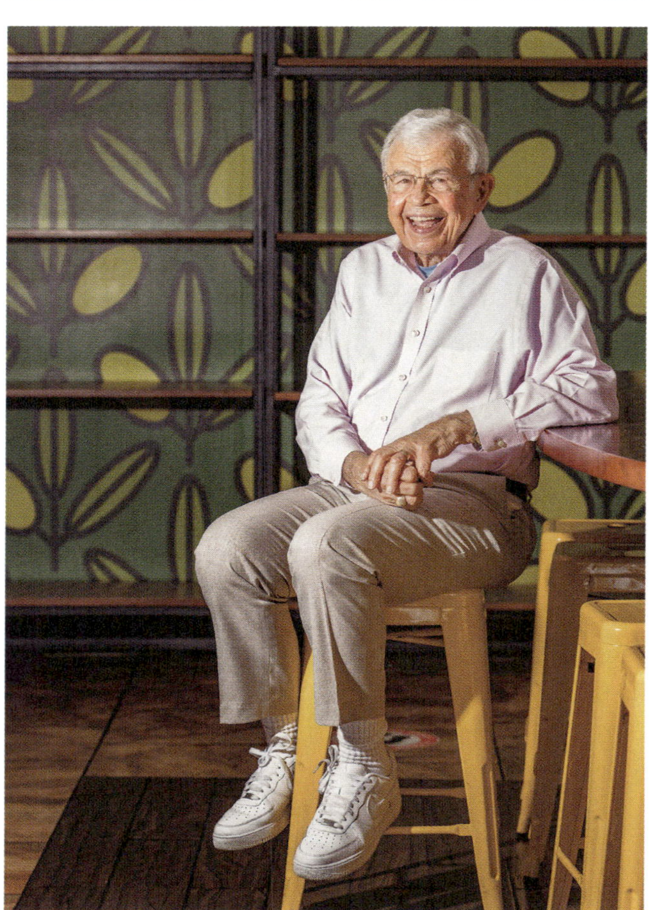

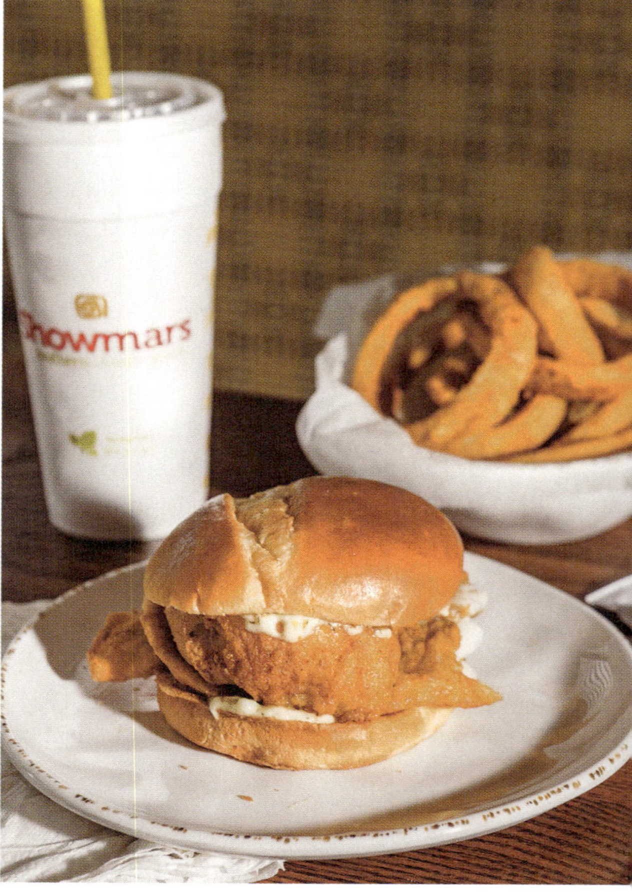

the distinctive arrangement of mill houses, originally company owned and leased to workers, around large brick buildings that once were factories. Trendy neighborhoods like NoDa, South End, and even the outer edges of Dilworth started as places where you lived *and* worked.

While large cities in the North like Chicago and Pittsburgh attracted thousands of immigrants, postwar poverty in the South deterred immigration. But Charlotte's textile mills did begin to attract Greek immigrants who came in increasing numbers throughout the first half of the twentieth century. Manufacturing was also critical to the beginnings of a working-class African American community in Charlotte. Both groups shaped Charlotte's distinctive food cultures, a culinary history grounded in the city's dynamic narrative of labor and industrialization. Charlotte writer and historian Chuck McShane says, "If you think about the early twentieth century, once you got outside the center city, the landscape was dominated by factories, by textile mills and other industrial factories. It was definitely heavy manufacturing in general. The high-end restaurants are a relatively new thing. They're definitely a part of Charlotte's atmosphere today. But you're more likely to see the Greek-owned diners and meat-and-threes."[1]

The Greek Way

In 2017, while working as the food editor of the *Charlotte Observer*, I made a list of the ten oldest restaurants in Charlotte that were still in operation. Because of a tie, there were actually eleven, and nine of them were either started by or still owned by Greek Americans. The oldest, the hot-dog café Green's Lunch, was started by Robert Green in 1926 but has been owned by the Katopodis and Sikoitis families since 1945. The lineup of Greek-owned restaurants shows the staying power of everyday places. Almost all of the venues are diners, drive-ins, or burger or hot dog stands. And even though most of the owners complain about the pressures of higher and higher taxes and operating costs, particularly for places known for affordable food, many have managed to stay open since the 1950s.

Constantine Kokenes was fourteen years old when he arrived in America in 1905, speaking no English and with a small sign around his neck: "Send this boy to Charlotte." Constantine became known as Gus and found work in Greek-owned food businesses in Charlotte. By 1914, he went back home to Greece, returning to Charlotte with his new wife, Vasiliki Gekas Kokenes. The Kokeneses ran the Star Diner uptown and had five children. In 1952, sons Speros and Steve launched the Open Kitchen, named so for its kitchen at the front of the drive-in restaurant. It remains famous as the first place to serve pizza to eager

FACING PAGE: ***Top*, Hot dog "all the way" with beef chili, mustard, and onion, hamburger with bacon, cheeseburger, chili cheese fries, Brooks' Sandwich House, Charlotte, North Carolina; *bottom left*, George Couchell, Showmars, Charlotte, North Carolina; *bottom right*, "World Famous Fish Sandwich," Showmars, Charlotte, North Carolina**

Charlotte teens. It's still *open* and owned by family members, and it still serves Italian (but very Greek-tinged) food, including Mama K's supreme pizza (ground beef, sausage, peppers, onions, mushrooms, and salami) and herby bottles of Mama K's salad dressing, both named for Vasiliki Kokenes.

"As late as the early eighties, when I came to Charlotte, almost every restaurant was Greek-run, and you might be able to get souvlaki. You might be able to get baklava for dessert. Even if it was called the Athens Restaurant, it served cheeseburgers and the meat-and-three—a meat main and sides reminiscent of the things that people grew in their gardens—pinto beans and onions, collards, and green beans."

—**TOM HANCHETT, historian, Charlotte, North Carolina, April 26, 2019**

The typical story of Charlotte's Greek food entrepreneurs is a story of building on small starts: opening a food cart or stand, stepping up to a diner, and bringing family members over from Europe to work. Elaine Tatsis Haskell remembers growing up in Dilworth in the 1960s, where cousins from Greece slept on the couch while they looked for work. "When I was growing up, everybody was family," says Haskell, whose father and uncle owned Kofinas' Snack Bar on Trade Street. "Most of the Greek people, they would come over, learn the language, get their driver's license, and go to work."[2]

Much of that work was in manufacturing, such as at the Lance Cracker Company, famous for its slim packs of cheese crackers that filled the lunch boxes and shirt pockets of blue-collar workers across the South. (Nabs was the trademarked name for competitor Nabisco's snack crackers and was later adopted as a generic term for cheese crackers.) Greek immigrants also worked in small restaurants where you didn't need to speak English to learn how to make simple American-style food, such as beef tips on rice or meat loaf specials. Those venues included flavors and preparations from Greece, too, such as Greek-style baked chicken flavored with lemon and oregano, burgers stuffed into pita pockets with tzatziki (a fresh yogurt sauce), and classic Greek salads piled with feta, Kalamata olives, and beets, served at the Old Pineville Premium Pub, owned by the Politis family; Pressley Park, in the warehouse district near Charlotte-Douglas International Airport; and at George Couchell's local chain, Showmars.

Charlotte restaurateur Andy Kastanas grew up in the Sedgefield neighborhood, one of the areas where many Greek families put down roots. Most of the families around them worked either in restaurants or for Lance—now Snyder's-Lance and a subsidiary of Campbell Soup.

"Growing up, it was always, 'What restaurant is your family?'" he remembers.[3]

Pressley Park is a classic southern-style meat-and-three where your lunch special comes with a free bowl of the lemon and chicken stock soup known as avgolemono, while Old Pineville is a working-class place where you can get buffalo wings or pita burgers. But Showmars is a different kind of success story, a study of southern fried meets Greek flavors. Owner George Couchell was a boy when his family left Greece after World War II. Starting with a small diner opened by his family, he went on to create the Showmars chain, with more than thirty locations across Charlotte. The restaurants range from large sit-down locations to tiny take-out counters, all with long menus of pita sandwiches, fried fish platters, and Greek salads.

Soulful before It Was Soul

In his 1998 book, *Sorting Out the New South City* (a revised edition was issued in 2020), on the urban development of Charlotte, historian Tom Hanchett explains that nineteenth-century Charlotte was a "salt-and-pepper" place, where Blacks and whites lived in proximity or even in the same neighborhood.[4] Through the early twentieth century, the arrival of manufacturing and early suburbs led to more segregated housing. For African Americans in Charlotte, housing was shaped by two kinds of districts: There were so-called rim villages, including Greenville/Irwinville, Dulstown, Blandville, and Myers Quarter, later renamed Cherry. These were usually located near white neighborhoods, such as Myers Quarter near Myers Park, and provided housing for Black housekeepers and other service workers employed by middle- and upper-class white homeowners—the bankers and white-collar professionals of Charlotte's industrial-financial economy.

The most significant rim village was Biddleville, started in the late 1860s along the corridor that is now Beatties Ford Road, which stretches from uptown along Charlotte's west side, passing by African American neighborhoods started in the 1950s until it finally reaches a rural area near Latta Plantation with buildings that date to the colonial era. Biddle Institute is now Johnson C. Smith University, a historically Black college founded by the Presbyterian church in 1867 for the education and training of freed Blacks. Many of the homes in Biddleville were substantial, where college administrators and professors lived, creating a thriving Black middle-class district by the 1910s.

The largest and most important Black district, though, was Brooklyn. Before beginning its outward sprawl into suburbs and neighborhoods, central Charlotte was divided into four districts, called wards, with Fourth Ward dominated by upper-class white homes. Second Ward was an area originally called Logtown, where free Blacks and enslaved workers had begun to settle on inferior, poorly drained land near the center of town. By the early 1900s, Logtown emerged as a town within a town, a place where Blacks could both own and patronize segregated businesses, including restaurants and cafés. People in the neighborhood, attracted by news of Brooklyn, New York, emerging as a fast-growing area in the shadow of Manhattan, gave Logtown the name Brooklyn, in honor of that idea. The Black business district wasn't accepted by many white business leaders. In a 1902 story in the *Observer*, according to Hanchett, city official E. M. Shannonhouse came out against the rise of Black-owned businesses so near the white business district—"the nasty little negro restaurants on East Trade Street"—and called for them to be taxed more heavily so they'd be forced to close. It didn't work. Hanchett explains, "By the 1920s, Brooklyn was home to Black restaurants, grocers, drugstores, barbers and hairdressers, shoemakers, undertakers and the Palace movie theater."[5]

Until it was destroyed by urban renewal in the 1960s and 1970s, Brooklyn wasn't just the Black business center of Charlotte: it was the solid center of Charlotte's African American community. North Carolina Representative Kelly Alexander has long ties to Charlotte. He remembers growing up in Brooklyn when kids went to a small store called Phillips for comic books, candy, and packaged sandwiches heated on a press. One of the most substantial buildings in Brooklyn was the Mecklenburg Investment Company, called the MIC, built to provide office space for Black professionals, including doctors, dentists, and lawyers. On the first floor, there was a drugstore, Issler's, that had a lunch counter. It didn't matter whether you were Black or white, Alexander remembers. Anyone could eat in Brooklyn. "The color to get in and do business was green," he jokes today.

Another Black-owned restaurant many people who lived in Brooklyn remember was El Chico's, at Third and McDowell. No one today remembers the origin of the name—El Chico didn't serve Mexican food. "El Chico served everything, including ice cream cones," recalled Gwen Moore Lucas, seventy-one, a retired nurse who grew up in Brooklyn. In a 2019 article in the *Charlotte Observer*, she was one of six people who shared their memories of the neighborhood. "They had a sandwich called 'Mix Ham,' which was really nothing but a thick slice of bologna, fried, with chili, mustard, ketchup and slaw. People would go there on Sundays when they left church to eat dinner."[6]

FACING PAGE: ***Top left*****, Subrina and Greg Collier, Leah & Louise, Charlotte, North Carolina;** ***top right*****, Leah & Louise, Charlotte, North Carolina;** ***bottom*****, Aries Zodiac Punch, Blacka Jacks (popcorn mix), River Chips (fried chicken skins), Mud Island (blackened catfish), Leah & Louise, Charlotte, North Carolina**

Because Charlotte had Black professionals, many Blacks came to the city to do business, helped by a Black-owned hotel, the Hotel Alexander at McDowell and Ninth Streets, that was cited in the yearly editions of *The Green Book*, the Jim Crow–era travel guide that advised Black travelers of businesses that would serve them. Even when restaurant seats weren't available, Brooklyn found ways to feed the community, Alexander remembers. His family's house was a community gathering spot where his mother often welcomed travelers coming to Charlotte for business, with "a good, wholesome, home-cooked meal."[7] "Because of segregation, there was a lot of food just served at home," says Alexander.

"Now, you'd take people to restaurants. But there weren't a lot of restaurants if you were Black."[8]

Church fellowship halls and cafeterias like the ones at the United House of Prayer for All People were important pieces in the Black food system in Charlotte. The United House of Prayer was founded in 1919 by Bishop C. W. Grace, a railroad porter who put on gospel revivals in towns where he stopped. Although the church is now based in Washington, D.C., it is still a huge presence in Charlotte, known for its long and exuberant worship services and cafeterias that dish up food including falling-off-the-bone turkey wings and freshly cooked greens.

Black-owned restaurants found ways to serve the community, too. Romeo Alexander, who died in February 2020 at the age of ninety-eight, owned several restaurants in Charlotte, including a small place called the Oak Lawn Terrace. His best-known restaurant, though, was Razades on Statesville Avenue. While it served simple country-style food at lunch, including soups, stews, cornbread, and biscuits, it was a stylish place located in a modern building, a rarity for African Americans in the South.

Charlotte mayor Vi Lyles didn't grow up in Charlotte. She's from Columbia, South Carolina. But she had family members in Charlotte, and her parents often made weekend trips to Charlotte to attend shows at the Excelsior Club, a Black social spot on Beatties Ford Road. Romeo Alexander was the father of Lyles's first husband, the late Wayne Alexander, and she talked to him often about being a Black restaurateur in Charlotte. Restaurants like Razades may have served southern comfort food, but they weren't soul food restaurants, says Lyles. "Not soul food, not at all," she says. "While his restaurant was a casual place, there were opportunities to do bigger events. Tablecloths came out at some events."[9] For instance, during prom season, when Black teenagers couldn't go to white-owned restaurants, Romeo Alexander would arrange special dinners for Black students after their dances.

By 1963, most of Charlotte's working-class eating spots, such as lunch counters, had been desegregated. But the white-tablecloth restaurants and hotels, the places where business is done, didn't join them until a peaceful protest, led by minister and civil rights activist Dr. Reginald Hawkins, demanded equality for all diners. Starting on May 29 and continuing for two more days, white city leaders led by Mayor Stan Brookshire decided to defuse potential pushback by inviting their counterparts in the Black community to lunch at whites-only restaurants. The effort worked, and Charlotte restaurants, in theory at least, were desegregated by June 1.

When Brooklyn was razed for urban renewal in the 1960s and 1970s, not all of its restaurants disappeared. One example was Rudean's, famed for its chicken wings and southern-style food. Rudean Harris was sixteen years old when she opened the West Charlotte Drive-In at 2228 Beatties Ford Road, renting the building for fifteen dollars a week. The oldest daughter in a family of seven children without a mother, Harris started working in food service when she was twelve to help keep her family together. When she was offered $300 for the business a few years later, she took the money and opened Rudean's on McDowell Street in Brooklyn. When the neighborhood was bulldozed, Harris returned to the original spot, on Beatties Ford Road, and continued to operate until she finally retired and closed in 2016.

"We're cooking food that is Black people's food. I don't care how you paint it or how you look at it—this is your food. You don't have to cook fried chicken, but understand that this is yours. You don't have to cook field peas, but you do have to feel and know that your ancestors and forefathers created something that's so important."

—GREG COLLIER, chef/co-owner, Leah & Louise, Charlotte, North Carolina, April 22, 2019

Keeping the Fabric Together

Today the clacking of looms is no longer heard in Charlotte, but the historic brick mill buildings remain, and in an ironic twist, they're becoming food hubs. The old Highland Mill recently underwent a massive renovation, reopening as Optimist Hall, with offices for Duke Energy at one end and a food hall with small restaurant spaces at the other. Some of Charlotte's most popular food trucks, including the Dumpling Lady and Papi Queso, have shifted from parking outside workplaces to opening permanent spots in the cavernous mills turned food halls.

Two miles away, on Statesville Avenue, another massive complex is taking shape as a food hall. Camp North End, covering seventy-six acres and including a steam-generator building, water tower, and massive factory space, was originally an assembly plant for Ford's Model T automobiles and later became a military missile plant during the Cold War. Today the abandoned site is being developed into a retail hub that will include restaurant spaces.

The most successful is Leah & Louise, which the talented food entrepreneurs Greg and Subrina Collier opened in spring 2020. Although the opening was delayed by state restrictions during the COVID pandemic, the Colliers hung on by making part of the Leah & Louise menu available for take-out, including elaborate Sunday night suppers. The success of the Colliers, who started with a small breakfast café, the Yolk, in Rock Hill, South Carolina, marks a major turning point in the new visibility of African American chefs in Charlotte. The Colliers are two of the founders of Soul Food Sessions, a series of pop-up dinner events that have showcased Black culinary talent in Charlotte since 2016.

For Leah & Louise, the Colliers are using a juke-joint theme to showcase the culinary heritage they brought from Memphis, Tennessee, where they both grew up in low-income Black neighborhoods. Named for Greg Collier's late sister, Leah, and grandmother, Louise, the menu features his elevated takes on fried chicken skin, rice grits, and ham-hock jam. New visibility for a more expansive view of African American cuisine in a former factory seems fitting for Charlotte. The inaugural BayHaven Food & Wine Festival, organized by the Colliers, took place at Camp North End in the fall of 2021 and included more than seventy-five Black chefs, farmers, distillers, authors, and other hospitality industry leaders. In an interview with the *Charlotte Observer* in 2017, Collier noted that Charlotte may be unusual in developing new attention for Black cuisine that arose in a segregated, industrial city after the agricultural history of enslavement.

"Charlotte thinks it doesn't have an identity," he said. "It's evolving into what it is."[10]

Carolina Chili Sauce **KATHLEEN PURVIS**

Makes about 8 cups

1½ pounds ground beef (not too lean)
1 large onion, peeled and diced
1 (6-ounce) can tomato paste
½ cup ketchup
1 tablespoon chili powder
2 teaspoons Worcestershire sauce
1 teaspoon apple cider vinegar
1 teaspoon salt
½ teaspoon black pepper

Adapted from *Desperation Entertaining*, by Beverly Mills and Alicia Ross

In a large pot set over high heat, add the beef, onions, and 2 cups of water and bring to a boil. Reduce the heat to medium and stir to break up the beef. Add the tomato paste, ketchup, chili powder, Worcestershire, vinegar, and salt and pepper. Stir well until the tomato paste and ketchup are dissolved and the meat is broken up. Simmer the chili for 15 minutes, stirring about every 5 minutes. As the chili thickens, reduce the heat to medium-low if needed to keep it from sticking. Serve over hot dogs or hamburgers.

To store leftover chili: allow the chili to cool completely, then cover and refrigerate for up to 2 days or freeze in small portions (about ¼ cup) for later use.

NOTES

1. Chuck McShane, "The Story of Charlotte," *Charlotte Magazine*, 12-part series, 2014–15; McShane, interview by Kathleen Purvis, January 2020.

2. Kathleen Purvis, "Where Is All the Authentic Greek Food in Charlotte?," *Charlotte Observer*, October 22, 2018.

3. Purvis.

4. Tom Hanchett, *Sorting Out the New South City: Rise, Class, and Urban Development in Charlotte, 1875–1975* (Chapel Hill: University of North Carolina Press, 1998).

5. Hanchett, 130–31.

6. Tim Funk, "Brooklyn Was the Center of Black Life in Charlotte; Until the Bulldozers Arrived," *Charlotte Observer*, January 18, 2019.

7. Kelly Alexander, interview by Kathleen Purvis, December 5, 2019.

8. Alexander interview.

9. Vi Lyles, interview by Kathleen Purvis, December 16, 2019.

10. Kathleen Purvis, "Where Are Charlotte's Black Chefs?," *Charlotte Observer*, September 28, 2017.

To Be Rather Than to Seem

Creating a Food Life in the Foothills

Head west out of Charlotte toward the mountains on US-74 and you'll hit Shelby, North Carolina, an hour or so into the drive. Keep on and you'll hit Asheville an hour later. To get to where I live, hang a right on US-226, just past the Ingles grocery store, and take the back roads to the rural part of Cleveland County, where Shelby is less quaint township and more God's country.

I live in the foothills of the Blue Ridge Mountains with my husband, farmer and former chef Jamie Swofford. Our place is a rural swath of land in the center of family land three generations old. Our move back in November 2019 was the culmination of a long-held dream, one that required countless hours of farm and food service work, gritty resourcefulness (his), and freelance hustle (hers). As partners, Jamie and I have knit our collective experiences to jointly reimagine a life together. We've birthed new businesses in the North Carolina food economy, refined and expanded our roles within our food communities, and actively nurtured an evolving vision—to create a farm-based life that suits us and serves our community.

Food is where we work. It's our passion and our livelihoods, and it touches every facet of our personal and professional lives. The path has not been linear, nor has it been traditional. Far from it. Where we are today—juggling the roles of chef, farmer, writer, beverage maker, baker, and food entrepreneurs—is vastly different from where we began.

Jamie Swofford grew up in Shelby, a former textile hub and cotton mill town, on his family's farm in a little blue house directly across the docile two-lane road where we live today. He comes from good country people who kept gardens and loved Jesus. His maternal grandfather Johnny Hoyle worked as a sharecropper and later in the sawmills, while his wife, Willie Bea Hoyle, raised six children at home. A pot filled with pinto beans—enough to feed a crowd—roosted on the wood stove in her kitchen. Her deft hands were always able to turn out one more pan of skillet biscuits. On his paternal side, Jamie's grandfather John Swofford was a skilled welder but kept a small herd of cattle to sell when money

Keia Mastrianni, Milk Glass Pie Bakery, Old North Farm, Shelby, North Carolina; *background*, Keia's pecan pie

was needed. For a time in the late 1970s and early 1980s, John operated the largest single-house egg operation in Cleveland County. As a kid, Jamie swept a mile in the chicken house each morning, up and down four long rows, a quarter mile each. He didn't like farmwork much. Solace came for Jamie around the dinner table, in food and cooking. By the time he was seventeen, he left home, eager to escape rural life.

He discovered kitchens, first as a dishwasher and busboy, then as a line cook. By virtue of the $1.99 Grand Slam at Denny's—the infamous combo featuring two pancakes, a choice of two strips of bacon or two sausage links, and two eggs any style—Jamie found himself in front of a flat-top grill one day and the hook was set. He quickly found his way to the big city of Charlotte in the late 1990s. Back then, Charlotte had only a handful of chef-driven restaurants. The atmosphere in those days was close-knit but competitive, each chef vying for a small share of a growing dining demographic. As a burgeoning bank hub, Charlotte had an affinity for corporate steakhouses: thus its reputation as a meat-and-potatoes town. But a small revolution was underway. A number of chefs charted a path toward more imaginative American cuisine driven by French technique. Over time ingredients became more reflective of the city's Piedmont origins and the local landscape, and those were the restaurants where Jamie Swofford worked.

As most young cooks do, Jamie worked his way through a number of eateries, including Mimosa Grill, Upstream, Zink, and the Meeting House—fine-dining restaurants with distinct voices: upscale southern, Pacific Rim, new American, and farm to table—again bolstered by classic French methods. His early years in the industry were his culinary schooling. On his first trip to the farmers' market with a chef, Jamie realized that rural life had taught him a thing or two about fresh food. He eventually moved into positions of greater leadership and enjoyed a culinary career that spanned eighteen years. As he matured, he began to ask deeper questions of the food that arrived at the back door. How many hands had touched this produce? Did the growers use chemical fertilizers? Who grew these vegetables, and where did they come from? The questions nagged at him. In time, they became a calling. He thought, "What if I return home, to the family farm, and start growing fresh food for chefs?" Jamie's logic—he could affect more people and share the power of food more broadly by putting ingredients with a distinct sense of place and a history worth sharing into the hands of the region's best chefs.

And that's what he did, starting in 2011. Oddly enough, my food writing career was beginning at the same time, just as Jamie was transitioning out of the kitchen. We did not know each other yet.

My life in food was set in motion when I moved to North Carolina on a whim. It was an easy relocation. My mother had lived in the state since 1999, and there was a ready-made place to rent and freelance work on deck. I wasn't a food writer when I arrived in 2010, though I had always written and spent a decade in food service, serving tables at restaurants in every state that I lived—Florida, Georgia, and my first two years as a North Carolina resident. Until I moved to Charlotte, my food life had been largely theoretical. I knew fine food because of the restaurants in which I worked. I went to farmers' markets because it was novel, and only in the high season. I drank the Kool-Aid of the latest food fads. I shopped at Whole Foods and bought produce labeled organic but flown in from other continents. My interest was performative, purely intellectual, and completely self-righteous.

North Carolina is where I fell in love with local food and its people. At the farmers' market, growers introduced me to the value of eating seasonally. It wasn't about food trucked in from some distant locale. It was about buying food from real people, tied to a specific time and place. Food grown right here at home. With guidance from the farmers I met at market, I started my own little backyard garden. Every Saturday at the Davidson Farmers' Market, I peppered Brad Hinckley from Coldwater Creek Farm in Concord with questions about how to prepare kohlrabi and when to plant my collards. I became enamored of the people behind the food, curious about their production. Cooking at home became a regular practice, and slowly a passion developed. For a year and a half, I explored my food interests on a now defunct personal blog before raising the courage to pitch local publications. I befriended farmers, traveled to markets, cooked, gardened, and let my wheels take me as far across the region as possible.

"Food never stops moving and I have to be moving with it. For any ingredient, there is a specific moment in time where it is absolutely perfect and that is a space of great responsibility. There must be a reverence for the place that we are and the time that we are."

—JAMIE SWOFFORD, Old North Farm, Shelby, North Carolina, November 29, 2020

By 2011, I was a regular contributor to the local alternative weekly newspaper and later developed two columns, one about local producers and another, "Keia Is Hungry," about notable dishes in Charlotte. As I became more involved in Charlotte's food scene, I got to know the growing community of chefs, producers, and food advocates. I explored Charlotte's restaurant history and researched the backstory of a city that was trying to find its voice. As is the life of a freelancer, I took odd jobs—working at the farmers' market for friends who raised heritage breed chickens, helping out in the catering kitchen at the PNC Music Pavilion, and serving as a part-time cheesemonger at the local cheese shop. I wrote for nearly every food publication in Charlotte and expanded to more regional writing throughout the South, which stoked my curiosity and expanded my regional understanding of foodways.

When I met Jamie Swofford, I was on assignment for *Charlotte Magazine*. I had pitched Jamie's story—a former chef turned prodigal farmer who was now growing food for Charlotte's best chefs. I was told that he grew pristine, often unusual, heirloom varieties of vegetables. Based on conversations with chefs, Jamie's edge was that he spoke their language, thought like they did, and grew food with the finished plate in mind. His vegetables arrived chef-ready—clean and ready to use. When I reached out to him, already on deadline, in December 2013, he sheepishly declined my interview request. Later, he told me it was because it was winter, and most farmers don't have much going on in the winter.

We finally did meet (persistence wins!) in January 2014, and I wrote two stories about him. The second piece, a feature for *Edible Charlotte* entitled "The Chef's Farmer," won the Critics' Choice award among the publication's readership, and the story title became the name by which Jamie is known in our food community today. Since then, our lives have been as intertwined as a Piedmont-woven plaid, a partnership that straddles the agricultural and culinary worlds in our small corner of North Carolina.

I don't usually fall in love with my subjects. This was a rare exception.

When Jamie and I became partners, our professional identities transformed, unearthing a deeper interpretation of our food lives that I can only describe as gestalt. Fueled and encouraged by new love, I began baking with fervor. A pie class in the mountains of western North Carolina with baker Tara Jensen gave me the confidence to lean into pie making. I baked for Jamie—buttermilk pie was the first. I baked for friends. I "popped up" for the first time inside a friend's clothing boutique and sold everything I brought with me—potato and Gruyère galettes, slices of salty honey pie, muscadine pie with rye crust, and classic buttermilk pie.

Our first Christmas together, Jamie gave me a pie book. The inscription on the inside cover read: "Love is Pie!" When I finally named my side hustle, Milk Glass Pie, it came with the apt tagline, "Love is Pie."

About this time Jamie was doing exploratory work with local brewers and brothers Jeff and Jason Alexander, who were on the cusp of opening Free Range Brewing in Charlotte's NoDa (North Davidson) neighborhood. Jamie had worked with the Alexanders before, providing foraged ingredients for their small-batch beers. With the brewery slated to open in 2015, the Alexanders asked Jamie to create a nonalcoholic beverage to serve on tap in their family-friendly establishment. He landed on shrub, an old-timey vinegar-based beverage that dates back to the colonial era. At its essence, shrub is fruit, vinegar, and sugar. But

Jamie, a former chef and North Carolina boy, crafted the beverage to include locally sourced fruit and botanical ingredients. The result, when carbonated, is a refreshing beverage with complex, well-rounded flavor profiles. He called it Old North Shrub, and within a year of the brewery's opening, he began bottling it for individual and retail sale. Soon after, it was winning prizes, including *Our State*'s "Made in NC" Award.

As these new endeavors took off, we continued our own work and sought ways to bridge the distance between us. I would leave Charlotte to spend half the week in Cleveland County, where Jamie lived, to help him in the garden. He would accompany me on assignment to eat at restaurants, his palate and commentary a welcome asset and a pleasure. Then a funny thing happened. Tendrils of my work began to spread like crabgrass into Jamie's work life, and vice versa.

The more time I spent with Jamie, the more I learned about southern ingredients, agriculture, and methods of preservation and cooking. Jamie is an avid fermenter and pickler, and his deep culinary knowledge and connection with the natural world shifted my thinking about food once more. I learned about eating root to leaf and the fascinating growth cycle of crops. I experienced the exhaustive joy of a hard day's work. I got a farmer's tan. My farmwork led me to partner with a fellow writer on an agricultural 'zine called *Crop Stories*. My pie pop-ups grew in frequency and Jamie's shrubs joined in. We called our collaboration the Sweet & Sour Pop-Up, and shrub became a secret ingredient in my pie fillings.

In our spare time, we cooked for ourselves in a way that opened my eyes once again. When you eat what you grow, seasonal eating looks different than it did when I was a casual market goer. I learned to cook turnips, sweet potatoes, tomatoes, and squash a hundred ways. I became adept at incorporating greens into everything and found creative ways to process, preserve, and eat all the ugly vegetables. Eating seasonally became more practical obligation than noble gesture. Resourcefulness replaced superfluous trips to the grocery store. We hosted dinner parties, too, and began dreaming of a farm life together. Jamie had spent eight seasons growing on a small plot of family land, but we talked of having our own.

I finally took the leap and moved out of Charlotte in 2015. That first year out of the city, I committed to working a full season on the farm. The soil will change you, Jamie said.

Living closer to the land put me in touch with the actual work of feeding ourselves. I began to think about food as it relates to humanity, labor, culture, and place. Those notions took my writer self to Harkers Island, a small fishing community on the coast of North Carolina, to document oral histories for the Southern Foodways Alliance. It took me

Top, Jamie Swofford, Old North Farm, Shelby, North Carolina; *bottom*, Gastonia; *background*, Ruby Streaks mustard greens growing in the field

inside immigrant-owned businesses to hear stories of migration, loss, and success. It took me into the homes of families from distant corners of the world who hold fast to the food traditions of their home countries. It taught me about Appalachian traditions and rural life.

Jamie and I collaborated on community-based food events from fundraisers to bake sales, working with folks like our friends at Free Range Brewing, restaurateurs Greg and Subrina Collier, fellow bakers, and the Piedmont Culinary Guild—a broad network of individuals and organizations who amplify community over the individual. Our currency was, and remains, food. We juggled farmwork and writing assignments, pie season and pop-ups, grant writing and one weighty cookbook project. We slowly pushed toward our vision of an autonomous life on the farm.

In ecological terms, the space where one ecosystem transitions to another is referred to as the edge, and it is said to be the place that teems with the greatest biodiversity. Jamie and I exist in this liminal edge, where we do the work of both farmer and chef, craftsperson and storyteller. It's a fluid space that moves between the culinary and the agricultural. In contrast, the majority of chefs we know do not toil in the fields for the food they prepare, and most farmers don't do the work of a chef. *We do.* At the intersection of our passions, community work, and making a living, we have found purpose and meaning in both places.

What we do may sound quaint, and perhaps romanticized, but amid political turmoil, global climate crises, a pandemic, and seemingly endless uncertainty, our work grounds us, connects us to the communities in which we live, and tethers us to an honest living. However big or small, this work affects our local communities for the better. In the literal and metaphorical sense, it helps us get by.

"When I eat your food, I want to know who you are. That's really what I want to know. And I want your heart to be on the plate."

—**KEIA MASTRIANNI, Shelby, North Carolina, April 25, 2019**

I've been thinking a lot lately about the superficiality that dominates mainstream food culture and how my feelings about food, land, and community have changed drastically since I first got here. Add a pandemic and the dissolution of food media as I've known it, and a complete reimagination feels requisite. My partnership with Jamie and my experiences up until now have turned lofty theory into practical application. It's a practicality that can't be intellectualized over Twitter or conveyed rightly on the pages of a glossy food magazine. At least not in its fullness. I'm learning that a true dedication to food means occupying spaces less visible and, perhaps, more important.

Our move farther into the rural county begs new questions. How can we find common ground with our rural neighbors? How do we live our values in community? How can we make lasting contributions to the local food economy? What does a life in food look like now, and what must be given up to embrace it fully?

After many seasons, we are in a place to live the answers. The vision we had conceived from a distance is front and center, and it's time to dig in.

The two-acre patch of land next to our home is slowly coming to life; first crops are in the ground and small structures have been erected. This season, though, has been mostly quiet, internal, filled with drafting the bones of what's to come. Many hours at the coffee table have yielded a vision we hope will carry us into the future. Of course, we press on with our amalgam of obligations. As Jamie says, food never stops moving. We recently spoke to students at Cleveland Early College High School about farming and sustainable food systems. The day after, Jamie planned a six-course fundraising dinner for the Uptown Shelby Association. I made the dessert, an apple stack cake twelve layers high. That same weekend we hosted a meeting in our new home for the North Carolina Herb Association. After that, we cranked out dozens of pies—brown sugar buttermilk pie and brown butter apple—for delivery, together.

> *"Be patient toward all that is unsolved in your heart and try to love the questions themselves, like locked rooms and like books that are now written in a very foreign tongue. Do not now seek the answers, which cannot be given you because you would not be able to live them. And the point is, to live everything. Live the questions now. Perhaps you will then gradually, without noticing it, live along some distant day into the answer."—Rainer Maria Rilke,* Letters to a Young Poet *(1929)*

Strawberry Pie KEIA MASTRIANNI

Makes one 9-inch double-crust pie

FOR THE CRUST

2½ cups plus 2 tablespoons all-purpose flour
1 teaspoon kosher salt
1 tablespoon granulated sugar
1 cup (2 sticks) unsalted butter, cubed and chilled
2 tablespoons apple cider vinegar
Ice water
1 egg yolk
2 tablespoons heavy cream
Demerara sugar, for sprinkling

FOR THE FILLING

2 pounds strawberries, trimmed and hulled
½ cup plus 3 tablespoons granulated sugar, divided
1 baking apple (such as Honeycrisp, Winesap, or Pink Lady), peeled and grated
Zest of 1 lime, finely grated
¼ cup lime juice
1 tablespoon orange juice
½ teaspoon black pepper
½ teaspoon kosher salt
½ cup light brown sugar
¼ cup plus 1 tablespoon tapioca flour

In a large mixing bowl, whisk together the flour, salt, and sugar. Add the chilled butter cubes and begin to cut the butter roughly into the flour with a bench scraper or pastry blender. Once the largest pieces have been cut into the butter, use your hands to start pinching and flattening the butter, continuously coating the butter with the flour. The mixture will begin to look like fine crumbs with small, pea-sized pieces of butter scattered throughout. In a measuring cup, add the apple cider vinegar and then add enough ice water to equal ½ cup total liquid.

Add the ice-water mixture, a little at a time, to the flour-butter mixture. Toss to incorporate. The mixture will become shaggy but never tacky. Once it comes together, form the dough into a disk, then cut it in half to form into 2 smaller disks. Wrap the disks and refrigerate them for at least 1 hour or overnight.

Roll out 1 disk of dough into a circle that extends 1 or 2 inches past the circumference of the pie plate. Transfer the dough onto the pie plate, leaving about an inch of overhang. Roll out the second disk of dough into a large rectangle. Using a ruler and a paring knife, cut out 6 lattice strips, each 2 inches wide. Lay the strips on a baking sheet lined with parchment paper and refrigerate until ready to assemble the pie.

Slice the strawberries and add them to the mixing bowl. If the strawberries are large, slice them into quarters. If small, halve them. Sprinkle 3 tablespoons of the sugar over the strawberries and macerate them for 30 minutes. Strain the excess liquid, then add the grated apple to the strawberries. Toss the fruit with the lime zest, lime juice, and orange juice. Combine the remaining ½ cup of granulated sugar with the pepper, salt, brown sugar, and tapioca flour. Toss the mixture together with the strawberries. Note: combine the tapioca mixture right before you assemble the pie; if the mixture is left to sit, it will develop too much liquid.

Set the oven to 425°. Whisk together the egg yolk and cream to make an egg wash. In the pie shell lined with dough, add the strawberry filling. Top with 3 vertical strips of lattice. To weave the lattice, fold the center vertical strip down and lay 1 horizontal strip across the center of the pie. Return the vertical strip to its original position. Next, fold 2 outside vertical strips down and lay another horizontal strip. Return the vertical strips to their original position. Repeat this process to add the final horizontal strip.

Using a pair of scissors or a paring knife, trim the lattice edges so that they are flush with the edge of the pie tin. Take the overhang of the bottom crust and roll it up and over the edge to cover the lattice edges and create a crust. Press the edges to seal and then crimp as desired. Place the pie in the freezer for 10–15 minutes. Remove it from the freezer and brush the egg wash over the entire pie. Sprinkle the top with Demerara sugar and place the pie on a parchment-lined baking sheet.

Bake on the lowest rack for 20–25 minutes, until the pastry sets and begins to turn golden. Lower the heat to 375° and finish baking on the center rack, about 30–35 minutes more. The pie is done when the crust is golden and the filling is bubbling. Allow the pie to cool completely before slicing.

Tasting Change in Global Charlotte

In today's South, traditional food doesn't just mean barbecue, collard greens, and cornbread. It's also pan dulce, cevapi, banh mi, shawarma, and much more. Since the 1990s, in big cities and small towns, a wave of new immigrants has added global flavors to our regional foodways. The east side of Charlotte, North Carolina's largest metropolis, offers a case study. In 2017 its diverse food cultures attracted scholars from the Southern Foodways Alliance, who recorded oral histories of immigrant entrepreneurs.[1] What had drawn the newcomers to Charlotte? How did they launch businesses? What foods did they offer? How did they interact with other immigrants and with the wider city? How have foodways changed—especially as younger family members raised in the United States find their way into food-related businesses?

Immigration still feels like a new thing in Charlotte. The city has boomed in recent years, riding the growth wave experienced by much of the urban South. Mecklenburg County, containing the city and its principal suburbs, doubled in population from 500,000 in 1990 to 1 million circa 2015. Once a regional textile town, it is now America's second-biggest banking headquarters. In 1990 less than 1 percent of Charlotte residents were foreign-born. By the end of the 2010s, that figure surpassed 15 percent.[2] Of those, Mexico sent the largest number, 16 percent, followed by India at almost 13 percent, Honduras at 9 percent, El Salvador at 5 percent, and Vietnam at 4 percent.[3] Add those up and it is less than half of the total—an indication of how varied the immigration flows were. People arrived from Bosnia and Serbia after the breakup of Yugoslavia; from Bhutan and Nepal in the wake of ethnic cleansing; from Congo, Ethiopia, and Eritrea to escape civil wars; and more.

Immigrants here do not cluster in ethnic neighborhoods. America's previous era of high immigration around 1900 saw distinct Little Italys and Chinatowns in big cities. Across the nation today's foreign-born settlement is more suburban and more intermingled.[4] Helping drive this new pattern were the 1968 U.S. Fair Housing Act and the 1977 Community Reinvestment Act, which made discrimination on the basis of race and ethnicity illegal. A 2017 map of Charlotte showed foreign-born residents at every point of the compass. Concentrations were high in the vicinity of South Boulevard to the south and Central Avenue to the east, where many 1960s and 1970s era apartment complexes provided affordable housing—but also around Mallard Creek Road in the more recent suburban fringe to the northeast. Even in the upscale edge city of Ballantyne on the southern loop of new Interstate 485, immigrants made up 15 percent or more of several census tracts.

The Central Avenue corridor, Charlotte's best-known concentration of international markets and eateries, offers many opportunities to explore the city's changing foodways. National studies repeatedly show that immigrants outdo United States natives in starting businesses. "Despite making up just 15.1 percent of the population, immigrants made up 16.4 percent of business owners in the county in 2017," reported UNC–Charlotte's Urban Institute.[5] On or near Central Avenue you'll find the city's first Mexican bakery, first Honduran/Salvadoran restaurant, first Vietnamese sandwich shop, first Ethiopian grocery, and first Bosnian market, as well as many more recently launched enterprises. All intermingle in a late twentieth-century suburban landscape of shopping plazas, ranch-style houses, and slightly worn apartment complexes.

"There's progress and excitement here when it comes to food. In cities like Raleigh, Durham, Greensboro, Charlotte, and Asheville, there's food from other places. People are moving here from around the world—and you can find their food in metropolitan areas in North Carolina, which is very, very healthy for a food scene."

—MIKE MOORE, chef/owner, Jack's, Wilson, North Carolina, September 11, 2019

Coming to Charlotte, Launching a Business

Desperation pushes some immigrants. Opportunity pulls others. Dino Mehic, a refugee from Bosnia, and Zhenia Martinez, who came with her parents from Mexico, personify those two extremes.

Dino bustles back and forth from his tiny Bosna Market down a step and through a door into his ten-seat Euro Grill. He takes special pride in his cevapi, the sandwich of stubby sausages that's wildly popular in Bosnia. He's got a smile and a wry sense of humor, but there's an underlying sadness, too.

"My Bosnia was a beautiful country," he says. "I left because of the war. In 1995, I lost my father in Srebrenica." The notorious mass killing there wiped out more than 7,000 Bosnian Muslims, mostly men and boys. "I lost him. And he"—Dino's son Mesa, who joined us for this interview—"was born in 1996. He took my father's name."

Dino fled to Germany, then to Charlotte. His wife found work in a local warehouse for a drugstore chain. "Then," Dino explains, "somebody must take care of Mesa, take him to school, pick him up from school. Somebody must take care of our daughter, our home." Was there a way for Dino to be a stay-at-home dad? "Can we open something, or do something and take care of our kids?

"When I came here I had no idea what I would do. I didn't speak

OPEN
HALAL
حلال
3117-A
ROTISSERIE
CHICKEN
FALAFEL
LAMB
SHANKS

English, I needed a job, I needed to make some money. I had two family members [a wife and son, and a baby girl on the way]. All my life I am in the restaurant business and groceries, and that was my first idea, can I open a small grocery?

"The first year I went every Friday morning to Atlanta and brought stuff here. When we were beginning, I bought a van. I remember I paid twelve hundred dollars and prayed to God, 'Come on, do not stop, please. I need you, I need you, I need you.' That first year, every Friday I woke up at three o'clock in the morning to pick up the stuff."

Soon Dino found a tiny storefront in a shopping plaza on Central Avenue. "All refugees, almost, were around here in Central Avenue apartments, the first two, three years. Our apartment was found for us by the refugee office; it was on Green Oaks Lane [off Central Avenue]. Many Bosnian refugees were in these apartments and the Morningside Apartments. That's the reason why we opened on Central Avenue.

"Central Avenue at this time, it was scary. So much crime. It was not nice. There's a lot of change. Now it's great."

In these same years a few blocks farther out Central Avenue, Aquiles Martinez founded Charlotte's first *panaderia*—Mexican bakery. While Dino Mehic had food experience in his previous life to draw on, Aquiles Martinez completely reinvented himself. A government bureaucrat in Mexico, he took what work he could find in menial labor after arriving in the United States. Later, a construction-related accident pushed Aquiles to learn a new trade as a baker.

"He was from a family that liked knowledge and sought knowledge," his daughter Zhenia remembers. "In his twenties he put himself through college, studying economics. He always had books around him. In all the houses where we lived in Mexico, we had at least one wall completely covered from floor to ceiling with books. He loved politics as well. He held various jobs in government while we lived in Mexico."

Aquiles and his wife, Margarita, a government secretary, worried for their children's future in impoverished Mexico. "My mom said, 'My god, how are my kids going to find a job here?' So that's when they decided to move us to the U.S."

They settled first in Columbia, South Carolina, where a relative ran a Mexican restaurant. "They worked as cooks. They did the prep work and line work and even, when necessary, dishwashing. I don't think they ever saw it as bad work. It was an honest way to make a living and feed your family.

"They came here with visas, but they overstayed their visas. Luckily, with President Reagan's amnesty program in 1986, they got papers.

FACING PAGE: ***Top, left to right*:** **La Shish Kabob, Central Avenue, Charlotte, North Carolina; falafel, Lebanon salad, ful mudammas, pita, mansaf, La Shish Kabob, Central Avenue, Charlotte, North Carolina.** ***Bottom, left to right*:** **banh mi, Le's Sandwich Shop, Central Avenue, Charlotte, North Carolina; cevaps, Euro Grill, Central Avenue, Charlotte, North Carolina**

No Mask-No
እባክዎ ማስክ

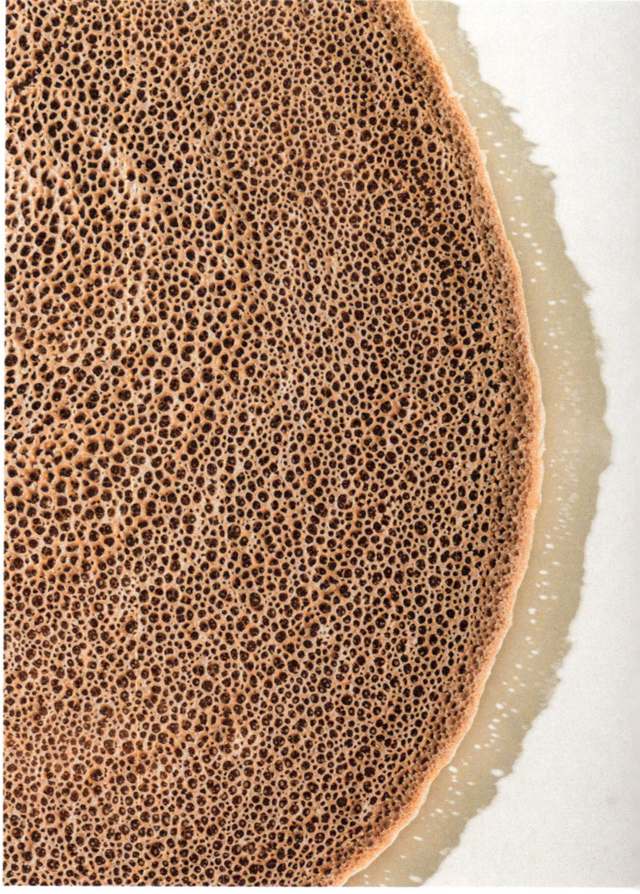

That's when they brought us. My brother and I stayed with my maternal grandmother in northern Mexico for about a year.

"My dad found work in construction; my mom worked in a factory. While my dad was working, he fell from a second floor. He couldn't keep working in construction. In his fifties, he had to find another way to make a living.

"He started selling Mexican products out of a van. He had driven through the small farming towns of North Carolina and South Carolina. He saw a growing Latino population.

"One of the things he bought was pan dulce," the sweet pastries beloved in Mexico. "When he saw how much people looked forward to that, he decided to open a bakery."

But neither Aquiles nor Margarita Martinez knew anything about commercial baking.

"They went to Mexico to Chihuahua to a small bakery which still had a brick oven. They said, 'We want to learn. Will you teach us?' They were there for six months, and they learned everything that they could about pan dulce.

"The variety of pan dulce, it's crazy. I'm trying to grasp a number—maybe about a hundred different ones? There are ten doughs, and from those doughs you make the different breads. The thing about pan dulce is that it's artisan made. You could never make it with a machine. It's so artful. Anyone that underrates the pan dulce should spend a day trying to make it and have it come out beautiful. Everything has to be shaped by hand."

Where to launch their shop? Charlotte's Latino population was growing rapidly in 1997, and there was an inexpensive space for rent on Central Avenue. Aquiles and Margarita Martinez named their new bakery Las Delicias, in honor of Margarita's Mexican hometown of Delicias. "That was the first Mexican bakery in Charlotte. I remember the first spring they opened, my aunt was here, my father's sister. We literally sat at the door waiting for customers, because nobody would come in."

The customers eventually did come—not only Mexican immigrants but migrants from every part of Central and South America. Today the panaderia is known as Manolo's, led by Manolo Betancur, who is from Colombia. Zhenia Martinez reflects, "What started out as a Mexican bakery is now a Latin American bakery. In Charlotte as we're growing so intertwined, we're seeing the influx of other cultures and the sharing that results. We're growing as a global culture and as a global business. We do not tailor our business to just one customer but rather to everyone."

FACING PAGE: ***Top, left to right*:** **marranitos de piloncillo, Manolo's Latin Bakery, Central Avenue, Charlotte, North Carolina; Zhenia Martinez, Manolo's Latin Bakery, Central Avenue, Charlotte, North Carolina.** ***Bottom, left to right:*** **Tsige Meshesha, Nile Grocery, Central Avenue, Charlotte, North Carolina; injera, Nile Grocery, Central Avenue, Charlotte, North Carolina**

Shaping a Menu, Building a Community

As Zhenia Martinez suggests, immigrant food establishments function as coming-together places. As such, they embody shared food history while also reflecting the social changes taking place in this new land. Time does not stand still. Neither do traditions.

Izzat Freitekh's La Shish Kabob restaurant is a favorite east Charlotte meeting place. People of all races, ethnicities, religions, and styles of dress step up to the busy counter to place an order with Izzat.

"My son, he came to UNCC, the university. It was not easy to live in Jerusalem in this time. There were war problems every day, and I have a big family. He told me that Charlotte is quiet, nice. August thirteenth, 2008, we came here. Our life began again." Izzat Freitekh's first job was frying wings in the food court at the dying Eastland Mall, but he longed to re-create the restaurant he'd owned in Jerusalem, Abu El Ezz Sandwiches.

In 2009 he opened La Shish Kabob a few blocks off Central Avenue in a narrow storefront that has tripled in size over the years. It was the first place in Charlotte to offer shawarma—chicken on a revolving vertical spit, slow roasted in the Middle Eastern manner. There's hummus, tabouli, and baba ganoush with pita bread, falafel wraps, and lamb shank cooked in yogurt sauce. During the month of Ramadan, he offers a sumptuous buffet each night for the faithful who come after breaking their daylong fast. But he also contributes meals to a nearby Christian church and happily hosts visits from Jewish leaders.

"I don't care about the religion. How you talk with me, that's your religion. You talk with me nice, that's your religion. You talk with me bad, that's your religion. I don't care about your color. How you talk to me, how you go with me, that's you. I thank God.

"We have a lot of friends, nice people. What does the customer need? A smile in his face, give him good food, and don't take a lot of money. That's it.

"I make the original. When you go to Jerusalem, you taste the same taste.

"But I serve American food, also—the Philly steak, the burger, the wings. I don't have just food from Jerusalem. The Philly steak, the Philly chicken, the Philly lamb, I don't have it in Jerusalem, but I serve it here—because I need all the people coming here.

"I need all the people. I need the world."

Walk two doors down from La Shish Kabob in the same unremarkable shopping plaza and you have traveled from Jerusalem to Ethiopia. Tsige Meshesha and her husband, Zerabruk Abay, welcome you to Nile

Grocery, a market with spice-laden shelves plus a row of restaurant booths along one wall.

"In Ethiopia, I worked in an office. I am an accountant," explains Tsige. "When I came here, to raise my kids, I never bring them to a babysitter or daycare. I decided to raise them in my home. So, I started to bake the injera at home." The spongy griddle bread, made with a gluten-free flour called teff, is the staff of life in Ethiopia.

"I sell a lot of injera."

The couple dreamed of opening a business. "This was not easy in terms of finance," Zerabruk recalls. "And we made some mistakes. Some people tried to cheat us. Finally, with God's help, with the help of our community—even though they were few in number, there was a very strong Ethiopian community here, even one small Orthodox Church—we managed to finish the project."

Once open, Nile Grocery, in turn, became a place of community. People come to buy food but also to visit. As she chats, Tsige roasts coffee beans in a brass pan, then pours small cups of coffee from a slender clay pitcher. In Ethiopia this ritual occurs several times a day; here it happens less often, but it does not disappear. Says Zerabruk, "The coffee ceremony, it's not like coffee drinking, it's like social therapy. It's more than drinking the coffee. It's very important for them to come here, to sit down, to talk to one another.

"We are fourteen thousand kilometers away from our home. It's not easy to get all these seasonings, snacks, and the rest—just like home. To sit together, to have Ethiopian food, to have Ethiopian coffee, to have conversation.

"This is a community service—not only a business."

> *"I think you can use Charlotte almost as a stand-in for what the American South is trying to figure itself out to be."*
>
> **—JOSEPH "PIKO" EWOODZIE JR., sociologist, Davidson College, North Carolina, April 23, 2019**

The Next Generation

Growing up in one of Charlotte's immigrant food businesses carries a special weight of responsibility. Many families arrived with young children more than a decade ago—and those youngsters are now coming of age. They grapple with how to live adult lives that honor their parents' work while also staying true to their own spirit.

Tuan Nguyen—most of his friends call him John—grew up in his parents' Le's Sandwich Shop, the city's first business selling the Vietnamese sub sandwiches called banh mi. His mother and father came to the United States as refugees in the 1970s following the Vietnam War. With the assistance of her husband, Minh Nguyen, Le Nguyen took the lead in building the family business.

"I was pretty young in our first shop, child labor, you know," Tuan chuckles. "I think I was probably ten or eleven, in the back of the kitchen, cutting carrots, peeling carrots. I watched what Mom was cooking. I guess that's a good start.

"Then I went to school, got my degree in graphic design, and worked for International Paper for about eleven years." It felt like a secure career with reasonable hours and creative work on a computer in an office.

But then Tuan's parents announced that they were ready to retire. Would Tuan take over Le's Sandwich Shop? "I grew up in the business, and I've seen what it entails. Hard work, long hours."

He came back as an apprentice, laboring side by side with Minh and Le. "The first thing I had to learn was all the recipes, even the way she organizes things, to make sure that we keep the flavors of our shop consistent. It's hard work, just to try to remember all the recipes—and come up with new ones."

"I want to experiment also. So, with my mother's help, there's new foods. She'll give me thumbs up and thumbs down if I make anything that's not good."

When the Southern Foodways Alliance interviewed Tuan in 2017, he was still not fully settled in his path.

"Thinking about how hard my parents worked to create this, I couldn't see it go to waste. I want to get my hands on it and see if I can actually do it, keep up with it."

"And, it's a Charlotte thing," he said with quiet pride. "It's something that we brought to Charlotte—I just want to think that we brought something to Charlotte."

Marranitos de Piloncillo (Molasses Pig Cookies)

ZHENIA MARTINEZ *with* TOM HANCHETT

Makes about 2 dozen cookies

3.4 ounces (about 7 tablespoons) water
7 ounces (about 1¼ cups, or most of a piloncillo cone) grated packed piloncillo (you can find piloncillos—little pressed cones of unrefined sugar cane—in the international aisle of your grocery store or at Mexican markets)
2½ cups all-purpose flour, plus more for rolling out the dough
½ teaspoon baking powder
½ teaspoon salt
½ teaspoon baking soda
¾ cup vegetable shortening or lard
2 eggs, divided

In a small saucepan set over medium heat, combine the water and the piloncillo and boil until the sugar has completely dissolved. Allow to cool.

In a large bowl, combine the flour, baking powder, salt, and baking soda. Slowly add the piloncillo syrup. Whisk 1 of the eggs and add it to the mixture. Next, add the shortening and mix until a soft dough forms. Cover and chill the dough for at least 1 hour to make it easier to handle.

Set the oven to 350° and line a baking sheet with parchment paper. Generously dust your work surface with flour. Roll out the dough ¼-inch thick or less and cut out the cookies with a pig-shaped cookie cutter (or any shape you prefer). In a small bowl, beat the remaining egg to make an egg wash. Carefully transfer the cookies to the baking sheet, brush with the egg wash, and bake until they puff up and the tops become slightly crinkled, about 15 minutes. Cool before serving.

NOTES

1. This chapter draws on interviews conducted by Keia Mastrianni at La Shish Kabob, Nile Grocery, and Le's Sandwich Shop and by Tom Hanchett at Bosna Market/Euro Grill and Las Delicias/Manolo's Bakery, all in Charlotte, N.C. See *Oral History: Charlotte's Central Avenue Corridor*, Southern Foodways Alliance, April 19, 2020, www.southernfoodways.org/oral-history/central-avenue-corridor/.

2. Laura Simmons and Katie Zager, "Our Population Is More Concentrated in Cities—and Increasingly Diverse," UNC Charlotte Urban Institute, November 15, 2019, https://ui.uncc.edu/story/carolinas-urban-rural-connection-demographic-shifts.

3. Ely Portillo, "Immigrants Play a Big Role in Charlotte's Growth, New Study Shows," UNC Charlotte Urban Institute, July 8, 2019, https://ui.uncc.edu/story/immigrants-play-big-role-charlotte's-growth-new-study-shows; "New Americans in Charlotte," New American Economy Research Fund, June 19, 2019, https://research.newamericaneconomy.org/report/new-americans-in-charlotte/. For more about Charlotte's recent growth, see the preface to Tom Hanchett, *Sorting Out the New South City: Race, Class, and Urban Development in Charlotte, 1875–1975*, 2nd ed. (Chapel Hill: University of North Carolina Press, 2020).

4. Tom Hanchett, "A Salad Bowl City: Food Geography of Charlotte, North Carolina," in *The Larder: Food Studies Methods from the American South*, ed. John T. Edge, Elizabeth Engelhardt, and Ted Ownby (Athens: University of Georgia Press, 2013), 166–83; John T. Edge, "In Indianapolis, the World Comes to Eat," *New York Times*, February 22, 2011.

5. Portillo, "Immigrants Play a Big Role in Charlotte's Growth"; "New Americans in Charlotte."

KATY CLUNE

The Flavor and Spirit of Laos in North Carolina

"It looks like Laos! A lot of trees, a lot of mountains."

—DANIL PHRAKOUSONH, speaking of her home in Morganton, North Carolina, September 2014

With a twelve-hour time difference and 8,000 miles between Laos and the United States, this small southeast Asian country feels, and is, worlds away from North Carolina. Yet through an extraordinary set of circumstances and people, I was introduced to Laos in Morganton, North Carolina. I took part in temple ceremonies and house parties, and I recorded interviews in kitchens in Vientiane and Luang Prabang in Laos and in High Point and Raleigh in North Carolina. What I learned about culture and spirituality, relationships and community, demonstrated the power of sharing traditional foods in new contexts. Laotian restaurant owners in North Carolina and across the United States are bringing these two countries closer together with each meal they serve.

My story begins in 2013, when I drove from Chapel Hill to meet Toon Phapphayboun at a Hmong New Year's festival in Hickory. A former colleague gave me Toon's email; I had just moved to North Carolina for a graduate program in folklore. Toon was a leader in the area's Laotian American community and a Spanish instructor at Western Piedmont Community College. I asked her questions about Laotian culture. This was partly fieldwork, but I was also eager to learn about the world where my parents had just moved. My father, a career Foreign Service officer, had been appointed United States ambassador to Laos earlier that year.

When I told Toon about my connection to Laos, she invited me to dinner at her sister's restaurant, Asian Fusion Kitchen, in nearby Morganton. Toon sat down with me at the back table reserved for family and VIPs. Her sister, Daraphone Phrakousonh, served us fried kaffir lime leaves and flaky-skinned peanuts and asked if I wanted a BeerLao, a light lager beloved in Laos. (Her dad would later urge me to "drink BeerLao like water!" before I left for Vientiane for the first time.)

That night I could see that Asian Fusion Kitchen was carefully, lovingly assembled, from the photos of famous Laotian monuments and musical instruments hanging on the wall to the monk's alms bowls and

Daraphone Phrakousonh, Pho Lao, Morganton, North Carolina; *background*, bamboo hat

elaborately woven *sinh* (skirts) displayed in the adjacent grocery store. Dara was acting as a kind of ambassador with every decor and menu choice she made, and with the careful way she invited her customers to try something new, "You need to encourage them." She told me: "Everybody says, 'Hey, you Chinese.' Laos never exists! That's why I said I'm going to open a restaurant or grocery store one day and I'm going to tell them I'm not Chinese, I am *Lao*."

For the next two years, I partnered with the Phapphaybouns to tell the story of how they "lived Laos" in rural North Carolina. This meant reckoning with a painful, little-known history. Most Laotians and Hmong who left Laos for America came as a result of the United States' Secret War, a covert conflict parallel to the Vietnam War. In an effort to keep the Pathet Lao Communist Party from overthrowing the Royal Lao Government, the United States launched a massive top-secret bombing campaign and conscripted some 30,000 Hmong (an independent ethnic minority) to fight against Laotian communist forces. Between 1964 and 1973, the United States dropped more than 2 million tons of bombs on Laos—equal to a planeload dropped every eight minutes, twenty-four hours a day, for nine years. Laos is one of the most heavily bombed countries in global history. Today, some seventy years after the first American planes entered Laotian skies, roughly one third of the explosives dropped remain undetonated in the landscape, posing deathly risks to anyone who might find one of these "bombies."

Despite this clandestine show of force, in 1975 the Lao People's Democratic Republic was established. Anticommunists and intellectuals were persecuted and sent to reeducation camps. Khamsi Siluangkhot, Toon's stepfather, served six years in one of these camps, where he was forced to perform manual labor and suffered from malnutrition: "We ate expired canned food from the war, and the rice was full of insects." The so-called bamboo curtain dropped and effectively cut Laos off from the rest of the world for two decades. Between 1975 and 1985, 10 percent of Laotians left the country as refugees. Toon, like so many others, fled Laos for Thailand during the difficult years following the war in a leaky boat across the Mekong River. She was fourteen years old. With economic and educational opportunities at a standstill in Laos, each of her immediate family members also left, bringing to America a sense of exile and a deep reverence and love for their home. The Phapphayboun family settled in Morganton, a city of roughly seventeen thousand in the foothills of the Blue Ridge Mountains, in the early 2000s.

As I spent more time with the family, I absorbed their love for Laos. By the time I first arrived in Vientiane in 2014, the Phapphaybouns had taught me a foundational vocabulary of flavor and spirit. For every intricate spirit house on the streets of Vientiane decked out with sticky rice balls and other offerings to appease the *pi* (local spirits), I remembered the shallow bowls of food the Phapphaybouns carefully placed at the foot of trees in their North Carolina yards. The elaborate banana leaf and flower offerings (*mak bheng*) in Vientiane were the full-color versions of the notebook-paper offerings Toon's mother folded for me in Morganton. She slipped these into my hand at Wat Lao Sayaphoum, the Buddhist temple the family helped establish in a double-wide trailer and converted carport. The markets in Laos had intriguing piles of bitter greens, but a few were already familiar—I knew them from Hmong farmers' tables at the Thursday morning flea market in Hickory. I had even already tasted padaek fermented by Toon's mother in her backyard with fish her son caught in nearby Lake James. Padaek is an acquired taste, and this pungent fish sauce is essential to Laotian cooking. (As Toon says, "Padaek is like makeup," meaning that a dish without it is incomplete, but if you overdo it, it is spoiled.) The Phapphayboun family wrapped me in deep friendship and generosity, teaching and teasing in equal measure. Food was how we conjured Laos together.

I felt at home in Vientiane. I peeked into open-air kitchens, tried recipes, and took photos of things I could not identify in markets to show Toon. By pure chance, the Phapphayboun family was in Laos while I was; it was Toon's first time home since 1988. I asked her: "What is the same as you remember?" Her answer: "The hospitality of the Lao people." I walked and looked and learned. I rode my bike to Wat Si Muang—the city's oldest temple—to observe offering rituals by families and office workers on their lunch breaks. I collected yarn ties on my wrists with pride; these were good wishes sealed with a knot during *baci* blessing ceremonies or by temple monks. Thick loops of orange and white yarn still hang from my car's turn signal.

I began to understand how Laotian spirituality is deeply intertwined with food and hospitality. For many Laotians, the act of cooking and offering food taps into a Theravada Buddhist worldview that deeply values giving to others, or making merit, in the karmic sense. This heart-offering may take the form of *tak bat*, the dawn almsgiving ceremony for neighborhood monks, bringing a deceased loved one's favorite food to the temple, or serving a generous meal to family and friends.

Sharing Laotian food and culture at Asian Fusion Kitchen empowered the Phapphaybouns to connect to Laos and represent themselves in their adopted North Carolina home. After so many years apart, family meals are joyous. Welcoming and feeding the community through their restaurant was satisfying work but also a deeply meaningful offering.

Purple sticky rice, spring rolls, chicken wings, summer rolls, mango and sticky rice, nam khao (rice balls and sour pork salad), yellow curry, pad Thai, Thai iced tea, Pho Lao, Morganton, North Carolina; *background*, Lao sticky rice steamer (mor neug khao huat)

Dara will soon open her second restaurant, Pho Lao. She sold Asian Fusion Kitchen in 2017 to another Laotian family and took a couple years away from the kitchen before debuting this new concept. There is a groundswell of community as well as civic support for her to return. In 2019, as part of a local business-support initiative, the City of Morganton granted her $10,000 toward her new business. When I asked her what she was most looking forward to about returning to restaurant life, she said, "To make new family. People miss my cooking!"

Pho Lao is located three miles south of downtown Morganton, in a strip mall that also includes Rural King, a popular farm supply store. This time, Dara's canvas is bigger. There are carved wooden clocks from Laos, thip kao (sticky rice baskets) hanging above the windows, and large portraits of the Buddha, all carried back on her visits home or sent to the United States through friends and family. She is still finalizing the menu, but the penciled draft she shared with me features noodle dishes named for each of the seventeen provinces of Laos. "Pho Luang Prabang" is actually the northern Laotian dish khao soi: rice noodles and ground pork with tomatoes and fermented soybean paste in a light, tangy broth. Dara is expert at welcoming new customers by first sharing a dish they know (pho) and then slowly introducing unfamiliar flavors: "You know in this area there are not a lot of people who will open up to new cultures, so you kind of have to be gentle, blend yourselves in a little bit. . . . I don't want to go out there and say 'Eat this, eat that.' You need to encourage them and see what they really want to eat." This time, however, it was very important to her to have Laos in the restaurant's name, no longer fearing that it might be unfamiliar to potential diners.

In recent years, Laotian restaurateurs around the United States have made significant headway in increasing cultural awareness and understanding between our two countries. Last year *Bon Appétit* named Khao Noodle Shop, owned by Donny Sirisavath in Dallas, Texas, number two on its list of America's best new restaurants. Renowned Washington, D.C., area chef Seng Luangrath renamed her beloved Bangkok Golden restaurant in Falls Church, Virginia, Padaek in 2017. *Washingtonian* magazine wrote about the name change, noting this confident claim of her cultural identity. (We celebrated my dad's U.S. Senate confirmation with Laotian sausages at Bangkok Golden, which despite having a Thai name always had a "secret" Laotian menu.) Chef Seng has since appointed herself leader of a national #laofoodmovement and with her chef son, Bobby Pradachith, has opened three more popular restaurants around D.C.: Thip Kao, Hanuman, and Sen Khao. "We are so shy about our identity, ashamed of what we eat because it's too spicy, too stinky, too strange for other people to embrace it. . . . I can be proud of it now, instead of hiding under another culture," Seng told Crystal HyunJung Rie of the DC Oral History Collaborative.[1]

Restaurants have put Laos on the map for many North Carolinians. The entranceway of Lao Restaurant+Bar on South Elm Street in downtown Greensboro does so quite literally. As you step inside, you are greeted by a wall-size painted map of Laos. This minimalist, contemporary restaurant opened in 2018 and is just half a block away from the International Civil Rights Center & Museum in the historic Woolworth's where one of our country's most important sit-in protests took place in 1960. Chef Seng, who has added consulting to her expanding portfolio, assisted with its grand opening. Its sibling owners Vonne Keobouala and Matt "Jit" Lothakoun take the "Bar" part of the name seriously. In addition to elegant bites such as seen lod (crispy oven-dried, seasoned beef strips, a.k.a. Laotian beef jerky), you can order drinks including the Laotian 75 (Greensboro-made gin, prosecco, white pepper simple syrup, lemon juice, cucumber, radish, and Thai basil leaves).

No essay on Laotian foodways in North Carolina would be complete without acknowledging the influence of Bida Manda and its sister business, Brewery Bhavana, in Raleigh. "When I was growing up in Greensboro, I could have never imagined there would be a Lao restaurant on Elm Street," Vansana Nolintha shared with me recently. My work in Morganton led me to meet Van and his sister Vanvisa in 2014, just two years after they opened Bida Manda, an upscale Laotian restaurant in downtown Raleigh. The name means father and mother in Pali, the language of the foundational Theravada Buddhist scripture, and the siblings consider the restaurant an homage to their parents. As a result of severely limited educational opportunities in Laos, Amphone and Sompheng Nolintha made the gut-wrenching decision to send their two children to the United States. Van moved to his aunt and uncle's in Greensboro in 1998, and Vanvisa followed a year later. My friendship with Van grew as we spent time together with our parents in Laos: a magical dinner at the Nolintha family home in the northern Laotian city of Luang Prabang, shopping at the morning market together, tea at my parents' house in Vientiane.

In Bida Manda, a large, black-and-white wedding portrait of the Nolintha parents hangs in the entryway, while photos of monks in Luang Prabang line sculptural bamboo walls. Bida Manda has been featured in the *New York Times*, *Condé Nast Traveler*, and *Garden and Gun*. Brewery Bhavana opened in 2017. This starkly beautiful tap room–florist–bookstore serves Laotian-inspired small plates and dim sum. Shortly after opening, Brewery Bhavana was nominated for a James Beard Award for best new restaurant in the country. (Following personnel issues in summer 2020, the Nolinthas left their leadership positions in the company.) The Nolinthas have inarguably raised the profile of Laotian dining in North Carolina and in the United States. They set a table for others, including Lao Restaurant+Bar and Pho Lao, to follow.

I AM DEEPLY PROUD of my father's work during his time in Laos. He successfully advocated for increased funding to assist in the removal of the unexploded ordnance (UXO) dropped by American military planes. He led preparations for President Barack Obama's 2016 visit to Laos, the first by a sitting U.S. president. During this visit, the president stated, "From the anguish of war, there came an unlikely bond between our two peoples."

"To see vegetables from Southeast Asian countries make their way into the soil here and then into restaurants here—that's pretty great. Seeing the diversity of what can be done here will continue to redefine what southern cooking is—what it has been, what it will become."

—AARON VANDERMARK, chef/owner, Pancuito, Hillsborough, North Carolina, June 4, 2019

Diplomacy is ultimately yielded by conversation, understanding, and negotiation. Conviviality through food and ceremony are critical to this process. Across the South and throughout our country, Laotian restaurateurs are raising our cultural awareness of Laos.

The first family from Laos was resettled in western North Carolina in 1976, with the help of a Baptist church. Today more and more Laotian families are moving to the American South from other parts of the United States as part of a second migration from longtime urban footholds in Wisconsin, Minnesota, California, Connecticut, and elsewhere. Some, like Toon, still remember the fear of escaping into Thailand across the Mekong River and the scarcity of refugee camps. Others, like Dara's son and daughter, both born in the United States, know Laos only through stories and North Carolinian incarnations.

Through my work with the Phapphaybouns, I sought to shed light on both our countries' little-known shared history and increase visibility of one of the state's fastest-growing populations: Asian Americans. These new North Carolinians are influencing the state in countless ways and will continue to do so as the first American-born generation comes of age. Of the million-plus voters to register since the 2016 presidential election in North Carolina, the majority are Latinx and Asian American, and many are young.

As North Carolina's Laotian American community continues to grow and expand its voice and impact, the bridges between our countries will span well beyond restaurants—but for now, we are closest to Laos when we taste padaek.

NOTES

1. Tara Bahrampour, "How D.C. Learned to Love Minced Alligator," *Washington Post*, October 7, 2018.

Khao Poon (Laotian Rice Vermicelli Soup)

DARA PHRAKOUSONH *with* KATY CLUNE

Makes 2–4 servings

1 (13.5-ounce) can unsweetened coconut milk, divided
2 tablespoons red curry paste (available in small jars at most grocery stores)
1½ cups vegetable or chicken broth
2 stalks lemongrass, trimmed and dry outer leaves removed
½-inch piece of galangal, peeled and thinly sliced (can substitute fresh ginger)
4 kaffir lime leaves
1 tablespoon fish sauce, such as 3 Crabs fish sauce
1 package rice vermicelli noodles
Sliced limes, cilantro, mint, beansprouts, and thinly sliced raw green beans for garnish

In a large heavy-bottomed pot set over medium-high heat, simmer a third of the coconut milk until it bubbles and thickens. Add the red curry paste, stir, and cook until fragrant, about 2 minutes. Add the remaining coconut milk and the broth, lemongrass, galangal, kaffir lime leaves, and fish sauce. Bring the mixture to a boil, then reduce the heat and simmer for 20 minutes.

Meanwhile, cook the rice noodles according to the directions on the package, drain, rinse in cold water, drain again, and set aside to cool.

Before serving, taste the broth and add more fish sauce to taste.

To serve, ladle the broth over the cooled rice noodles. Garnish with the cilantro, mint, beansprouts, and thinly sliced green beans.

Note: this dish can be supplemented with cooked shredded chicken, cooked ground pork, or raw fish or shrimp added to the broth at the final simmering stage.

RONNI LUNDY

Crafting Asheville's Foodtopia

Two Decades in the Mountain South

In the early 2000s I moved to Asheville, where I found myself on the cusp of a burgeoning food scene unlike any other I'd encountered—rooted in tradition but exuberantly extending its boundaries with a powerful creative streak. I lived three years in that city, and when I finally returned in 2013 to dig deep roots in nearby Burnsville, in a sweet little Mamaw house with a porch where you can rest your eyes easy on the nearby mountains, I discovered that this nascent movement in Asheville had grown into what local promoters were calling a full-blown Foodtopia.

This is the story of how that came to be in the words of those who were there.

In the fall of 2003, the Southern Foodways Alliance (SFA) focused its sixth annual symposium on the foodways of the mountain South. It was arguably the first gathering to observe and limn the people and culture of this specific region, past and contemporary, through the lens of food. Two months before the symposium, the SFA, under the guidance of its incoming president, Elizabeth Sims, hosted an introductory field trip in southern Appalachia. Asheville and its environs were chosen as the focus for this hands-on experience because of the region's notably vibrant artisanal and small-scale agricultural traditions.

Five years later, in September 2008, Sims again was the driving force in the Biltmore Estate's Field to Table Festival, which brought together more than three dozen scholars, producers, farmers, restaurateurs, and artists whose work was connected to Appalachian foodways. Although panelists came from several southern Appalachian states, including east Tennessee, eastern Kentucky, West Virginia, southwest Virginia, and north Georgia, the overwhelming majority of food producers and purveyors were from the immediate Asheville region, representing its by then flourishing sustainable farm and restaurant movement.

A bit more than a decade later, in the fall of 2019, Asheville hosted its first major food event, Chow Chow, a three-day experience that highlighted the "city's table—from growers and farmers to brewers to chefs to crafts people and artists." At this moment, journalist Jane Black, writing for the *New York Times*, spotlighted Asheville as the epicenter of a surprisingly diverse and burgeoning Appalachian food scene. Earlier media, including another essay by Black, had already heralded the culinary coming of age of Appalachian food.[1]

"Maybe it was after we'd been open five or six years, it was clear, you certainly cannot have breakfast in Asheville without avocado."

—JULIE STEHLING, cofounder/former owner, Early Girl Eatery, Asheville, North Carolina, September 25, 2019

To understand why Asheville restaurants were suddenly lauded for serving vinegar pie, "leather britches," Indian dal served with collards and country ham, salmon cured with sumac, and fig and sorghum bagels—the foods of western North Carolina, both present and past—it's helpful to remember a bit of the region's agricultural history. Unlike other agrarian territories in the United States that had long ago converted to large-scale factory farming, Appalachian farms had remained—by virtue of topography, climate, and tradition—small and still practicing older, sustainable methods. This, noted John Stehling, then chef and co-owner of Asheville's Appalachian-focused Early Girl Eatery with his wife and partner, Julie, was a distinctive boon to the region's restaurateurs and farmers: "Restaurants in other places have to start the [farm-to-table] process a lot of the time. They have to prime the pump by getting small growers to start growing or encourage large growers to put in some specialties. But here in the southern Appalachians, it's *always* been a small farm world. And the farmers here have never stopped growing these things. They *bring* you things you won't see anywhere else, like this squash, this Candy Roaster. It's got a flavor that's deeper, with layers, and you'll start thinking of something new to do with it, just based on that taste. The place and its food has never died off, and it inspires me."[2]

Clearly it has inspired the dozens and dozens of other restaurateurs, food artisans, growers, and producers who have set up shop in this western North Carolina city in the past twenty years, virtually all of them, including the breweries, making a point of identifying their reliance on local sourcing as if required by law. The vibrancy of the tourism economy, which underpins the food economy (and increasingly vice versa), is physically visible in the mushrooming development of previously neglected West Asheville, the once abandoned now bustling South Slope and River Arts District, and the sheer vertical rise of hotels that has reshaped the downtown skyline dramatically in the past year. What was once a summer and fall seasonal tourist spot is now a thriving, year-round destination with an emphasis on its food and beverage scene.

With this booming tourist economy has come increased revenue flow more stably distributed over the year for local food service establishments, as well as the farmers and purveyors who provide them. That

Top, **John Fleer, Rhubarb, Asheville, North Carolina;** *bottom*, **Rhubarb's Red Wine Sorghum Vinaigrette;** *background*, **vinaigrette**

has attracted and nurtured a coterie of chefs regularly recognized by the James Beard Foundation and prominent food publications. It has also brought problems, including staffing restaurants in a town where many skilled food employees cannot afford to live, the loss of affordable entrepreneurial space to large-scale corporate development, and pressures on regional land use as business, shopping, hotel, and housing developments take over already limited farmland.

The city faced just such a dilemma in late September 2019 when it was disclosed that a hotel development project would possibly force out the highly successful and popular downtown farmers' market. After gaining preliminary planning approval, the project was unanimously rejected by the city council, which later legislated a temporary moratorium on further hotel development, a move many perceived as recognition of the economic and cultural importance of the regional farm and food scene.

Conversations with a selection of individuals who have worked in and observed the changes in Asheville's food scene over time add texture and nuance to understanding why Asheville, and western North Carolina, hold a unique place in the larger Appalachian food scene.

The Godfather

I met Mark Rosenstein in 1999 on a trip to Asheville to promote my recently released book, *Butter Beans to Blackberries: Recipes from the Southern Garden*. At that time, a book focused on vegetables but not expressly for vegetarians was rare, and even rarer was a book about the garden produce of the then-stereotyped hot biscuits, salty ham, fried chicken, and gravy South. Mark was asked to help me prep food for a television presentation because his Asheville restaurant, Market Place, was known for its fresh products from local farmers. In 1999 few people had heard the term "farm to table," and few restaurants focused so deeply on it, but even more remarkable was that Mark had been doing so since the early 1970s, when he established his first restaurant in Highlands, North Carolina. Mark was part of the counterculture movement, whose impact on the farming and foodways of the southern Appalachians was significant and little recognized then or now. What brought the twenty-year-old here from his home in Florida? He answers, "James Taylor, Bob Dylan . . . grab your sweetheart, and move to the mountains."[3]

Mark Rosenstein has long been recognized as "the godfather of local food in Asheville."[4] The network of producers and buyers he established more than forty years ago when he opened the Market Place in 1979 is still strong and influential today, including Mountain Food Products, a local company distributing fresh fruits, vegetables, and products from more than two dozen farmers within the Asheville area, and Hickory Nut Gap Farm, for which Mark was one of the first commercial customers. Early on Mark served Spinning Spider Creamery cheese in his restaurant but also introduced it to his peers in Europe. There were two sixty-five-gallon tanks in the walk-in so that Mark could stock trout from a farmer he worked with in Highlands. He was the first restaurateur to buy from the three-hundred-plus-acre student-run sustainable farm at Warren Wilson College in Swannanoa, which has had a near immeasurable impact on western North Carolina's food economy and culture.

Although Mark readily acknowledges his role as a groundbreaker, he stresses that the success of the contemporary Asheville food scene is the sum of many parts coming together.

"There's so many good things that have happened here. You have this whole local food thing. You have Warren Wilson College. You have ASAP, you have Market Place, the tourism development authority." He notes that the term "Foodtopia" was coined by Asheville's tourism creatives not long after that 2008 event, in recognition that the city had something distinctive to offer the culinary world.

ASAP, the Appalachian Sustainable Agriculture Project, was founded in 2000 to assist western North Carolina farmers as they transitioned from tobacco to food production. Mark says, "Their brilliance is to connect the farmers to the people who eat food. They realized, we don't need to teach the farmers how to farm, let's teach them how to market." In the past decade, the region has added 426 more farms growing fruits and vegetables to the western North Carolina region.

"We're one of the few regions in the country to have gained net farmland, because [ASAP] made it viable," Mark says.

Mark pinpoints that working for and with one another is an important aspect of mountain culture, and central to why the food scene is so vibrant, and why he has stayed in the region for almost fifty years, even after selling the Market Place in 2009.

"I consider myself to be mountain irregular, the highest praise you can give a person."

The Storyteller

In 2008, John Fleer had earned his place at the SFA Appalachian field trip for his work as executive chef at Blackberry Farm, the luxury resort in Walland, Tennessee. Fleer, as he is referred to by his peers, was recognized as the first contemporary chef to elevate the products and techniques of the region's foodways to fine dining. Producers such as

Benton's Smoky Mountain Country Ham, Cruze Farm's dairy, and Muddy Pond Sorghum credit Fleer with bringing them, profitably, to the attention of the larger culinary world. But Fleer notes that his purpose wasn't simply to promote stellar foodstuffs and serve the most delicious meals possible. He wanted his menu to provide "the people who came to Blackberry with an experience of a very particular place, to tell its story."

An example would be his velvety, intoxicating buttermilk cornbread soup, which triggers deep memories for mountain people who remember a simple summer supper of leftover cornbread crumbled into a tall glass, covered in tangy buttermilk, and topped with chopped green onion. He was turned onto the dish by a young, Smoky Mountain–born dishwasher "who couldn't believe I'd never eaten it."[5] Converting the dish to an elixir for the professional dining room was, for Fleer, a way of not only sharing those distinctive flavors "but of sharing the Appalachian story of simplicity and resilience."

When it came time for Fleer to open his own restaurant, one that explored the region's foodways even more deeply, he chose to do so in Asheville and western North Carolina, a region unusually rich in ingredients and story.

"That is one of the things about our community—the quality level of the products we use is beyond incredible: flavor-wise, vegetable-wise, beer-wise, it's unique.

"Some of it is a matter of the passage of time and the changes in the world, the existence of small farmers and people who are treating their land sustainably. Some of it is about the sea change that has happened over the last couple of decades broadly. But I'm pretty sure that Asheville has the best community of farmers and makers and creators of anywhere that I could ever have imagined living.

"Sometimes I've ascribed that to the Appalachian spirit of creativity and making the best of what you have and making those things sing, no matter what. It has always been a community of people who just are hell-bent on doing something interesting."[6]

Fleer established Rhubarb—his flagship restaurant—in downtown Asheville in 2013 with a menu that explicates both mountain and other southern traditions with contemporary flair. Soon after, Fleer was offered the chance to open the cornerstone restaurant in a new Asheville hotel. Slated for the downtown area known as the Block, the once thriving business and restaurant hub for Asheville's African American community, Fleer agreed to participate if the restaurant became a vehicle for telling that story.

"The vernacular history of Asheville tells us that this neighborhood was thriving, exciting, and had this same spirit of innovation that has created these restaurants and farms. . . . That same spirit was a part of the Block."

From its portraits of the African American women who cooked and created community on the Block to the dinnerware made by a western North Carolina African American master potter and to the innovative Affrilachian menu conceived by the restaurant's first executive chef, Ashleigh Shanti, with guidance from Hanan Shabazz (one of the godmothers pictured on the portrait wall and the restaurant's éminence grise), Benne on Eagle opened in 2018 and was soon on every food publication and website's list for top new venues. In 2019 *Time* lauded the restaurant for its delicious food but also, and as significantly, for broadening the story of race in Appalachia and the contributions of African Americans. "African American people existed here, in these mountains," Ashleigh explains. "My work is to make their voices heard."

Ashleigh has said that her work at Benne was inspired by *sankofa*, a word from the Akan language of Ghana which means that the past must be reclaimed if one is to move forward. Moving forward is what Ashleigh decided to do at the end of 2020 when she stepped down from her post at Benne and announced her intention to establish an Asheville-based restaurant group with multiple locations that will reflect and support even more diversity. "As a Black chef who's a woman and queer, it's vital to have some representation when it comes to restaurant ownership," she told the *Asheville Citizen Times*.[7]

Meanwhile, Benne will continue to tell the story of the Block and the Affrilachian experience with newly named chef de cuisine Malcolm McMillan.

The Husbandman

Attendees at the 2003 SFA mountain field trip in Asheville had the opportunity to visit a trout farm, a cheese maker, a winery, and Hickory Nut Gap Farm, established at the 1918 site of an old inn on the Drover's Road. There they met Jamie and Amy Ager, then recent graduates of Warren Wilson College's farm and business programs, and the fourth generation of Agers to work this family property. For their senior project at Warren Wilson, Jamie and Amy wrote a business plan to take Hickory Nut Gap sustainably into the future.

At the 2008 Biltmore event, Hickory Nut Gap represented a local farm success story with the couple's pasture-raised pork and chicken and grass-fed beef found on Asheville's best restaurant menus. Today Jamie Ager credits their success to Asheville's "perfect storm"—its loyal

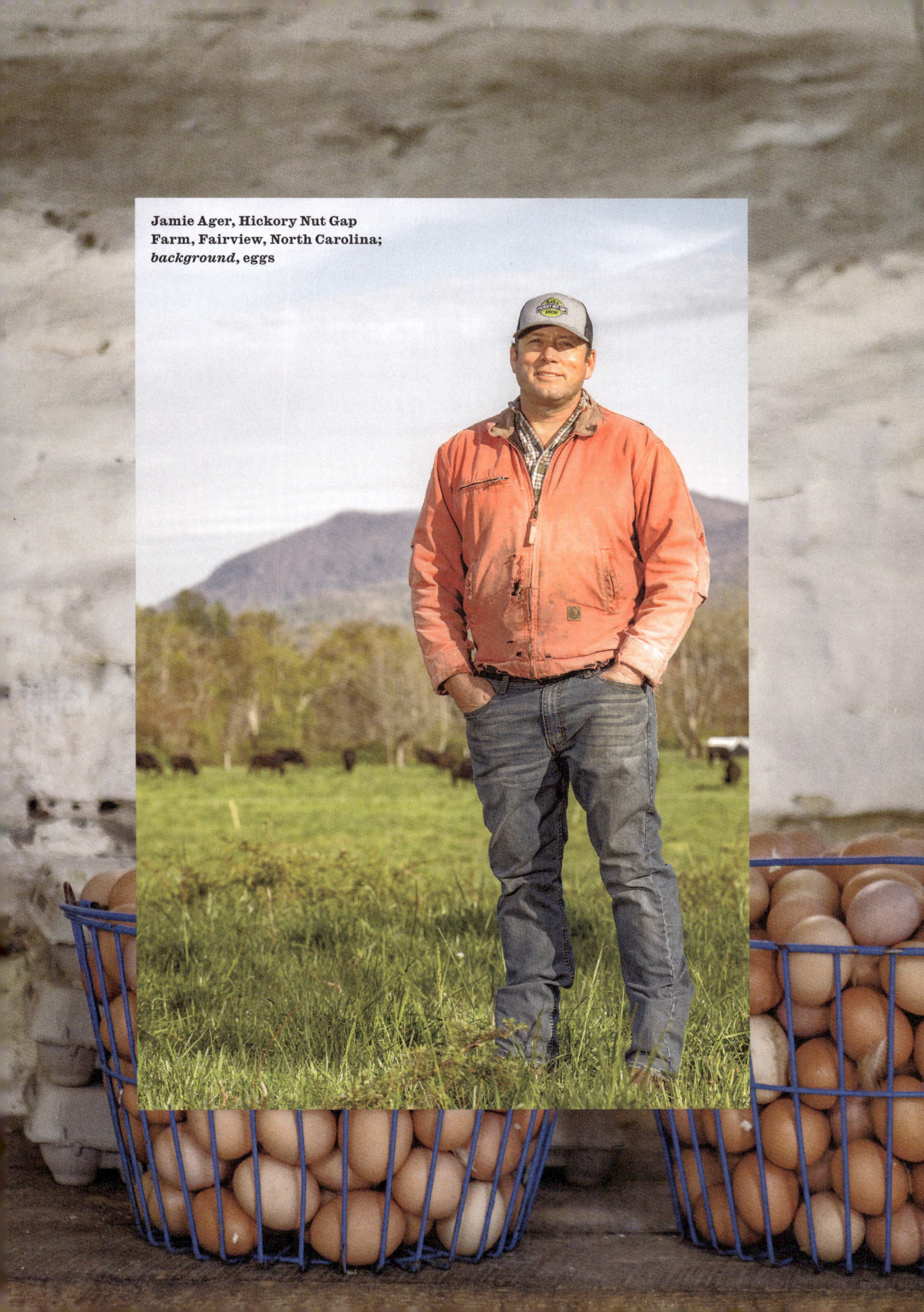

Jamie Ager, Hickory Nut Gap Farm, Fairview, North Carolina; *background*, eggs

consumers who support local food and sustainable production, and the region's long history of small farms and good husbandry. These factors have enabled Hickory Nut Gap to expand in ways that will positively affect the future of food sovereignty in western North Carolina.

Hickory Nut Gap Farm was placed in a conservation easement with the Southern Highlands Conservancy in 2008, and in addition to its meat business, the family operation includes Jamie's cousins Annie Louise and Isaiah Perkinson's Flying Cloud Farm, fourteen acres of organically grown vegetables. Hickory Nut Gap hosts classes and seasonal events such as whole animal butchery, fermentation, sausage making, stargazing, and contra dancing. They also operate a farm store and popular restaurant on-site. But their greatest achievement, as yet, is the formation of a cooperative of more than thirty southeastern farms that supply pastured pork and chicken and grass-fed beef to stores and restaurants.

"We've got the ability to produce year-round grass from the mountains of West Virginia and southern Virginia to western North Carolina. We have water here that's a real resource. We are sitting on this geographically appropriate place to be growing a lot of high-quality beef and cattle in a manner that ultimately is good for the environment."

—JAMIE AGER, Hickory Nut Gap Farm, Fairview, North Carolina, March 4, 2019

Jamie notes that some of their employees "even think of us as this boutique-y company, but we're an agriculture company. We're focused on changing agriculture. Restaurants are fantastic partners, and we tell our story together, we build value together. But at the end of the day, there's nothing wrong with adding more farmers and giving more farmers opportunity. And this is what we really do. And if that's what we stay focused on, then we're going to be successful as an impactful company."[8]

The success of Hickory Nut Gap has given Jamie and his Appalachian partners an effective position to encourage sustainability.

"How do we continue to build models that are better for climate change? And how do we build the political scene around something that is farmer friendly? As we move forward in that debate there is so little conversation between the rural agriculture people and the more urban conversation around climate change. And in a larger sense, that disconnect between urban and rural is just growing and growing. All the economics are driven toward urban opportunity, and rural is just commodified.

"I understand the concept of sustainability, and now the question is, how do you build a sustainable company? At the end of the day, you can only do so much as an individual. But if you can organize yourself as a team, then you're going to be a much stronger organization that can drive a much larger level of change.

"I think that's going to be our generation's [and the region's] political narrative—how you build a political reality and make change."

The Rainmaker

Elizabeth Sims was born and grew up in middle Tennessee, yet because of her eastern Kentucky–born father, she spent summers and holidays with her grandparents, great-aunts, and great-uncles in the foothills of the Appalachian Mountains.

"There was something magical about that place and their lives that just resonated with me, and when I moved to Asheville in 1985, I felt as if I'd come home."[9]

Food played a large part in Elizabeth's identification with the mountains: "When I was at my grandmother's, I know I ate my weight in country ham, and she made wonderful jams and jellies. She was a biology teacher and a botanist and a forager, so we had ramps every spring. And gooseberry pie. I remember her telling me that the trouble with gooseberries were rattlesnakes loved them as much as we did, so you had to be careful picking them."

As a marketing professional Elizabeth saw foodways as a particularly evocative way to tell the stories of her Asheville clients, which have included, among others, Biltmore, the John C. Campbell Folk School, and Tupelo Honey Cafe, whose three cookbooks she has authored.

"There's so much to be proud of when it comes to Asheville food, but planning the SFA field trip in 2003 I felt I had been charged to make sure what we did was authentic to the mountains, to western Carolina's culture, and that it also revealed how connected the past and present are. By the time we organized the Biltmore Field to Table event in 2008, the local food scene was growing so fast, we put together eleven days of panels, demonstrations, and meals. We had John Fleer and Sean Brock, Robert and John Stehling, and Alan Benton. It felt like Asheville was on the cusp of something huge."

So huge that in 2016 Elizabeth and a small group of food, beverage, and arts professionals began to envision the gathering that would become Chow Chow, an Asheville culinary event.

"Asheville is unique in that people see us as a city, but we also have a rural, mountain identity and resources—generational farms, bakeries, glassblowers, pottery. When you see Asheville today, you see those key 'ingredients' on the table at dinner."

Elizabeth believes that Chow Chow can be, among other things, a way to show how those things come together. "It's important to make a distinction that it's a collaborative effort between all kinds of creative people. It's more than just food. What we're trying to demonstrate isn't just about one thing happening here and another over there, but that collaborative effort between chefs, farmers, artists, and artisans that makes up Asheville's story. It's about synchronicity and the mystical power of the western Carolina mountains to attract and inspire such creativity, from the period of Native American settlement to the present. That's what our story is about, past, present, and I believe well into the future."

Rhubarb's Red Wine Sorghum Vinaigrette

JOHN FLEER *with* RONNI LUNDY

Makes about 1½ cups

1 tablespoon chopped shallots
¼ teaspoon chopped garlic
½ teaspoon crushed green peppercorns
½ teaspoon kosher salt
¼ cup red wine vinegar
⅛ cup Banyuls wine vinegar (can use sherry vinegar)
1 teaspoon Dijon mustard
1 cup hazelnut oil
⅛ cup sorghum syrup

Combine the shallots, garlic, peppercorns, and salt with the vinegars and let sit for 10 minutes. Whisk in the mustard, then the oil, then the sorghum. Pour into a container with a lid and store in the refrigerator. Whisk or shake again before using.

Serving notes: At Rhubarb, for each salad, they dress ½ cup radicchio chiffonade and 1 tablespoon julienned fresh strawberries with this vinaigrette and a dash of salt. This marinates while the chef sears a slice of fresh goat cheese in olive oil to caramelize each surface. The salad is served with goat cheese in the center and a thin slice of warmed country ham accompanied by cornbread croutons. A blackberry balsamic reduction and a bit of sorghum syrup are drizzled on top of the cheese.

NOTES

1. Jane Black, "The Next Big Thing in American Regional Cooking: Humble Appalachia," *Washington Post*, March 29, 2016; Jane Black, "Long Misunderstood: Appalachian Food Finds the Spotlight," *New York Times*, September 11, 2019.

2. Ronni Lundy, *Victuals: An Appalachian Journey with Recipes* (New York: Clarkson Potter, 2016), 21–22.

3. Mark Rosenstein, interview by Marcie Cohen Ferris, September 25, 2019.

4. Mackensy Lunsford, "Asheville's Original Farm-to-Table Restaurant: The Market Place Celebrates 40 Years," *Citizen Times* (Asheville, N.C.), May 1, 2019.

5. Ronni Lundy, "Melting Pot: Buttermilk Soup in Asheville," *Our State*, December 19, 2017.

6. John Fleer, interview by Marcie Cohen Ferris, September 25, 2019.

7. Mackensy Lunsford, "Ashleigh Shanti Steps Down from Benne on Eagle with Plans to Create Restaurant Group," *Citizen Times* (Asheville, N.C.), November 20, 2020.

8. Jamie Ager, interview by Ronni Lundy and Marcie Cohen Ferris, March 3, 2019.

9. Elizabeth Sims, interview by Ronni Lundy, February 12 and March 11, 2019.

COURTNEY LEWIS

Native Food Sovereignty

As I thumb through the elegant layouts in such magazines as *Southern Living* and *Garden and Gun*, I see the Indigenous stories that lie beneath recipes portrayed as quintessentially southern, from cornbread to pecan pie. I also see the millennia-old ingredients of the American South omitted from these recipes: rich ᏐᏂ (sohi; hickory nuts), tart and sweet ᎤᏩᎦ (uwaga; passionflower fruit), and earthy ᏫᏍᏂ (wishi; maitake mushrooms). While recent work has brought to light the voice and labor of African American men and women in the development of southern cuisine, the southeastern Indigenous peoples' foundations of southern food remain hidden. Although these gaps contribute to the historical and contemporary erasure of Native Nations from the culinary narrative of the South, in many ways, their lack of recognition by non-Native society may also be their salvation—a lesson that I learned one day in a courthouse.

My passion for Indigenous food justice was sparked on November 23, 2009. That day, I sat in a courtroom in Bryson City, North Carolina, and watched George Burgess, an Eastern Band of Cherokee Indians (EBCI) citizen, defend a practice that was thousands of years old: the gathering of wild green onions called ᏩᏍᏗ (wasdi; ramps) in an area of historic Cherokee land known currently as the Great Smoky Mountains National Park (GSMNP). Cherokee people have lived in the southeastern United States for tens of thousands of years, but the EBCI used a combination of strategies to stay in North Carolina during the federal government's Removal era. They continue to live on a portion of this homeland adjacent to the GSMNP called the Qualla Boundary. Today the EBCI are one of three federally recognized Cherokee nations, alongside the Cherokee Nation and the United Keetoowah Band of Cherokee Indians, both located in Oklahoma.

The EBCI community gathered that day in November to support Burgess, and the courtroom bustled with folks ranging from the chief and council members to elders and children. As the case progressed, my frustration grew as I learned that Cherokee people were being punished for their gathering of ramps due to a new East Coast restaurant fad—the mass wild harvesting of so-called forest delicacies like ramps

Bean bread with fatback, fried chicken, potatoes and cabbage, beans and hominy, ramps and scrambled eggs, Cherokee Indian Fair, Cherokee, North Carolina; *background*, wishi (mushrooms), Cherokee, North Carolina for foraging dinners. Chefs are supplied largely by harvesters and food vendors with no knowledge of, or interest in, sustaining the ramp populations—a truth evidenced by devastated ramp patches throughout the mountains.[1] The National Park Service (NPS) responded to this attack by banning all ramp harvesting, which ignored the Cherokee people's reliance on this important first green of the early spring. The case revealed additional issues with NPS official studies regarding plant harvesting; for example, the park service's expert on ramp harvesting had neither consulted with, nor had any knowledge of, Cherokee ramp harvesting techniques. These skills have been honed over time by Cherokee people to maintain sustainable ramp populations. The final outcome in court that day penalized Cherokee people for the personal gathering of one of their most valued native foods.[2] I have written about this case in the decade since it first went to trial, and while there is movement for the EBCI on other plant-gathering rights in the mountains (for example, ᏎᏣᎾ; sotsana; sochan, a type of coneflower also eaten as an early spring green), the burden of legally reinstituting these rights through mandated sustainability studies falls on the shoulders of the EBCI, who bear the significant financial and labor costs of this process. For sochan alone, this cost was approximately $68,000, and after this study the GSMNP granted the EBCI only thirty-six permits. Because of these mandates, it may be many years before the required study on ramps (a notoriously slow-growing onion) can be funded and completed. This is only one of many stories in the continuous fight for Indigenous agricultural, foodways, and health rights.

"I had a great grandmother that lived to be one hundred and fourteen. She walked everywhere she went. She raised her own garden. . . . She had to carry corn in a sack on her back to the miller to have it grinded into cornmeal. Everything else she gathered and made or even did without. So, we're a strong nation. The Cherokees are strong. We're strong women. We can do just about anything we set our minds to do."

—JOHNNIE SUE MYERS, citizen, Eastern Band of Cherokee Indians, April 20, 2020

When Europeans first arrived in what is now known as the United States, they believed they had found a "pristine Eden."[3] Lush, extensive forests, brimming with plants and wildlife, thrived. At the time, European writers assumed that this was a natural state of the land and forests.[4] However, these rich landscapes were the direct result of thousands of years of complex agricultural and agroforestry techniques used by American Indian peoples, including the Cherokees in the southeast United States.[5] The process of European settling is known as settler-colonialism and includes not only the removal but also the erasure of Indigenous peoples in order to claim land for ongoing settler use. Like the NPS erasure of Cherokees in ramp harvesting, here we see settler erasure of American Indian forest cultivation.

At the time of contact, Cherokee territory included Alabama, Georgia, Tennessee, South Carolina, North Carolina, and some of Kentucky and Virginia.[6] Cherokee people's productive farming techniques, in addition to their intensive and long-standing agroforestry methods, produced the bountiful food needed to feed their large population. The most well known of these in gardening culture today is the three sisters companion planting method of growing corn, beans, and squash together. Although I am focusing here on the Cherokee people as a whole as well as the Eastern Band of Cherokee Indians, it should be noted that many of these foods, agricultural techniques, and experiences are shared by other Native Nations throughout the South and the United States.

The Cherokee Nation grew economically and politically throughout the nineteenth century, but settler-colonial interventions and aggressions took their toll on Cherokee populations and the lands they cultivated. Tracts of Cherokee land were illegally claimed by settlers in western North Carolina, with much of the land being cleared for homesteading and increasingly lucrative lumber. Other natural and human-generated disasters followed. The year 1816 was known as the Year without a Summer due to the volcanic winter caused by the 1815 Mount Tambora (Indonesia) eruption.[7] Crops tended by farmers in cooler locations, including the Cherokees in the Appalachian Mountains, were ruined by frost. Starvation followed. Although little has been published about this time period, Cherokee people relied on their community stores of food, their extensive trade and commerce networks, and a movement from home farmwork to wage labor (that is, work for pay) to keep their nation fed. Following this, the period 1830–38 marked the federal government's genocidal forced marches of southeastern Native Nations, including the ᏅᏃᎯ ᏚᎾᏠᎯᎸᏱ ((Nvnohi Dunatlohilvyi), the Cherokee Trail Where They Cried). The Eastern Band of Cherokee Indians employed many political strategies to remain in North Carolina but were then left to manage their remaining southeastern Cherokee lands and forests without the support of the collective Cherokee Nation.[8]

At the turn of the century, these forests were further, and forever, altered by another impact of settler-colonialism in the form of a blight. Until the twentieth century, it is estimated that at least one in four trees in the Appalachian Mountains were American chestnut (*Castanea dentata*); these represented nearly 45 percent of the canopy trees in southern Appalachian forests.[9] A single mature chestnut tree could produce 6,000 nuts.[10] This plentiful and delicious nut was a staple of the Cherokee diet. Due to their thin skin that contained no tannins, chestnuts were easily processed and used for roasting, boiling, or ground into a flour. Of equal importance, they were a vital resource for the wild and domesticated animals eaten by Cherokee people.[11]

A massive chestnut blight began in 1904, caused by a fungal pathogen that first appeared in New York City.[12] This blight is the largest recorded ecological disaster in the United States; by midcentury, nearly none of the estimated 4 billion American chestnut trees remained on the

East Coast.[13] At this same time, the federal government's policies emphasizing forest fire suppression resulted in the outlawing of prescribed burning and, along with it, the Cherokees' yearly agroforestry technique of controlled burns each fall.[14] These burns previously increased the abundance of chestnuts in the southern Appalachians.[15] Within the Cherokee community, many believed that federal fire suppression policies contributed to the rapid spread of the chestnut blight. Another federal policy, the prohibition against allowing domesticated animals to feed in the forests, further crippled the Cherokees' ability to best use their agricultural resources.[16]

The loss of the American chestnut tree had a catastrophic impact on Cherokee foodways. Following the blight, the EBCI rallied, using valuable chestnut lumber to create revenue for its people and provide food for their tables.[17] Throughout each challenge, the EBCI and its citizens responded quickly, and in some cases proactively, to attenuate the effects of these issues. From astute political actions to community-based support efforts, Eastern Band people have actively continued to protect the Qualla Boundary for future generations.

Today, although mature American chestnut trees are rare, we still see the chestnut's importance in Cherokee foodways. For example, one of my favorite dishes is the hearty and dense Cherokee chestnut bread. Instead of the small and flavorful American chestnut, Cherokee people now use nuts from the blight-resistant Chinese chestnut tree, which are larger, but bland, necessitating added flavoring, such as a pinch of sugar. This popular dumplinglike bread is made with cooked chestnuts and unbolted (unsifted) cornmeal, shaped into patties, wrapped in hickory leaves or corn husks, and boiled. Chestnut bread is highly versatile and can be eaten as is or drizzled with fatback and grease and served with greens, such as ramps. Although considered plain in taste by those unfamiliar with it, chestnut bread is relished by many Cherokee people. During the chestnut blight, Cherokee cooks turned to other versions of this bread that have since gained prominence, including bean bread and sweet potato bread.

These special breads are sold at public events and gatherings in Cherokee, North Carolina, the longest running of which is the Cherokee Indian Fair each fall. The fair was officially opened to the public in 1912 and today is one of Cherokee's signature annual events. The fair hosts national and local American Indian musical acts; Cherokee games, such as chunky (a game of skill played with a javelin and a small ring rolled on the ground) and marbles; large stickball tournaments; annual competitions such as the Miss Cherokee pageant; and craft contests, including the art of creating vibrant ribbon skirts, delicate jewelry making, and intricate basket weaving. Throughout the day and into the night, the fair fills with people as the sounds of children on rides mixes with music from the main stage and cheers from the crowds at the Cherokee games, overlaid with the voices of community members under the large white food tents, chatting in both Cherokee and English. However, the most anticipated highlight of the fair—second only to stickball rivalries—is the food.

> *"We were always told, 'You're the next generation. You need to go off and get educated, come back, and make a difference.' . . . Now I'm feeding back into the cycle, getting to work with the youth, the community members and seniors, absorbing all their knowledge. . . . You see the cyclical nature of how we operate."*
>
> **—JOEY OWLE, secretary of agriculture and farming, Eastern Band of Cherokee Indians, Cherokee, North Carolina, October 21, 2020**

After the stickball games, we walk to the fairgrounds, where long lines form in front of family food vendor booths. There are the standard fair foods of burgers and chili cheese fries, but the Indian dinners are why people wait in line for a half hour and longer. These meals vary depending on which family is cooking and what ingredients are seasonally available, but each dish tells its own story of Cherokee foodways and history.[18] The typical Indian dinner includes bean bread often served with fatback, fried chicken or local fried trout, potatoes and cabbage, beans and hominy, and, if you are lucky, ramps (frozen since the spring harvest) mixed into scrambled eggs. The smell of fried chicken, simmering hominy, and pungent ramps intensifies as you wait in line, slowly edging closer to the booths. For dessert, I head across the fairgrounds lawn for strawberries at the North American Indian Women's Association (NAIWA) kitchen, a group that also hosts the Qualla Boundary's Annual Cherokee Strawberry and Blueberry Festivals. At the fair, NAIWA serves modern dishes, such as strawberry shortcake, which can be served en masse, quickly and easily. At other events, the extraordinary women chefs offer samples of older recipes, like ᎧᏔᎦᏟ ᏗᎬᏂ (kanugatli digvni; blackberry dumplings). The fairground Indian dinners provided by such vendors as Nana's Kitchen are also enjoyed at fundraisers for families in need (Calhoun's Cherokee Frybread is known for these, in addition to its fair booth), EBCI event catering (Granny's Kitchen is the usual supplier for this), and at restaurants in the town of Cherokee on select days, such as the Hungry Wolf Deli & Fresh Market, the Little Princess, and Newfound Lodge.

The ability of Indigenous peoples to access their own foods, such as the ramps and chestnuts served at the Fall Fair, and to control their own foodways is the central concern of the Indigenous food sovereignty movement. Begun as a grassroots farmer's movement, the first global forum on food sovereignty was held in 2007 in the Republic of Mali. The declaration created there defines food sovereignty as "the right of peoples to healthy and culturally appropriate food produced through ecologically sound and sustainable methods, and their right to define their own food and agriculture systems."[19] The American Indian food sovereignty movement supports the reclamation of American Indian foods—and

Fry bread, Cherokee Indian Fair, Cherokee, North Carolina

therefore American Indian health—at several levels.[20] First, individuals support these efforts by accessing and propagating native seeds and plants at home, then saving the seeds for further use and community dispersal. Second, Native Nation governments help by funding seed-saving programs, providing support for home farmers, and even leasing land to their citizens, specifically for home agricultural purposes. The EBCI government does all three through its EBCI Center of the North Carolina Cooperative Extension on the Qualla Boundary. The EBCI's emphasis on food sovereignty begins early for its youngest citizens in the newly built Cherokee Central School (K–12), which has its own garden. While growing native plants, students reclaim their language as they learn the Cherokee vocabulary of gardening. Third, collaborative nonprofits, such as Native American Food Sovereignty Alliance, focus on "restoring, supporting and developing Indigenous food systems through best practices and advocacy that place Indigenous peoples at the center of national, Tribal and local policies and natural resources management to ensure food security and health of all future generations."[21] Fourth, several programs hosted by colleges and universities promote food sovereignty. The Indigenous Food and Agriculture Initiative located at the University of Arkansas is increasing student enrollment in food and agricultural studies; creating new programs in food and agricultural studies; and providing strategic planning and technical assistance to Native Nation governments on infrastructure, finance, health, and intellectual property rights policies.[22]

It is crucial that all of these elements work together to address the issues of food sovereignty as the stakes continue to grow. The Standard American Diet (SAD, a low nutritive diet composed of processed foods, meat, and added sugars, salts, and fats, usually eaten due to low cost and convenience, especially by those in poverty) has critically affected the health of American Indian peoples, who experience high rates of all associated conditions, from obesity to hypertension. Diabetes, in particular, continues to disproportionately affect these communities. American Indian and Alaska Native adults have a 2.3 times higher chance of being diagnosed with diabetes as compared with non-Hispanic whites, while children have a 9 times higher chance.[23]

On a global scale, climate change is also robbing Indigenous peoples of their foods and foodways. The shifting of growing zones has already reduced the growth of southern plants such as ramps, as well as fungi, including the much sought-after wishi mushrooms of the mountains. While at the 2019 Cherokee Indian Fair, I could find no wishi mushrooms for sale, nor were they present as I searched for them on my walks on the local mountain trails. I left my coat behind as the temperature reached seventy-six degrees. The week before it had been a staggering ninety-one degrees. The average high temperature for an October day in the past had been about sixty-five degrees. That fall, streams were low due to the heat and lack of rain. Plants that should have been almost dormant wilted instead. Providing sustenance, pleasure, and medicine, such plants are growing scarcer as their native environments become increasingly hostile.

For me, food sovereignty is one part of a holistic movement of cultural reclamation that weaves together and strengthens the foundations of Cherokee societies: food with art with nation-building with economic stability. For the EBCI, enacting food sovereignty policies also represents only the latest actions in its history of supporting and protecting the EBCI nation and its citizens. These efforts fuel the broader southern Indigenous food sovereignty movement, which seeks to protect not only the endangered plants and foodways that are enjoyed by southern American Indian peoples but *all* native foods that have been adopted by *all* southern cooks. These shared foodways come with shared stewardship obligations. By actively encouraging these efforts and supporting Native Nation rights to food access, we can help ensure that the beloved core ingredients of the American South—foods such as strawberries, pecans, and grits cultivated and eaten by the first southern cooks, American Indian people—will continue to thrive for generations to come.

Ꮜ Ꮩ Ꮥ Ꮜ Tuya Gadu (Bean Bread) COURTNEY LEWIS

Makes 2–4 servings

½ cup dried pinto beans (use heirloom brown beans if available)
2 cups unbolted (unsifted) white cornmeal
Optional: self-rising flour (wheat is a colonially introduced ingredient)
Optional: baking soda (baking soda is a colonially introduced ingredient but is used regularly today)

Cook the beans on the stove or in a crock pot using your favorite recipe (be sure to omit the salt). Note: do not use canned beans because you'll be using the hot bean stock later.

In a large bowl, combine the cornmeal, flour (if using), and baking soda (if using). Add 2 cups of the cooked beans to the cornmeal and mash them with a potato masher or the tines of a large fork. Add hot bean stock, a tablespoon at a time, until the dough holds together and is slightly sticky but not too wet.

Bring a large pot of water to a slow boil. Set a bowl of cold water handy to cool your hands. Working with the bread dough while it is still hot, form thick 1½-inch wheels about the size of your palm (do not make them too thin or they will break when they boil). Gently drop the shaped dough into the boiling water and cook until they float, about 15–20 minutes, depending on their size. Remove the little bean breads from the water, drain them, and wrap them in tin foil to keep warm. Enjoy them as you would biscuits or other breads served with a main dish, topped with gravy or a condiment of your choice.

NOTES

Do not use salt in the bread or in the bean water or the bread will dissolve.

Unbolted cornmeal is not sifted, so it is variously sized and usually unenriched local cornmeal. Masa harina can be substituted for accessibility, but fine or coarse cornmeal will alter the texture significantly.

The bread dough is generally made with equal parts cornmeal and cooked beans with about ¼ of the bean stock. Adjust as necessary.

Bean bread is traditionally wrapped in hickory leaves or corn husks after cooking.

NOTES

1. Lisa Lefler, "Ramps: Appalachian Delicacies That 'Smells God-Awful, but Cures What Ails Ya,'" in *Southern Foodways and Culture: Local Considerations and Beyond* (Knoxville, Tenn.: Newfound Press, 2013).

2. Courtney Lewis, "The Case of the Wild Onions: The Impact of Ramps on Cherokee Rights," *Southern Cultures* 18, no. 2 (2012): 104–17.

3. William M. Denevan, "The Pristine Myth," *Annals of the Association of American Geographers* 82, no. 3 (1992): 369.

4. Charles C. Mann, *1491: New Revelations of the Americas before Columbus* (New York: Vintage Books, 2006), 5, 314, 326.

5. "Agroforestry Practices," U.S. Department of Agriculture, www.fs.usda.gov/nac/practices/index.shtml; Cynthia T. Fowler and Evelyn Konopik, "The History of Fire in the Southern United States," *Human Ecology Review* 14, no. 2 (2007): 168–70.

6. Theda Perdue, *The Cherokee Nation and the Trail of Tears* (New York: Viking, 2007), xiii.

7. C. Edward Skeen, "The Year without a Summer: A Historical View," *Journal of the Early Republic* 1, no. 1 (1981): 51–67.

8. Will Chavez and Finger-Smith, "EBCI Ancestors Remained East for Various Reasons," *Cherokee Phoenix*, March 25, 2016, https://www.cherokeephoenix.org/Article/index/10143.

9. John R. Finger, *Cherokee Americans: The Eastern Band of Cherokees in the Twentieth Century* (Lincoln: University of Nebraska Press, 1991), 77; Charles R. Burnham, "The Restoration of the American Chestnut: Mendelian Genetics May Solve a Problem That Has Resisted Other Approaches," *American Scientist* 76, no. 5 (1988): 478; D. B. Vandermast, D. H. Van Lear, and B. D. Clinton, "American Chestnut as an Allelopath in the Southern Appalachians," *Forest Ecology and Management* 165, no. 1–3 (July 2002): 173.

10. "Hybrid American Chestnuts," Penn State College of Agricultural Sciences, https://agsci.psu.edu/research/extension-centers/erie/grape-non-grape-crops/hybrid-american-chestnuts.

11. Julia Reed, "Thinking Multidimensionally: Cherokee Boundaries Above, Below, and Beyond," in *The Power of Maps and the Politics of Borders*, APS *Transactions*, vol. 110, part 4 (2021).

12. Catherine Keever, "Present Composition of Some Stands of the Former Oak-Chestnut Forest in the Southern Blue Ridge Mountains," *Ecology* 34, no. 1 (1953): 44.

13. John Holusha, "Hope for Chestnut Found in Virus That Fights Blight," *New York Times*, October 20, 1981.

14. William T. Sommers, Stanley G. Coloff, and Susan G. Conard, "Synthesis of Knowledge: Fire History and Climate Change," U.S. Joint Fire Science Program (George Mason University, 2011), 88; Cynthia T. Fowler and Evelyn Konopik, "The History of Fire in the Southern United States," *Human Ecology Review* (2007), 171–72.

15. Vandermast, Van Lear, and Clinton, "American Chestnut as an Allelopath," 180.

16. Barbara R. Duncan and Brett H. Riggs, *Cherokee Heritage Trails Guidebook*, (Chapel Hill: Published in association with the Museum of the Cherokee Indian by University of North Carolina Press, 2003), 88.

17. Finger, *Cherokee Americans*, 77.

18. Duncan and Riggs, *Cherokee Heritage Trails Guidebook*, 45, 58–59.

19. "Declaration of Nyeleni," Forum for Food Sovereignty, February 27, 2007, www.nyeleni.org/spip.php?article290.

20. D. N. Cozzo, "The Effect of Traditional Dietary Practices on Contemporary Diseases among the Eastern Band of Cherokee Indians," in *Under the Rattlesnake: Cherokee Health and Resiliency*, ed. Lisa J. Lefler (Tuscaloosa: University of Alabama Press, 2009), 79–101.

21. "About NAFSA," Native Food Alliance, June 2, 2015, https://nativefoodalliance.org/about/.

22. "Our Work," Indigenous Food and Agriculture Initiative, December 14, 2018, www.indigenousfoodandag.com/what-we-do.

23. "Diabetes in American Indians and Alaska Natives: Facts at-a-Glance," Indian Health Service, Division of Diabetes Treatment and Prevention, 2017, http://keepitsacred.itcmi.org/wp-content/uploads/sites/5/2016/05/Fact_sheet_diabetes.pdf.

MAIA SURDAM; BAXTER MILLER, *Photographer*

Making the World We Want through Food

A Visual Tour of Western North Carolina

Western North Carolina has long been a center of food and farming traditions. Yet in recent decades, residents of the Blue Ridge Mountains are transforming local foodways to meet the needs of the twenty-first century. The six western North Carolinians profiled here are making the world they want to inhabit. They are chefs, a miller, growers, a seed saver, a potter, and a flower farmer who claim these mountains as home—by birth and by choice. Their backgrounds and identities vary, as do their skills and entry points into North Carolina's food economy, but all are visionaries in their own way. A quest for quality food is the connective tissue that unites their stories. Through their leadership, persistence, creativity, and hopefulness, they are bringing flavorful mountain-grown food within more people's reach. Some have been on this path for decades, while others have just begun. Although some may not see themselves as activists, their life choices and actions reveal a dedication to fostering change and making positive impacts. Chef Kikkoman Shaw, for example, is part of a coalition that offers local, high-quality food—the type too often reserved for high-paying customers—to the under-resourced residents of Asheville's public housing communities. And Chris Smith, a seed saver in Leicester, seeks to address climate change by building a more robust regional food system that emulates the generosity and diversity of plants. These individuals are pursuing personal passions that also engage the broader, pressing needs of their communities, state, and region—even our global neighbors.

Many of these individuals engage deeply and directly with history. They draw lessons from the past that allow them to innovate and create things anew. Carolina Ground founder Jennifer Lapidus, for instance, drew on her studies of the Industrial Revolution as she forged a new regional grain economy that is reconnecting farmers, millers, and bakers throughout the South. In Madison County, Emily and Josh Copus

John Dugan, Ty Bushyhead Boyd, and David Anderson, Kituwah, Swain County, North Carolina; *background*, pickled ramps

named their grocery store after another entrepreneurial couple, "Zadie" and Emma Ponder, who sold groceries in the area during the Great Depression and inspired the Copuses' path forward as modern grocers. And, in the far western mountains of North Carolina, tribal members of the Eastern Band of Cherokee Indians are protecting and preserving their most sacred site, Kituwah, reintroducing its history into their school curriculum, ceremonies, and community programs to ensure that it will sustain future generations in their collective goal of caring for one another.

These profiles offer a taste of the profound flavors that permeate North Carolina's mountains. Freshly milled wheat is baked into nutty sourdough loaves. Savory vegetables, bright herbs, and local fish, pork, and poultry are transformed into new expressions of the Appalachian table at the hands of culinary wizards like Ashley Capps and Travis Schultz. But as the following stories demonstrate, the ways that food enriches our bodies, enlivens our spirits, and fuels our economies always depend on their human contexts. As Josh Copus puts it, "The people are making this place.... Without the people, none of it really matters."

Cherokee Growers

Near the Tuckasegee River, in Swain County, a gentle mound rests in the center of a mountain valley. Its subtle appearance belies its remarkable historical significance. To the Cherokee, this site is called Kituwah—"the Cherokee Mother town, the center of everything." For thousands of years, the Indigenous people of this region recognized this place as sacred, a birthplace bestowed by the creator, connecting diverse peoples across an extensive area.

Generations of white colonization and land seizures by the U.S. government threatened Kituwah and its history. The "mother mound" once stood seventy feet in height but grew smaller as nonnative people farmed it and mined it for artifacts. But all is far from lost. In 1996, the Eastern Band of Cherokee Indians bought back 300 acres of the land, beginning a process whereby tribal members "teach, reteach, and recognize what actually happened here," Ty Bushyhead Boyd, a younger tribal member, explains: "Now that we have a central place that's recognized . . . it creates pride. It creates identity." Tribal members gather at the mound for ceremonies and celebrations. They lease plots of land in the adjoining fields to grow food to feed themselves and community members and to use for local businesses.

Kituwah connects contemporary Cherokee people to the past and provides a path to the future. John Dugan, Ty Bushyhead Boyd, and David Anderson are among many tribal members who grow food in the

Jennifer Lapidus, Carolina Ground, Asheville, North Carolina; *background*, Appalachian white wheat

valley. Dugan, a lifelong farmer, has mentored younger growers and supported youth garden projects. He is proud of that work, especially of the kids who "got hands-on experience. . . . Plus, the spirits come to them here," he says. "There's a feeling here whenever you're out there in the dirt and it's good."

Kennebec potatoes, mountain sweet watermelons, Cherokee flour corn—these plants and more thrive in the fertile valley soil. Their flavors astound, and the superb taste is one community benefit among many. At the nearby Tribal Greenhouse, horticulturist David Anderson grows up to 100,000 plants in a season and supports tribal citizens through his work. On any given day, he sees elders, students, people in recovery, and aspiring entrepreneurs, all eager to learn, connect, and grow. "Food's important," Anderson says. "Food brings people together more than anything in the world."

Jennifer Lapidus

When Jennifer Lapidus moved to these mountains in 1998 to start a small wood-fired, brick-oven bakery in Walnut, a small community in Madison County, there "wasn't much of a bread presence" here. Nearly twenty-five years later, things look (and taste) very different. Tailgate markets abound, naturally leavened breads are plentiful, and bread bakers more often use wheat grown in the Carolinas and milled nearby. In large part, we have Lapidus to thank for this dramatic change. Her leadership helped to build a southern grain revolution. Carolina Ground, her regional stone-ground milling business in Asheville, was both a result and a conduit of this transformation.

Hardly a solitary endeavor, this process rested on Lapidus's ability to revitalize a core relationship that had been nearly lost to industrialization. She has reconnected the baker, miller, and farmer. Each has their own needs when it comes to grain. Farmers must consider yield and bakers need consistent performance. The miller sits in between, turning plant matter into a useful ingredient. And a stone-ground miller, eschewing more efficient technology for the ancient practice of grinding whole grain between two stones, reintroduces "nutrients and flavor" into the conversation.

A student of history raised in Miami in the 1970s and 1980s, Lapidus believes in "reclaiming the parts of our past that shouldn't have been lost in this idea of progress." She also welcomes innovations that help us adapt to our current moment. Only recently did public plant breeders develop the Appalachian White Wheat variety, for instance, a hard wheat suited to the humid climate of North Carolina. Tony Horton, a

Ashley Capps and Travis Schultz, New Stock, Asheville, North Carolina; *background*, strawberries, Flying Cloud Farm, Fairview, North Carolina, and Bear Necessities Farm, Barnardsville, North Carolina

farmer in Zebulon, grows it and Lapidus mills it and ships it to customers. It has a "buttery flavor profile" and "a lovely application" that suits not just bread but cookies and cakes, too.

Lapidus has lofty goals for her small mill. "This is about us growing together," she explains, but "we don't want to get that big. We want to be sustainable. . . . There's another level of being fed when community comes together and creates its own food."

Ashley Capps

On the cusp of opening a restaurant in Weaverville in early 2020, chef and North Carolina native Ashley Capps performed "a quick turnaround" when COVID-19 struck. Facing unemployment, Capps and her partner, Travis Schultz, thought creatively and launched a "weekly curated meal box" service for the Asheville area called New Stock. They deliver to their customers' homes and provide convenient pickup locations. Their meals center on seasonal and local ingredients. When planning their menus, Capps explains, "The first question is always, 'What's in season?' What do our farmer friends have . . . that they need to sell?"

Every week the meal box contains the same five elements—entrée, salad, bread, dessert, and beverage—but each version offers a unique culinary adventure, something like a "restaurant experience at home." For an autumnal meal, they begin with Chinese broccoli and cilantro from Lee's One Fortune Farm in Marion, sweet potatoes from the Sleight Family Farm in Pleasant Garden, and eggplant from Gaining Ground Farm in Leicester. These ingredients become a Thai green curry entrée inspired by Schultz's travels through Southeast Asia. A salad consists of freshly cut greens and a vinaigrette, such as the green goddess dressing with ramp purée they made in March. Local baker Gus Trout makes a naturally leavened loaf of bread, and their buddies at Bad Art Beverage Company create mixers, such as shrubs or syrups, that can be added to cocktails or teas. And the desserts, prepared by Capps, are always delightful. Her peaches-and-cream pie boasts a buttermilk custard with four varieties of local peaches, all encased in a flaky cornmeal pastry of heritage grains milled at Farm and Sparrow in Mars Hill.

Capps reflects on this moment honestly: "This year was a giant experiment. . . . It's working. We're surviving and we're doing good work. . . . What are we going to become? We don't know." No matter how the business grows, they "want to make sure that the quality of our food never lowers." The financial side of running a business feels uncertain, "but cooking all the food? That's what we know. . . . We're not nervous about that. I can say that with confidence."

Emily and Josh Copus, Old Marshall Jail, Marshall, North Carolina; *background*, Carolina Flowers Farm and Florist

Capps approaches this project with nearly twenty years of culinary experience and a deep commitment to collaborative relationships. She prioritizes working with small-scale food producers, growers, millers, and innovative professionals. People like photographer Nicole McConville, whose high standards match those of New Stock, "make us want to be better," Capps explains. "I love the creative process of transforming raw ingredients into something delicious and beautiful," she says. "It is about the product, but it's also about the people whose business it is. I care about these people. I don't want them to go away. I want them to keep living their dream, and I can help by buying what they make and making it shine."

Emily and Josh Copus

Josh Copus makes pots and bricks from clay that he digs by hand. He hails from a commune in the mountains of Floyd County, Virginia, and now owns land near Marshall, North Carolina. "I've been building places for flowers to go for a long time, just waiting for the right person to grow them there," he says. Emily Copus, a reporter turned flower farmer who grew up outside of Atlanta, eventually started her first business, Carolina Flowers, on that property. Married in 2018, there is a dreamy sheen to the "flowers and clay utopia" the couple is building together in picturesque Madison County. But that is not the whole picture. The two work incredibly hard and have learned to collaborate in ways they never imagined.

Their joint venture is a grocery store called Zadie's Market. Its home is in Marshall, a small mountain town located on the French Broad River. Initially a virtual store that offered free delivery, they decided to launch the business earlier than planned because of the coronavirus pandemic. Zadie's has now settled into its permanent spot inside the Old Marshall Jail, a historic building the couple owns with a group of friends that also includes a small boutique hotel. When deciding what to do with the space, they thought, "What's going to get the biggest number and different types of people in here? Food. And not just any kind of food, groceries. Lettuce, sandwiches, bread. The staples." A farmer herself, Emily sources as much produce as possible from the area's surrounding farms, in hopes of strengthening the regional food system.

Josh oversees the building's renovations with an eye turned to both the past and the future. After buying the building, they "started interviewing people," those from "both sides of the bars" of the former jail, to learn about its complicated legacy. While shopping at Zadie's or staying at the hotel, customers and guests support the local economy while also learning about the town's history, for Josh literally embedded

Kikkoman Shaw, Hanan Shabazz, Tarell Burton, and Alvin Scales, We Give a Share Culinary Team, Southside Kitchen, Asheville, North Carolina; *background*, cabbage and turkey soup, We Give a Share

townspeople's stories into the brick-lined walls. This project honors the past, yet it is no backward-facing museum. "The narrative is not over," Josh says. "Right," adds Emily, "we're just picking up the thread."

Kikkoman Shaw

Kikkoman Shaw is a revolutionary force in the kitchen. "I'm the type of person that whatever I set my mind to do, I'm going to give it my all," says the Southside Kitchen chef. Currently, he is set on bringing love, compassion, and peace of mind into this kitchen, all while providing delicious and healthy food to people in his community who face food insecurity. Shaw is a key player in the We Give a Share program in Asheville. Launched in April 2020 amid the COVID-19 pandemic, this groundbreaking collaboration among local farmers, chefs, volunteers, and donors brings "high-end, quality food" to people in need, many who are elderly or homebound. Veteran chef Mark Rosenstein, who has been an important culinary mentor to Shaw, spends time in the kitchen and helps to organize volunteers. Anne and Aaron Grier of Gaining Ground Farm regularly deliver their produce and check in with the kitchen crew, too. These folks "are hands on," Shaw says. "That's the beauty of it."

Each meal includes an entrée, side dish, and dessert, with plentiful portions that sometimes provide leftovers. On a November day, for example, Shaw prepared a penne trout salad with fish sourced from Sunburst Trout Farms, alongside cauliflower, broccoli, and zucchini, and with a Pink Lady apple from nearby Creasman Farms for dessert. Volunteers often make homemade desserts to share, so Shaw likes to alternate the fresh fruit with something sweeter, such as cookies or cake. "We try to keep it a healthy balance."

Shaw, and most of the other Black chefs who work with him, grew up in Asheville's public housing communities. "I have family members that get these meals," he explains. They tell him, "Oh, that was so good! What are you having tomorrow?" This is especially meaningful to Shaw because he experienced difficult times as a young person, and his family and community were a source of support. "Now I try to pay it back with my cooking," he says. A few months into the pandemic, Shaw had an opportunity to return to his former job cooking at a high-end restaurant downtown but decided to stay at the Southside Kitchen instead. Preparing meals for his own community is an act of love. "To see a smile on somebody's face? That makes me feel good."

The pandemic turmoil has presented unexpected opportunities for growth and connection. "It brought a lot of people together that would

Chris Smith, The Utopian Seed Project, Leicester, North Carolina; *background*, edible dahlia

never, ever bumped heads," Shaw reflects. Many in the Black community "understand what struggling is all about and [know] how to take a little bit of nothing and turn it into something." In 2020, with that sense of insecurity spreading, Shaw provides leadership for how to navigate those troubling waters. "I take pride in what I do," he says. But the astounding success of this program? "It isn't about me," he insists, "it's about us." He relies on his core kitchen crew: Hanan Shabazz, Tarell Burton, Gary McDaniels, and Alvin Scales, each person brings something important to the table. "We produce a lot of meals. . . . At the end of the day, I can't excel if I don't bring somebody up with me. That's what I'm all about, bringing other people with me."

Chris Smith

"The climate is going south quickly, and we've got some big challenges ahead of us," says writer and activist Chris Smith. Known for his James Beard Award–winning book, *The Whole Okra*, Smith runs a nonprofit in Leicester called the Utopian Seed Project. When he moved from England to the United States about ten years ago, Smith was disturbed by the American factory farming system he encountered. His initial impulse was to "disengage" and simply grow his own food. But landing a job at Sow True Seeds in Asheville connected him with people, networks, and seeds that propelled him in a different direction. He believes that if we "change the way people think about . . . experience, and interact with food, then we change the world and its trajectory."

Smith's goal is to create a network of microregional seed hubs that can aid in global transformations of climate, nutrition, and food security. Each seed hub, like the Utopian Seed Project that he oversees, will "manage and preserve [seed] varieties, conduct research and trials to identify new varieties, and then redistribute the food to the local people." Since every place has different growing conditions to consider and resources to draw on, each seed hub will be unique. "Once we've got seed hubs in every single region, then we connect the networks and we can have trade . . . [and] information and resource sharing" among them.

Put more simply: at Utopian Seed Project, they grow, educate, and celebrate plants, as well as "the diverse people behind the food." This process began with okra, an adaptable plant and a versatile food that grows well in these mountains: Smith grew more than seventy varieties in 2018. Originally from Africa, okra has been embraced by people and cultures throughout the world. (In the foreword to Smith's *The Whole Okra*, culinary historian Michael Twitty calls okra "a globetrotter" for a reason!) Using podcasts, public presentations, community events, and social media, Smith shares his platform with people who tell the histories and stories of these foods. While it may surprise many to learn that there are dozens of delicious varieties of collard greens or that dahlia tubers are edible, Smith is careful to note that he is not "discovering" these things once used by generations before us and still eaten in other parts of the world. "We're not learning new things. We're relearning things."

Afterword

A Road Map to Edible Equity

The making of *Edible North Carolina* occurred during the tumultuous months of 2020 and 2021 as our nation experienced pandemic-related lockdowns, climatic extremes, a volatile presidential election, the violent assault on the U.S. Capitol, and more tragic mass shootings of innocent Americans. Following the murder of George Floyd, we witnessed a transformative turn in the nation's long civil rights movement as thousands of people went to the streets to demand justice and racial equality for Black Americans. There can be no food history or contemporary food movement in North Carolina, the American South, and our nation that does not acknowledge race and racism within the coercive structures of capitalism and colonization that forged the core food cultures we know and eat today.[1] Our diverse food cultures in North Carolina, including our historic foodways—how, why, and what we eat—and the evolving contemporary food systems that will enrich our communities, animals, and the environment, are all at stake today as we chart a path forward. The writers, places, and issues gathered here in *Edible North Carolina* speak of the revolution underway in our state's food systems at this groundbreaking time. Their work honors North Carolinians who are committed to antiracism, equity in food workplaces, reinvigorated, interconnected regional food economies, and the building of a sustainable food infrastructure that bridges the state's small-scale farms, fisheries, food entrepreneurs, and its urban and rural peoples.

Throughout the pandemic we witnessed the fraying and dissolution of foundational American institutions from public health to food production. In North Carolina, we saw both the resiliency and the implosion of food economies across the state. North Carolina's local food systems rose to the challenge as national food supply chains dissolved with the closure of much of the economy during the pandemic. When restaurants and bars were shuttered because of mandated closures, chef-owners and business leaders launched curbside food pick-up, home delivery, outdoor dining, and innovative food hub models such as Carrboro United, which allowed Chapel Hill and Carrboro customers to order food from local restaurants, purveyors, and farmers that was delivered weekly at one central location. North Carolinians viewed food relief lines in our communities, euthanizing of livestock due to COVID-19 outbreaks in meatpacking facilities, and dumping of food destined for shuttered commercial institutions. The problem lay in the tightly concentrated agribusiness sectors that control American food production and distribution.[2] When one piece of the sector fails, it fails big, as seen in the frequent national recalls of *E. coli*–contaminated produce and meat. Initial coronavirus-related government relief funds were inadequate and short-term. Many restaurants closed permanently, unable to pay rent, expenses, and payroll without the steady income from daily customers. The stress on food businesses, their employees, and their families was shattering.

The pandemic revealed massive fault lines across America that reverberated in North Carolina, from the overwhelming impact of the virus on African American and Latinx communities to systemic fractures in how this nation feeds itself. For low-income North Carolinians with so-called underlying conditions—high blood pressure, obesity, heart disease, diabetes, chronic lung disease, and stress-related illness—the crisis existed long before the pandemic began. When asked why Black people are sick in America today, sociology professor Sabrina Strings answers, "Slavery."[3] In July 2020, the board of commissioners in Wake County, where Raleigh is located, acknowledged that systemic racism is a *public health crisis* and pledged as a county government to address it.

"We need to support people so that everyone in North Carolina has the opportunity to sit down with their family and have a meal together at the end of the day."

—SARAH BOWEN, sociologist, North Carolina State University, May 1, 2019

From the first months of the pandemic to this writing nearly two years later, North Carolina's small-scale family farms and farmers' markets saw a substantial increase in business from both first-time and regular customers who were avoiding grocery stores yet still seeking fresh produce. Because of their size, diversification, locations across markets, and face-to-face relationships with consumers, small farmers, food hubs, and food entrepreneurs could respond quickly in times of crisis. For many Americans, COVID-19 was a harsh introduction to the fact that we *have* a food system, and industrial agriculture is the engine of that system.[4] Jamie DeMent Holcomb of Coon Rock Farm in Hillsborough observed a pandemic-related wake-up: "Folks who live on our road and have driven past our place for years, suddenly realized what we actually *do*."[5] In their farm newsletter, Jamie and her husband, Richard Holcomb, encouraged new customers to embrace local food for the long term: "As we start to open up again our hope is that many of you have discovered the value and joy of eating locally and sustainably produced veggies, eggs and meat, and will continue to cook meals at home with family and friends using what's local and in season."[6]

Local food remains out of reach for most North Carolinians, who are distanced by geography, cost, and predominantly white farmers' markets. Described as food apartheid, this scenario reflects the absence of food sovereignty—the right to affordable, high-quality, locally grown, nutritious food of their choosing. Shorlette Ammons identifies the basic principles of food sovereignty: "People who work and steward the land act as decision-makers as to how that land is used, what is grown for the community, and operate under a culture of shared use and resources needed to grow and distribute food as medicine."[7] Creating opportunities for people of color to build wealth within the local food scene in North Carolina is crucial to food sovereignty. This shift will require land ownership, investment, and both individual and family financial return.

Author and journalist Mark Bittman argues that "the way forward" is a sustainable and equitable food system for all grounded in the principles of agroecology and food sovereignty.[8] Agroecology "regenerates the ecology of the soil instead of depleting it, reduces carbon emissions, and sustains local food cultures, businesses, farms, jobs, seeds, and people instead of diminishing or destroying them."[9] Small-scale farmers, like-minded food entrepreneurs, consumers, and food system activists in North Carolina increasingly address land reform, salary equity, fair and safe working conditions, empowerment of women and people of color, animal welfare, environmental stewardship, and community access to affordable, local, seasonal food. Although this is not the predominate model in North Carolina, we see more and more examples of food that is grown and marketed sustainably across the state. Greater opportunities now exist to study and work in agroecology, sustainable food, and agriculture at our colleges and universities. North Carolinians who can afford to participate and have access to a local food system seldom support industrial agriculture, big-box retail stores, and corporate-owned supermarkets, but for the majority of North Carolinians, that is the only food system they know.

"Food is a right, not a privilege."

—ALISHA STREET, founder, The Bulb mobile market, Charlotte, North Carolina, July 5, 2019

To build a vital statewide, equitable, healthy, local food system for all will require far more than white shoppers who support farmers' markets. Real change must be based on activism, protest, coalition building, and legislation that supports sustainable agriculture.[10] Climate change and severe weather events that challenge our local food systems and the daily lives of North Carolinians disproportionately harm those whose lives are already diminished by poverty and racism. We can turn this tide through renewable energy options that protect our air, water, and food resources and through increased support for low-income and working-class Americans—programs projected to be a part of President Joe Biden's massive infrastructure plan announced in the spring of 2021. We must end hunger where we live. Often hidden from view, North Carolina has the tenth highest rate of food insecurity in the nation, which means that one in four children in our state lacks adequate food. Local organizations like TABLE, PORCH, the Inter-Faith Food Shuttle, and the Food Bank of Central & Eastern North Carolina are among many hunger relief programs across the state that provide food to those in need. We should expect to pay more for our restaurant meals, knowing that price increases reflect fair, living wages and basic benefits for all staff members.

The immigration crisis, as Bittman explains, is really a crisis of food and labor in Mexico, intensified by climate change and industrial agriculture that forces people to leave home to find work here in our fields and restaurants.[11] These eligible undocumented workers and their families deserve a compassionate path to legal status.

We must support the important work of BIPOC-owned farms, CSAs, food businesses, and markets in North Carolina, like LaTonya Andrews's Soul City Farm in Norlina and Tonya Council's N.C. MADE, which curates gift boxes made from North Carolina's best artisanal foods. Andrews farms land first purchased by her great-grandmother Suzi Valentine Andrews in the 1940s.[12] Tonya Council grew up in Chapel Hill, where she watched her grandmother Mildred "Mama Dip" Council create her iconic restaurant, cookbooks, and food products. In Charlotte, a contemporary generation of young Black chefs, restaurateurs, food makers, writers, and photographers are creating one of the most vibrant food communities in the state. In May 2021, Nigerian-born, southern-raised journalist Emiene Wright examined "food of the African diaspora" in a powerful *Charlotte Observer* series highlighting the city's Black food entrepreneurs.[13]

If North Carolina politicians do not address our local food economy and food justice, we can either educate them to support these crucial issues or vote for those who do. Healthy, local, affordable, delicious food is a human right, as are humane workplaces in fields, food processing plants, and restaurants. The 2021 passage of the $1.9 trillion COVID-19 Relief Bill includes $5 billion to provide debt relief, grants, and land access supports to Black farmers long harmed by systemic racism in all aspects of agriculture, as well as a $28.6 billion Restaurant Revitalization Fund for independent restaurants and bars to compensate them for revenue lost during the pandemic and the recovery period. Although these funds cannot fully repair the massive losses—economist William Darity Jr. estimates the loss to Black farmers due to U.S. Department of Agriculture policies and white land appropriation at $250 billion to $350 billion—these new funds reflect the unrelenting work of coalition members, congressional leaders, and a president dedicated to rebuild the economy and address the long history of racism and racial harm experienced by Black Americans.[14] North Carolina chefs and restaurant leaders from Asheville to the Outer Banks—Katie Button, Ashley Christensen, Kait Goalen, and Cheetie Kumar—are important voices in the Independent Restaurant Coalition (IRC), which fought for the relief funds voted into law in March 2021. Katy Kindred and Wes Stepp mobilized grassroots efforts in their regions of the state. A year earlier, the IRC was organized during a phone call with eighteen people from the restaurant and beverage community to determine a course of action on pandemic-related relief from Congress. That phone call became a nationwide movement.

In these critical times where practically every food decision we make shapes the lives of our children and the future of the planet, activism must focus on direct political action and programs that rebuild and reinvigorate local food systems. While it is important to change our individual acts of consumption in North Carolina, we must make a difference that affects more than our own personal health and well-being. We must make a commitment of time and money and working with people beyond our tight circles.

During the months following the COVID-19 outbreak, farmers, restaurants, churches, volunteers, and nonprofit organizations across North Carolina provided hot meals, boxes of fresh produce, medical support, and financial aid for laid-off food workers.[15] Several of these relief programs became nonprofit organizations that support local food economies and community members in need. Feed Durham NC, a Durham-based mutual aid collective founded by filmmaker Katina Parker, provides nutritious, *delicious* meals to students, seniors, and families.[16] In a temporary outdoor kitchen, volunteers prepare trays of smoked chicken, rice and beans, and seasonal vegetables like braised butternut squash. Feed Durham also helps build collaborative vegetable gardens, shares local cooking skills, and organizes against hunger. In Asheville, farmers Aaron and Anne Grier provided produce to We Give a Share, the community-supported meal program established in Asheville during the pandemic. Aaron Grier stated, "The plate of the Tailgate Market Shopper, and the plate of the diner at a downtown restaurant, and the plate of someone living in affordable housing can all have the *same quality* ingredients on any one night. As farmers, being able to connect that dot that we haven't been able to reach is something that is inspiring to all of us."[17]

Feast Down East (FDE, 2006) was created as a UNC–Wilmington research initiative in response to massive job loss and high poverty rates in southeastern North Carolina. FDE aggregates fresh, seasonal food from local small farmers at its food hub, which is located in the historic train depot in Burgaw. The program distributes produce, eggs, honey, meats, and goat cheese to local restaurants, grocery stores, markets, and institutions. FDE also distributes locally sourced food through a mobile farmers' market that visits Wilmington neighborhoods with limited access to fresh food. At these markets customers can purchase a variety of products from local farmers at affordable prices and SNAP/EBT purchases are matched dollar for dollar. During the pandemic, FDE organized weekly deliveries of farm-fresh products to vulnerable senior citizens and quickly transitioned to a CSA model to make local food available to the larger community when restaurants and schools were closed. In 2022 the Wilmington Food Bank will open a new location in the south side of the city. As part of this project FDE will operate a brick-and-mortar farmers' market where it will offer fresh, local products, also reasonably priced. FDE will work closely with the Wilmington Food Bank and their new facility, which will include a community learning farm and a commercial kitchen to prepare meals during community emergencies, such as recent devastating hurricanes.

The extraordinary leaders of the contemporary food movement and the issues explored in *Edible North Carolina* offer a road map for the food choices we make every day. The unique food cultures of contemporary North Carolina are a sacred trust for its people. We must honor that trust and those whose history, labor, sacrifices, creativity, and vision nurture the food we eat today and future generations will enjoy. We must embrace the power of regional and local food knowledge as we contemplate our place on this fragile planet, as we cherish the distinctive flavors of this state, and as we address racial justice and food sovereignty for all. There could be no more important time to savor and sustain the food of North Carolina's soil and waters, to express gratitude, and to support those who bring that food to our tables.

A Higher Form: A Cocktail in Honor of North Carolina's Women in Food

GARY CRUNKLETON

Makes 1 drink

2 ounces Conniption Navy Proof Gin from Durham Distillery in Durham, N.C.
¼ ounce Luxardo Maraschino Liqueur
¼ ounce Tempus Fugit Crème de Noyaux Liqueur
¾ ounce fresh lemon juice
¾ ounce simple syrup (2 parts sugar to 1 part water)
1 egg white
Lemon peel for garnish

In my opinion, women are of a higher form than men. They are intelligent and practical. They are strong. They know how to get things done while remaining true to themselves. I used gin to create this drink celebrating the women who work in food in North Carolina. Gin is a spirit that is limitless, enduring, refined, and authentic. It can hold its own in a state full of whiskey fans. The many women in this book integrate their values in the food they create and steward each day. I raise a toast to them here.
—Gary Crunkleton

Pour all the ingredients except the lemon peel into a Boston shaker filled with cubed ice. Shake vigorously to chill, mix, and aerify the drink. Using a Hawthorne strainer atop the mixing tin, pour the drink into a cocktail coupe. Garnish with a swath of lemon peel.

NOTES

1. Janine Jackson, "Our Food System Is Very Much Modeled on Plantation Economics," Counterspin Interview with Ricardo Salvador, Union of Concerned Scientists, May 13, 2020.

2. Jackson.

3. Sabrina Strings, "It's Not Obesity; It's Slavery," *New York Times*, May 25, 2020.

4. Ligaya Mishan, "The Activists Working to Remake the Food System, *New York Times*, February 19, 2021.

5. Jamie DeMent Holcomb, conversation with Marcie Cohen Ferris, May 29, 2020.

6. "Notes from Coon Rock Farm," email newsletter, June 5, 2020, Coon Rock Farm, Hillsborough, N.C.

7. Shorlette Ammons, "A Case for a 'New Normal' in the Wake of Two Pandemics," *Southern Cultures*, June 2020, www.southerncultures.org/article/food-sovereignty/.

8. Mark Bittman, *Animal, Vegetable, Junk: A History of Food, from Sustainable to Suicidal* (New York: Houghton Mifflin Harcourt, 2021), 267–68.

9. Bittman, 267.

10. Bittman, 296–97.

11. Bittman, 263.

12. Martha Quillen, "Covid-19 Relief Bill Offers Long-Denied Aid to Black and Other Minority Farmers," *News and Observer* (Raleigh, N.C.), March 16, 2021.

13. Emiene Wright, "The Skillet: How Black Cuisine Became America's Supper," *Charlotte Observer*, May 23, 2021.

14. Laura Reiley, "Relief Bill Is Most Significant Legislation for Black Farmers since Civil Rights Act, Experts Say," *Washington Post*, March 8, 2021.

15. Ammons, "Case for a 'New Normal.'"

16. Katina Parker, "Nourish and Flourish: From Cookouts to Raised Beds, Feed Durham NC Works to End Hunger," *Gravy* (Southern Food Alliance), Fall 2021.

17. Aaron Grier, Gaining Ground Farm, Leicester, N.C., *We Give a Share*, Kinetiscape Media.

Acknowledgments

Edible North Carolina represents the voices, hands, and labor of hundreds of North Carolinians, and I am deeply grateful for their generous participation and support of this work. This book began at the University of North Carolina at Chapel Hill in my courses focused on North Carolina's diverse food cultures, team-taught with colleagues Elizabeth Engelhardt and Sharon Holland, and coordinated by social entrepreneur and educator Laura Fieselman, a graduate of UNC's American Studies–Folklore program. While chair of the American Studies Department, Bernie Herman supported this project with a Southern Studies course development grant.

I want to express my deep admiration for the talented students with whom I explored North Carolina's food cultures together in our class. Especially inspiring was the manifesto written by Carolina undergraduates Claire Hannapel and Maddy Sweitzer-Lamme, now food writers and policy activists, which began, "WE CALL ON THE CITIZENS OF NORTH CAROLINA." Their key points included: "To know that food is inextricable from place; to be aware that by repairing the local food systems of North Carolina, we're mending networks that have been broken by industrial agriculture; to cultivate relationships within the food system in order to sustain evolving North Carolina foodways—know your farmer, your chef, your neighbor; and remember that food tells stories."

I am indebted to the leaders of North Carolina's food community who shared their understanding of the state of the state's contemporary food landscapes. Filmmaker and *Southern Cultures* team member Ashley Melzer helped me navigate the technology as I recorded and filmed more than 160 interviews across the state. Bob Rudolph was, as always, indispensable for his adept computer support.

Most of the highlighted quotations showcased in these pages are from interviews I conducted, but a few are from other sources:

In Michelle T. King's essay, the quotation from Minyu Zheng is from an interview by Holt McKeithan. The quotation from Hannah Jian is from an interview by Victoria Tran.

In Victoria Bouloubasis's essay, the quotations from Charlie Ibarra and Moses Ochola are from interviews she conducted.

In Katy Clune's essay, the quotation from Danil Phrakousonh is from an interview she conducted.

In Courtney Lewis's essay, the quotation from Johnnie Sue Myers is from the "Policies and Plates" panel in the Native Foodpreneurs and the Food Sovereignty Movement series, chaired by Courtney Lewis, at Davidson College on April 20, 2020. The quotation from Joey Owle is from an interview conducted by Maia Surdam.

The talented team behind *Edible North Carolina* are my extended family, and I thank each of them for their unwavering commitment to excellence and their perseverance in such challenging times. Katherine "K. C." Hysmith, associate editor for *Edible North Carolina*, was a working partner par excellence. Her insights as a rising food studies scholar, journalist, administrator, digital maven, and culinary star are reflected throughout this volume. Photographer Baxter Miller and her partner and collaborator, Ryan Stancil, captured the spirit, passion, and work of the varied food communities and people explored in *Edible North Carolina*. Their photography animates the breadth and depth of North Carolina's local food movement. The generous support of John Powell (UNC Class of '77) made the far-reaching photodocumentation featured in *Edible North*

Carolina possible. Our writing team represents North Carolina's finest authors, chefs, folklorists, educators, journalists, makers, mixologists, and scholars at this singular moment in our state's history. I am forever grateful to each essayist and to Vivian Howard, who wrote the foreword, for their exceptional, perceptive work.

Emma Patterson, my literary agent at Brandt & Hochman, offered strong support and counsel. At the University Press of North Carolina, I am especially grateful to Executive Editor Elaine Maisner, Acquisition Assistant Andreina Fernandez, Director of Editorial, Design, and Production Kim Bryant, designer Rich Hendel, and Assistant Managing Editor Erin Granville. Elaine's sharp insights, steadfast enthusiasm, invaluable guidance, and long friendship were an important foundation for this book. Thank you to the readers who provided crucial guidance in shaping this work. The interest and support of my cherished *Southern Cultures* colleagues—Emma Calabrese, Ayse Erginer, Tom Rankin, and Emily Wallace—mean the world to me. Dick and Sue Barrows, thank you for the many delicious meals from KITCHEN that sustained our household throughout this project.

Virginia, Chase, Fiona, Jamie, Huddy, Albe, and my Ferris family provided love and encouragement. Lydia Wegman's friendship and conversations kept me as sane as was possible. Bill Ferris, I love you and thank you for your constant cheer, for your belief in this work, and most important, for respecting the voices of women and the expressive power of food.

The territory we now call North Carolina belongs to the federally recognized Eastern Band of Cherokee Indians and the state recognized Coharie, Lumbee, Haliwa Saponi, Meherrin, Occaneechi Saponi, Sappony, and Waccamaw Siouan people. We are grateful for the food and nourishment this land, waters, and these people have brought forth for generations.

Contributors

SHORLETTE AMMONS | Community food systems outreach coordinator, Center for Environmental Farming Systems, North Carolina State University
Shorlette Ammons is a native of eastern North Carolina, where she grew up in a large family of farmworkers, cooks, and storytellers. At NC State's Center for Environmental Farming Systems, Ammons is the equity in food systems coordinator, core team lead, and an extension associate. Ammons was a 2011 Maya Wiley Fellow at the Center for Social Inclusion (now Race Forward) and a 2019–21 Castanea Fellow.

KAREN AMSPACHER | Executive director, Core Sound Waterfowl Museum & Heritage Center, Harkers Island, North Carolina
Karen Amspacher was born and raised in the Core Sound region of North Carolina, where she has tirelessly advocated for the maritime culture of coastal Carolina. She has served as the executive director of the Core Sound Waterfowl Museum & Heritage Center since 1992. Amspacher is a coauthor of *Living at the Water's Edge: A Heritage Guide to the Outer Banks* (UNC Press, 2017).

VICTORIA BOULOUBASIS | Journalist, food writer, filmmaker
Victoria Bouloubasis is an award-winning journalist whose work dispels myths about the Global South—its people and places—against the backdrop of complex social, political, and personal histories. She grew up in Winston-Salem, North Carolina, the proud daughter of Greek American restaurateurs. In 2014, Bouloubasis directed *Un Buen Carnicero / A Good Butcher*, a bilingual documentary produced by Vittles Films and the Southern Foodways Alliance.

KATY CLUNE | Director of communications, Duke Arts
Katy Clune is a folklorist and documentarian whose work focuses on cultural communications. She is director of communications for Duke Arts, Duke University's arts initiative, and a 2020 recipient of the Archie Green Fellowship, awarded by the American Folklife Center at the Library of Congress.

GABE CUMMING & CARLA NORWOOD | Working Landscapes
Gabe Cumming and Carla Norwood are cofounders of Working Landscapes, a nonprofit rural development organization based in Warrenton, North Carolina. The organization works to advance the economic and environmental resilience of the region. Cumming and Norwood each earned a Ph.D. in ecology at the University of North Carolina at Chapel Hill.

MARCIE COHEN FERRIS | Author, emeritus professor, Department of American Studies, University of North Carolina at Chapel Hill
Marcie Cohen Ferris is an author, educator, and scholar whose work focuses on the American South through its foodways, the southern Jewish experience, and material culture. She is an emeritus professor in the Department of American Studies at the University of North Carolina at Chapel Hill and editor for *Southern Cultures*, a quarterly journal of the history and cultures of the U.S. South. Ferris is the author of *Matzoh Ball Gumbo: Culinary Tales of the Jewish South* (UNC Press, 2005) and *The Edible South: The Power of Food and the Making of an American Region* (UNC Press, 2014).

SANDRA A. GUTIERREZ | Food writer, recipe developer, professional cooking instructor
Sandra Gutierrez is an author, food writer, and cooking

instructor. She is the former food editor of the *Cary (N.C.) News*. An expert in Latin cuisines, Gutierrez was born in the United States and grew up in Latin America, where she learned about its complex and delicious foodways. She lives in Cary, North Carolina. Her forthcoming book explores Latin American food cultures in more than twenty countries (Knopf, 2023).

TOM HANCHETT | Community historian
Tom Hanchett is a community historian interested in the history of urban place-making, often using Charlotte as a case study. For sixteen years, he served as the historian at the Levine Museum of the New South. Recognized as Charlottean of the Year in 2015, Hanchett was appointed the Charlotte-Mecklenburg Library's first-ever historian-in-residence in 2019. He is the author of *Sorting Out the New South City: Race, Class, and Urban Development in Charlotte, 1875–1975* (UNC Press, 1998; 2nd ed., 2020).

VIVIAN HOWARD | Chef, restaurateur, author
A native of Deep Run, North Carolina, Howard returned to eastern North Carolina in 2005 with her husband, Ben Knight, to open Chef & the Farmer, a farm-to-fork restaurant in Kinston. The PBS series *A Chef's Life* premiered in 2013 and was awarded Emmys, a Peabody Award, and James Beard Awards. Howard's first book was *Deep Run Roots: Stories and Recipes from My Corner of the South* (Little, Brown, 2016). Her current PBS series is *Somewhere South*, a culinary tour of the American South through cross-cultural dishes.

K. C. HYSMITH | Writer, Ph.D. candidate University of North Carolina at Chapel Hill, recipe developer, food stylist
K. C. Hysmith is a Texas-bred, North Carolina–based writer, food historian, recipe developer, food stylist, and photographer. With Chef Ricky Moore, she cowrote *Saltbox Seafood Joint Cookbook* (UNC Press, 2019). A Ph.D. candidate in American studies at the University of North Carolina at Chapel Hill, she focuses on the intersection of food, gender, and the digital landscape.

MICHELLE T. KING | Professor of history, University of North Carolina at Chapel Hill
Michelle T. King is a professor at the University of North Carolina at Chapel Hill in the Department of History, where she specializes in modern Chinese gender history and food history. She is the editor of *Culinary Nationalism in Asia* (Bloomsbury Academic, 2019). In 2020–21 King was awarded a National Endowment for the Humanities Public Scholars grant for her forthcoming book on Taiwan's beloved postwar television cooking celebrity Fu Pei-mei (1931–2004).

CHEETIE KUMAR | Chef, restaurateur
Cheetie Kumar is chef and owner of three venues in Raleigh, North Carolina—Garland restaurant, Kings music venue, and Neptunes Parlour—and the guitarist for Birds of Avalon. Her family and cuisine are both of and from India, the United States, and the American South. Kumar was a 2020 finalist for the James Beard Award for Best Chef: Southeast.

COURTNEY LEWIS | Associate professor of anthropology, University of South Carolina, Columbia
Courtney Lewis is an associate professor at the University of South Carolina–Columbia in the Department of Anthropology, where she specializes in Indigenous economic studies and food and agricultural sovereignty. Lewis is the author of *Sovereign Entrepreneurs: Cherokee Small Business Owners and the Making of Economic Sovereignty* (UNC Press, 2019). She is a citizen of the Cherokee Nation. Lewis will join the Department of Anthropology at Duke University in the fall of 2022.

MALINDA MAYNOR LOWERY | Cahoon Family Professor of American History, Emory University, Atlanta, Georgia
Malinda Lowery is the Cahoon Family Professor of American History at Emory University. Lowery's work explores American Indian migration and identity, school desegregation, federal

recognition, religious music, and foodways. Her most recent book is *The Lumbee Indians: An American Struggle* (UNC Press, 2018). She is a member of the Lumbee Tribe of North Carolina.

RONNI LUNDY | Journalist, food writer
Born in Corbin, Kentucky, Ronni Lundy has long chronicled the people of Appalachia through their music and food. She is the former restaurant reviewer and music critic for the *Courier-Journal* in Louisville, Kentucky, and the former editor of *Louisville Magazine*. In 2017, Lundy received a James Beard Award for her groundbreaking book, *Victuals: An Appalachian Journey, with Recipes* (Clarkson Potter, 2016).

KEIA MASTRIANNI | Writer, oral historian
Keia Mastrianni is a writer and the baker behind the small-batch pie company Milk Glass Pie. She and her farmer husband, Jamie Swofford, are proud owners of Old North Farm outside of Shelby, North Carolina.

APRIL McGREGER | Food writer, chef, entrepreneur
April McGreger is a writer and chef raised on a sweet potato farm in central Mississippi. She is the former owner of Farmer's Daughter, a farm-driven artisan food business based in Hillsborough, North Carolina, where she was a much beloved pickler and preserver at the Carrboro Farmers' Market. McGreger is the author of *Sweet Potatoes: A Savor the South Cookbook* (UNC Press, 2014).

BAXTER MILLER | Photographer
Baxter Miller's photography and documentary work spans North Carolina's diverse foodways, landscapes, and cultures. Together with her partner and collaborator, Ryan Stancil, she served as creative director and principal investigator for *Rising: Perspectives of Change along the North Carolina Coast* (2018), a multimedia exhibition focused on climate change and community resilience. Baxter and Ryan share a deep love and reverence for North Carolina and have collaborated with numerous chefs and restaurants, including Vivian Howard for her recent book *This Will Make It Taste Good* (Voracious, 2020).

RICKY MOORE | Chef, author
Ricky Moore is a chef, restaurateur, and writer born and reared in the North Carolina coastal town of New Bern, where catching and eating fresh fish and shellfish is what people do. He is the chef-owner of Saltbox Seafood Joint in Durham, North Carolina. Moore is the author of *Saltbox Seafood Joint Cookbook* (UNC Press, 2019).

KATHLEEN PURVIS | Food journalist
Kathleen Purvis is a food journalist, author, and the former food editor for the *Charlotte Observer*. She is a member of the Southern Foodways Alliance, the Association of Food Journalists, and the James Beard Foundation. Her most recent book is *Distilling the South: A Guide to Southern Craft Liquors and the People Who Make Them* (UNC Press, 2018).

ANDREA REUSING | Chef, author
Andrea Reusing is an author, the former executive chef of the Durham Hotel in Durham, North Carolina, and the chef and owner of the award-winning restaurant Lantern in Chapel Hill. In 2011, Reusing was a recipient of the James Beard Award for Best Chef: Southeast. Her book *Cooking in the Moment: A Year of Seasonal Recipes* (Clarkson Potter, 2011) was named one of the year's most notable cookbooks by the *New York Times*.

BILL SMITH | Chef, author
Bill Smith was born and raised in New Bern, North Carolina, and was the chef at Crook's Corner in Chapel Hill, North Carolina, for nearly three decades until his retirement in 2019. He now focuses on food writing and activism that supports racial justice and equity. Smith's most recent book is *Crabs and Oysters: A Savor the South Cookbook* (UNC Press, 2015).

MAIA SURDAM | Historian, baker, educator, gardener
Maia Surdam is a writer, historian, and baker. She is co-owner of OWL Bakery in Asheville, North Carolina, and the program director of the Partnership for Appalachian Girls' Education (PAGE) in Madison County, North Carolina. Surdam received her Ph.D. in history from the University of Wisconsin–Madison.

ANDREA WEIGL | Food journalist
Award-winning journalist Andrea Weigl worked at Raleigh's *News and Observer* for seventeen years, including a decade as a food writer and editor. She is a producer for two PBS series, *A Chef's Life* and *Somewhere South*, starring Chef Vivian Howard.

Index

Page numbers in italics refer to illustrations.

BOGUE SOUND
WATERMELONS
4031